APESICK

RITUAL EXCLUSION

AND

THE SEEDS OF FASCISM

BARTHOLOMY

APESICK

FOREWORD: THE COMPASSIONATE FOOL   I

BOOK I: REPRESSED AGGRESSION

THE SEEDS OF FASCISM

MASS HYSTERIA   9

THE WITCH-HUNT BELONGS TO MODERNITY   25

MUTUALLY DEPENDENT FICTIONS   35

WE DID IT, NOT "NUDGE"   43

HOARDING INNER POVERTY   57

WHAT IS LONG COVID?   63

OUR BODIES RESONATE WITH MALADAPTATIVE FRICTION   75

A LOVE LETTER TO THE NEWLY DISILLUSIONED   83

PSYCHOLOGY IS NOT YET BORN

REPRESSION AND THE UNCANNY   89

THE ART OF PERCEPTION   105

THE AUTODIDACT MAKES THE FUTURE   127

A HOSTILE TAKEOVER OF EVOLUTIONARY PSYCHOLOGY

INTERESTING DENTISTRY   141

HUMAN NATURE: EMBOLDENED BY ERROR   149

MAN AND WOMAN, CRIMINAL AND SLAVE   173

THE SOCIAL FUNCTION OF TRUTH   183

BOOK II: OPPRESSIVE REGRESSION

ILLS OF THE TRIBE

GREED: THE VICE OF THE OLD   199

ENVY: THE SOCIOLOGY OF ORDINARY WITCHCRAFT   221

HATE: THE DEVIL'S BUTTHOLE   245

SPIRITUAL SELF-DEFENSE CURRICULUM

NEUTRALIZING MORAL CENSURE   265

THE LEAGUE OF DIDACTIC WHITE BOYS   273

REDEMPTION OF THE TRIBAL CREATURE   279

THE TINY ABACUS   291

RITUAL EXCLUSION

THE BASAL TRIBAL INSTINCT   299

THE BRUTALITY OF CLOWNWORLD   339

AFTERWORD: THE MISANTHROPIC SAGE   371

FOREWORD: THE COMPASSIONATE FOOL

- 0 -

I don't expect this book to be successful for many years. It's primarily a manual for veterans of a long, secret war: just to declare this war, to finally map the contentious territory is healing enough. But those with hearts hard enough to hear me, don't read books like mine; while those who might read it, prefer to hide their clever calculating nihilism behind a feint of idealism, and therefore cannot afford the many uncringing assessments a book like this contains. I might stand a better chance of being heard, if I could package this sentiment in a divinely savage heavy metal album, or that gorgeously dark, eloquently furious hiphop track of my dreams, the one where I pry open cold hearts and pour in molten gold, the one where I finally prove the efficacy of my bluntforce attack of passionate inquiry.

- I -

In some ways this work represents a recovery from the insights of my previous book: a deepening, a ramification, yet also a recovery – but a recovery via an *even darker outlook*. How is that possible? Because by deepening the commitment to my own insight, I've found more freedom: the more I articulate the problem, the less responsibility I find in my column, and therefore the less bitterness remains, and the more I find the situation funny. Profoundly, sublimely funny, like Phineas Gage walking around with an iron bar through his skull, finally free to advocate for himself: that's the joy of *Apesick*, that's my big belly laugh with tears in my eyes, that's the mad weeping primate at the center of our soul.

- 2 -

That mad weeping primate knows what he is, what you are, what we have been pretending not to be in our costume balls, Sunday school *dramatis personae*, and professional headshot pucker. *The perpetual pucker of the good ape*: trying so hard to please, trying harder to hide his contempt of apenature, of his own schemes. Has no one until now seriously undertaken a psychology of the ape? Has no one dared look into the face of our simian ancestors and said, "Yes, I understand. Please go on." Compassion and love for the ape – a tough love, but a love nonetheless I cannot deny it. The longer I look at the problems of anthropology and everything that's been missing from philosophy and psychology since the axial age, I find the same lacuna: a lack of the evolutionary theory of our origin does not account for the millennia-long denial of our essential character. We are the scheming, shapeshifting, vicious, always-there-before-you apemind: misanthropy gets you only halfway to the full confession. A shapeshifting animal must have an essential nature – perhaps all the more so in lieu of strong instincts. We confuse the other animals because we have a mysterious mastery over our *lack of shape*: we are constantly both abjectly subject to nightmarish hallucination and suddenly masters at conjuring whatever spirit suits our whimsy. We are the animal which benefits more than any other, from the cascading neural tremor called *laughter*: fear, surprise, and rage sublimated into a substance divine, a fabric of sanity strong and pliable enough for almost any depth of insanity, frustration, and dysfunction...

- 3 -

Yet the recovery I'm speaking of cannot occur merely through the *pointing of fingers*: it's typical of my moral critique to heap blame in a single category, building up a profile of everything loathsome which resists daylight, only to reverse the roles and collapse the polarity at the last moment, demanding that we understand how we're all responsible for every bit of human nature – not one of us exempt, not one of us free of its best or worst qualities, not ever free to say, "I am not that". To be caught in the receding tidepool longings of a mendacious ape, half-aware of its wretchedness without being able to resist it, being compelled to behave shamefully before one's own witness, to fly off the handle even more thoroughly because of this silent witness, and reveal how petty one can be under the double pressure of an impotent self-consciousness: we misanthropes, we too have sufficient compassion to admit that we're all subject to these embarrassing revelations. But it's characteristic of my type, not to allow the *premature reconciliations of compassion* to interfere with the deeper reckonings of wrath. There is so much more clarity in anger than the muddy waters of pity. There is great potential for *a science motivated by wrath*, and very little for the lipsmacking flattery of compassionate story-telling: science requires as much hostility towards ignorance as curiosity for the unknown. In other words, this book is not about forgiveness, but understanding.

BOOK I:
REPRESSED AGGRESSION

I.1

THE SEEDS OF FASCISM

MASS HYSTERIA

Der Irrsinn ist selten bei Einzelnen — aber bei Gruppen, Parteien, Völkern, Zeiten die Regel: — und deshalb redeten bisher die Historiker nicht vom Irrsinn. Aber irgend wann werden die Ärzte Geschichte schreiben.

Madness is rare among individuals – but among groups, parties, peoples, and ages it is the rule: – and therefore the historians do not speak of madness. But at some time the physicians shall write history.

Nietzsche, *Nachlass* VII-1.72

- 4 -

I won't seek to prove something which any qualified reader knew long ago: the COVID crisis was a case of mass hysteria. The virus itself is very real but the pretense of fear surrounding it is histrionic, unconsciously strategic, and more demonstrative than genuine. An extremely virulent but *nondeadly* respiratory nuisance, a profound attachment to the fiction of a deadly pandemic, an enormous flood of misinformation, an extremely dangerous set of legal precedents, an encircling crowd of jackal-eyed economic and political opportunists, but never once a genuine threat to the collective human health on its own: yet out of all these minor disasters, I find the most pernicious element of COVID is the *willful ignorance* concerning the underlying reason for the hysteria. But willful ignorance is precisely one of the symptoms of hysteria: we would rather not know why, or *pretend we don't*.

But I believe the answer is very clear. We cannot see it because we swim through it, we breathe it, we take it for granted: *repressed aggression* caused COVID hysteria. Although I believe COVID and the year 2020 will in the end be only another baffling footnote in the long history of human error, COVID is an opportunity to analyze something the human race needs desperately to understand: what I will describe as *mass aggressigenic hysteria*.

- 5 -

What is "mass hysteria"? This term is tossed around like a deflated beach ball no one understands how to handle. Most often it stands for "unreasonable fear" and nothing more. But hysteria has a definite, discernible, and well-researched formula: where is this knowledge now that we need it? Those most to blame for this are the representatives of mainstream academic psychology: they have buried all real psychological insight beneath a tidal wave of moral posturing and political agenda, which is *suspiciously antagonistic* toward the analysis of hysteria in particular.

- 6 -

The mainstream consensus on mass hysteria is skewed toward a relatively minor syndrome which is easier to document, easier to dismiss, and does not threaten the moral norm. 21st century psychologists will generally only speak of "mass psychogenic illness". But "psychogenic" is a willfully stupid and evasive term. Everything in psychology is "psychogenic" else it's not the domain of psychology, and everything not an illness is not interesting. This is equivalent to saying "contagious crazies" and intentionally obfuscates the history and depth of early 20th century thinking concerning hysteria.

The proper term is *mass conversion hysteria*: this is the case of a psychosomatic symptom of disease spreading quickly through a uniform population: homogeneous groups of women and children under stress are known to be especially susceptible – thus its historical frequency in factories and schools. The famous "June Bug Epidemic" among the women of a dressmaking factory during a sweaty summer of 1962 serves as example. "Conversion" here means the conversion of some repressed impulse into a delusional symptom along a socially accepted trajectory: thus "conversion hysteria" is the best of the accepted terminology because it indicates its own heritage in the vital Freudian concept of *Verschiebung*, or *displacement* – which I'll discuss shortly.

But do not misunderstand me: COVID hysteria is not and never was primarily driven by anything like conversion hysteria. Despite its value as a diagnostic, mass conversion hysteria is a rare and relatively transient event. But with COVID we are dealing with a mass hysteria manifested in ideological, moral, and governmental terms, not short-lived nocebo effects. In order to analyze it we must turn to the older conception of what is properly termed *anxiety hysteria.*

- 7 -

The study of hysteria lies right at the heart of the best achievements of early 20th century psychology: this is a fact much obscured now by the armies of psychiatric pillpushers and academic yesmen, but the study of hysteria was the key to the discovery of *unconscious mechanics*, the knowledge of which all of us utilize in our speech and manner of thinking every day. Start a heated argument with any half-educated bloke, and eventually Freudian terms will be lobbed back and forth: "You're just projecting. You're so egocentric. He's so anal!" Freud is anathema, both sacred and forbidden: simultaneously enthroned via the implicit use of his vocabulary and excommunicated from contemporary science.

We must return to this forbidden source in order to understand what hysteria is. Freud is describing here how anxiety hysteria works:

> Die fliehende Besetzung wendete sich einer Ersatzvorstellung zu, die einerseits assoziativ mit der abgewiesenen Vorstellung zusammenhing, anderseits durch die Entfernung von ihr der Verdrängung entzogen war (Verschiebungsersatz) und eine Rationalisierung der noch unhemmbaren Angstentwicklung gestattete. Die Ersatzvorstellung spielt nun für das System Bewusstsein die Rolle einer Gegenbesetzung, indem sie es gegen das Auftauchen der verdrängten Vorstellung im Bewusstsein versichert, anderseits ist sie die Ausgangsstelle der nun erst recht unhemmbaren Angstaffektentbindung oder benimmt sich als solche.

> The retreating energetic investment devotes itself to a substitutive idea which, on the one hand, is connected by association with the rejected idea, and on the other, has escaped repression by reason of its remoteness from that idea – as *Verschiebungersatz*, a "displacing substitute" – and permits the still uninhibitable development of anxiety to be rationalized. The substitute idea now plays the part of an energetic uninvestment for the conscious system, by securing it against an emergence in consciousness of the repressed content. On the other hand it is, or acts as if it were, the point of departure for the release of

the affect of anxiety, which has now really become quite unin-
hibitable.

Das Unbewusste, §IV

⤙ "Energetic investment" refers to what is badly translated as "cathexis"
elsewhere: the quantum of psychosomatic excitation generated by the
activation of any given instinct, which may manifest as sexual or aggressive urges.

⤙ What is a "displacing substitute"? Any given object of an instinctual
urge can be displaced by another when social pressures demand it: but
the original ideational content does not disappear, it is *repressed*. This is
what it means when we say that someone is "anal" or "obsessed": they
employ some seemingly meaningless activity such as repetitive hand-
washing, to gratify some other urge, the content of which is repressed and
yet deeply connected to the substitute.

At this point I must insist the reader learn a little German – it won't hurt as
much as it seems. *Verschiebungsersatz* I translate literally as "displacing
substitute": *Verschiebung* can be quickly understood in English as
"shoving away", *schieben* having the same root as "shove". *Ersatz* is already
common in English and means simply "replacement", with a similar mor-
phological structure as the Latinate "re-place". Therefore
Verschiebungsersatz is "a substitute that displaces".

Finally, it's important to note that in this short passage Freud also
manages to touch upon the essence of the hysterical symptom: the *rationalization of anxiety*. This is generally what everyone already understands
about hysteria and all histrionic neurosis – that the fuss and bother must
really be *about something else*. To clarify this common knowledge is my aim
here.

- 8 -

This "substitutive idea" plays two roles simultaneously: the role of a
repressive force, by obscuring awareness of the true cause even while
hinting at it, and a *rationalized vector* for the release of anxiety behaviors.
One of the most important Freudian insights is that every displacement
can be traced along discernible semantic lines: the substitute is never
completely arbitrary, and it only takes a little practice in the art of untan-

gling semantic valence to learn to detect the clues leading backward to the original impulse.

Hysteria is the *exemplum magnum* of the mechanism of displacement and its analysis constitutes therefore the core of 20th century psychological insight – what is now called "conversion disorder" is in fact the last stump of Freudian thinking the psychiatrists have not managed to uproot, so stubborn and obvious is hysteria in telling us that some unconscious sleight-of-hand is going on. Sometimes it seems that the riddle of hysteria *wants* to be solved: it communicates as much as it obscures.

So obvious is all this, that if we analyze the commonest pop psychology concerning hysteria, we find traces of this latent knowledge. All over the Internet I see half-finished thoughts concerning the COVID hysteria: that most of the more draconic measures in local jurisdictions represent the revenge of petty bureaucrats; the curious way demonstrative fear of the virus disappears and reappears depending on social context; the overwhelming cognitive dissonance concerning the efficacy of vaccines – on and on.

And yet I don't see anyone qualified in the analysis of hysteria speaking up about how it works: imagine if Pasteur were as controversial and "disproven" as Freud is, and in the midst of an outbreak of salmonella nobody thought of doing the dishes...

- 9 -

The other mechanism central to the functioning of hysteria is *projection*: but what's projected? Not so much the fear of something environmental, but the danger represented by the *instinctual drive itself*. To want to do something which would cost too much in social terms: danger. To want to abandon your children and see your husband dead: danger. To want to be rid of grandma: danger. To want to set fire to the office: danger. To want to let go of the steering wheel and see your SUV packed with big mistakes careen into the oncoming lane towards that truck gleaming with deliciously threatening chrome: danger. To want to be *overtly aggressive* in an age extremely intolerant toward overt aggression: danger.

And when these urges cannot be acknowledged, they are repressed, find a substitute, and are projected: it's not that mum deeply resents her children and has elaborate fantasies about disappearing into the night, it's that the lawn has dandelions and junior dropped out of lacrosse. It's not that dad hates himself and everyone he allows to disrespect him on a daily basis in a swirling jacuzzi of regret and incrimination, it's that he has to drive the kids to school again. Examples are as cheaply obtained in the firstworld as fast food.

And yet what almost no one understands consciously, is that *hysteria is not driven by fear*, but by the need to express and *achieve* some other urge. By making a fuss about the house and becoming bizarrely attached to very selective aspects of her children's wellbeing which benefit nothing but her vanity, mum achieves her original aim: taking revenge on her family. This is called "the return of the repressed", and it is the secret behind the "helicopter parenting" so increasingly common.

Listen again to Freud:

> [...] daß durch den ganzen ins Werk gesetzten Abwehrmechanismus eine Projektion der Triebgefahr nach außen erreicht worden ist. Das Ich benimmt sich so, als ob ihm die Gefahr der Angstentwicklung nicht von einer Triebregung, sondern von einer Wahrnehmung her drohte, und darf darum gegen diese äußere Gefahr mit den Fluchtversuchen der phobischen Vermeidungen reagieren. Eines gelingt bei diesem Vorgang der Verdrängung: die Entbindung von Angst läßt sich einigermaßen eindämmen, aber nur unter schweren Opfern an persönlicher Freiheit.

> [...] by means of the whole defensive mechanism thus set in action a projection outward of the instinctual danger has been achieved. The ego behaves as if the danger of a development of anxiety threatened it not from the direction of an instinctual impulse but from the direction of a perception, and it is thus enabled to react against this external danger with the attempts at flight represented by phobic avoidances. In this process repression is successful in one particular: the release of anxiety can to some extent be dammed up, but only at a heavy sacrifice of personal freedom.

> *Das Unbewusste*, §IV

...Or with the sacrifice of the freedom of the group: hysteria is highly *socially* effective, and does much more than merely cope with personal anxiety. Hysterical anxiety has the power to generate *new opportunities for control*: anyone who's ever been seriously involved with an anxiety hysteric knows how much power over group priorities this kind of neurosis wields. This is no accident and not merely collateral damage: it is the return of the repressed and a vector for social power.

- 10 -

In the case of COVID, what are we told is the cause of the histrionic fear? The fear of death? I don't see fear: I see hunger for oppression, for sanctioned violence, to find someone to banish. At most I see fear of abandonment, fear of finding oneself outside the narrowing circle of exclusion.

Why therefore a fear of disease? Why did COVID seem to strike just the right note? Why is a fictional pandemic so well suited as a displacing substitute? My first answer is that COVID stands in the place of the *real pandemic* of which we do not want to be aware: an epidemic of chronic illness is all around us. It turns out we *are* in the midst of a health crisis: the health crisis of the 21st century firstworld is the collective degeneracy of the human race as we speed toward a global unity of chronically bad health. Endocrine disruption, an irremediably fouled microbiome, an unhinged and exhausted immune system that can only grind out chronic inflammation everywhere in this bloated modern body, obesity, increasingly sedentary habits, ubiquitous and logarithmically rising anxiety, dark secrets of depression, a careful tapestry of interwoven addictions, and psychosomatic disorders multiplying faster than they can be catalogued: this is the pandemic.

- 11 -

In an age of ubiquitous psychosomatic disease, are we to believe that our problems are "merely organic" and thus the body's fault? It's as though the further down this road of a chronic psychosomatic pandemic we travel, the more need we have of disguising the increasingly obvious etiology from ourselves. At most we are willing to talk of "stress", and the armies of biomedical pillpushers are more than willing to chase the symptoms of stress with their pharmacological savagery, but we seem increasingly unwilling to address the *causes of our mounting stress...*

And yet I believe COVID is about much more than this.

Again, the COVID debacle is *not* about conversion hysteria: if that were true, there would have been a few mass outbreaks of short-lived psychosomatic symptoms, obvious placebo and nocebo effects, and the whole episode would have been over years ago. But COVID hysteria is *not* merely "contagious panic": it is long-lived, long-brewed neurosis releasing the accumulated frustrations of our civilization.

I might concede that the COVID episode may have begun with some hint of a mass conversion hysteria, and thus "converted" the rising awareness of chronic illness into a suitable scapegoat – but COVID quickly took on a more sinister flavor and gathered other repressed content in its wake: it released the accumulated *repressed aggression* of our age. Therefore COVID demonstrates amply the morphology of what I wish to term *mass aggressigenic hysteria*.

Most readers of Freud assume that hysteria expresses a repressed *sexual* urge: we are much more comfortable with this idea and feel smugly superior to the Victorian age by dint of our sexual sloppiness. Yet early Freud said no such thing and this kind of assumption is probably the easiest way to dismiss him wholesale, as is so popular now.

I quote now from his first book, *Studies on Hysteria*:

> Eine Beleidigung, die vergolten ist, wenn auch nur durch Worte, wird anders errinnert als eine, die hingenommen werden musste. Die Sprache anerkennt auch diesen Unterschied in den psychischen und körperlichen Folgen und bezeichnet höchst charakteristischerweise eben das schweigend erduldete Leiden als „Kränkung". – Die Reaction des Geschädigten auf das Trauma hat eigentlich nur dann eine völlig „kathartische" Wirkung, wenn sie eine adäquate Reaction ist, wie die Rache. Aber in der Sprache findet der Mensch ein Surrogat für die That, mit dessen Hilfe der Affect nahezu ebenso „abreagirt" werden kann.

> An injury that has been repaid, even if only in words, is recollected quite differently from one that has had to be accepted. Language also recognizes this distinction in mental and physi-

cal consequences; it very characteristically describes an injury that has been suffered in silence as *Kränkung*, "mortification". The injured person's reaction to the trauma only exercises a completely "cathartic" effect if it is an adequate reaction – as, for instance, revenge. But language serves as a substitute for action; by its help, an affect can be "abreacted" almost as effectively.

Studien Über Hysterie, §I.2

This invaluable German expression says it all: *Kränkung* is literally "making sick", and yet in modern German it means "an injury to one's feelings" – just as "mortify" means literally "to deaden". *Resentment makes us sick*: when we have the humility to examine our own language honestly, we learn something.

Here is Freud, right at the beginning of his career expressing what has become so glaringly obvious and scrupulously silenced: *repressed aggression makes us ill.*

In an age of "safe spaces", which is an age of *maximally distributed policing*, which is an age in which morally charged and thinly disguised aggression is consistently rewarded while honest overt aggression will earn you banishment, a swarm of slandering social media flies, and nasty implications driven by the increasingly homogeneous crowds of cramped hungry bigots – is it any wonder that strategies of moral posturing are so popular? Everyone an activist, everyone an evangelist, everyone an actor, everyone adept at anticipating the slightest shift in group consensus: if you cannot feel the nausea at this point you have no hope of understanding what I mean, when I say that repressed aggression makes us ill. There are in truth only a few prepared to thrive in a milieu of maximally distributed policing: most are merely conformists and uninspired placeholders hoping to escape punishment; some of us only learn the game secondhand and hesitatingly; but most of us know the sting of a thousand poisoned paper cuts, and most of us carry around a half-dead bodymind tattooed with accumulated shallow scars, whether we know it or not.

- 13 -

"Aggression" is only a word for some of the many responses and urges a creature exhibits, the true origin and nature of which we do not hardly understand. It's less important to attempt a premature neurological catalogue of behavior or a taxonomy of instinct, especially in humanity where instinctual coherence has become so weak, than that we develop an intuition for the *mechanism of repression*. Exactly what's repressed in each case varies, and in mass psychology there can only be a vague description of the general character of this content – but the mechanism remains uniform and easily recognized. Therefore when I say "repressed aggression" one should call to mind one's own experiences of frustration, resentment, humiliation, and those many slights and subtle digs you accepted in the moment and lived to regret... It is the *accumulated collective resentment* of the human race, increasingly passive, clever, and noxious in its strategies, which drives us to respond so homogeneously en masse: misery makes unity.

- 14 -

To return to our formula of hysteria: a displacing substitute *both obscures and expresses* a repressed urge. Why does this post-menopausal woman lavish so much attention on her garden of gaudy flowers? Why does this dude who can't keep a girlfriend obsess with his gleaming "crotchrocket" of a motorcycle? Both displacements obscure but express the original impulse in unmistakable symbolic terms. Take this model and use it elsewhere: to imagine *frustrated aggression* in place of loneliness and desire is all that's needed to open up a surprising vista of insights into the gaudy vaudeville of moral posturing, political correctness, and petty politicking which everyone and their grandmother seems so attached to.

Therefore what does aggressigenic hysteria accomplish? It obscures the repressed aggression even while offering a rationalized vector for its exercise: which also happens to be one of the indispensable ingredients of a fascist enterprise. We seem bound to fall backward into a reinvented fascism with the same tired labcoat-disguise and a police-with-unclear-jurisdiction because we cannot afford to acknowledge the absurd misery of our privileged yet frustrated lives.

- 15 -

It's an almost trite observation that highly repressed people are *most subject to hysteria*: Freud mentions monks, nuns, old maids, and strictly raised children. Therefore all that's required to set your thinking straight concerning COVID hysteria, is to try on the assumption that we are, as 21st century citizens, *highly repressed*: wishing away aggression does not make it go away. It results in what I insist be termed *moral posturing*: just as neurotic perversity is the result of sexual repression, moral posturing is the result of aggressive repression – see my previous work for a detailed analysis of the "morality of morals"...

- 16 -

It's important to emphasize that the displacing substitute, the *Verschiebungsersatz*, does not merely function as rationalization for anxiety: it is chosen carefully in order to maximize the social benefit of this expensive emotional display. One exchanges a little self-respect for the rewards of moral posturing. The modern human creature is orders of magnitude more clever and effective in the construction and execution of its neurotic games than in any facet of its conscious life. Its mendacious self-congratulatory political attitudes may appear merely reactionary, but it is in fact highly calculating and attuned to the slightest changes in collective direction.

- 17 -

So if hysteria is the partial achievement of a repressed impulse via the leverage of anxiety, and if COVID hysteria is driven by *repressed aggression* alongside the overwhelming need to *create new criteria of exclusion*, as I assert it is, what are the gratifications this hysteria affords?

⌐ To see one's neighbors condemned to a petty hell of loneliness and futility: a hell the majority of those most "concerned" by COVID were already acclimated to.

⌐ To see the minority of the young, healthy, and active punished for the inequity of their happiness: revenge upon those who have successfully generated an industry of envy out of social media. That this lockdown-revenge seems to harm those less ostentatious and genuinely active young people is only sauce for the goose.

⌐ To displace blame and defer the reckoning with the specter of chronic illness: a collective sense of repulsion and dismay is accumulating and cresting just above the conscious horizon. Everyone and no one knows that something is deeply wrong with our health when one quarter of our children are obese, when the average age of the cancer patient is dropping steadily, when among the most privileged quarters it might be difficult to recall anyone over the age of 30 who does not suffer from some chronic and perhaps psychosomatic ailment.

⌐ To invert the concern with overpopulation and redirect the rising sense of claustrophobia and panic concerning planetary limits. One of the chief mechanisms of unconscious distortion is simple inversion: add a sign of negation to the formula and repression lifts. What do I see when I read, "Saving Lives"? I see the desire to crush vitality, to handicap fertility, to shackle children. One also obtains the right to fantasize that the necessary depopulation will follow along the lines of conformity to the COVID narrative: "may the unbelievers perish".

⌐ To distribute a one-size-fits-all politically correct mask for the exercise of morally justified witch-hunting. For the accumulated aggression of the average slob, COVID serves as an excuse for *anonymous violence*: one obtains the right to ugly illiberal attitudes toward the unvaccinated and to wish police brutality upon them. This means that one does not need to be black, or transgender, or any other politically privileged identity to obtain the right to morally justified aggression. COVID spills *the prize of victimhood* among the unremarkable white masses.

⌐ To create a stringent membership with criteria that disqualify precisely those whom one finds most threatening: the independently minded, those immune to hypnosis and willful stupidity, the creative, the robustly healthy. This is driven by the frustration of the great mass who are made painfully aware of their insignificance, who are seduced by celebrity status and the salacious fantasies of global capitalism, who belong nowhere, who daily devour the corn syrup magma from the teats of this monster and only grow more hungry... But this alienation and subdued panic of a lonely creature, like a mouse caught at daybreak too far from home, extends all the way up the chain of power: the mad thirst for a final secure membership that might end the unbearable and mysteriously emissive alienation which seems to permeate the 21st century – the age of "connectivity" and "social" media – is a force which no one, no matter how much wealth or power they obtain, seems able to escape. And of course the fact is that *privilege heightens the sense of cultural poverty*: it makes loneliness and meaninglessness seem yet more cruel, ironic, and hopeless. Most lottery winners succumb to their own emotional immaturity. It is largely toil, artificial scarcity, and a community of equally distributed misery that stabilizes the average human wretch: we globally suffer from the pangs of the nouveaux riches, prematurely freed from the life of honest labor which held together the repressed but highly functional psyche of our grandparents, and unwisely freed from the traditional strictures which gave a horizon and canon of values to the human creature. To the precise degree that the cosmopolitan future of a cushioned throne of ubiquitous yuppie self-absorption is achieved, the likelihood of COVID hysteria and neofascist measures increases: for example, Australians are more susceptible because they are more homogeneous, comfortable, and lacking in cultural loyalties – in other words, "emancipated".

Vaccination status wanted to be a passport to 21st century citizenship. Biomedical profiling may yet be exploited to institute a new pseudoreligious criterion of exclusion, with the power to excommunicate those who will not bow before a false idol: the people thirst for the certainty of a religious worldview. It has been taken from them and replaced with a shallow *cargo cult scientificality* – but give this cult enough time and it will gather all the elements of religiosity back under its spreading wings.

- 18 -

To return to our question: *what is hysteria?*

Hysteria is the discharge of instinctual frustration in the form of anxiety. But anxiety is *not* the motive force, nor merely a maladaptive accident, nor dysfunctional: *hysteria turns anxiety into leverage*. It is the first clever twist among the neurotic topologies: *Verschiebungsersatz* stands at the head of the class in the school of neurotic strategy. None of these mechanisms profit much without navigable societal hierarchy, without labile functions of compassion and more than a little confusion among mores. Now is such a time: the rewards of victimhood are a spilling cornucopia attracting a grasping gawking crowd – but as the scene becomes more obscene and farcical it begins to look more like a sloshing pool of vomitus on the schoolbus no one wants to address.

What's the evolutionarily adaptive value of "mass aggressigenic hysteria"? This pattern is too widespread through history to be a simple "cognitive error", a case of misinformation, or even a maladaptive syndrome: there is something highly effective and evocative at play – an ancient ritual everyone seems to silently understand. What does a witch-hunt accomplish? It creates new enemies, new targets of justified violence, new hierarchical lines and criteria of exclusion: it creates novel opportunities for political power, social prestige, and moral credit. When we look at the hysteria of COVID and the protofascist measures applauded over so much of the firstworld, I believe we are looking into the face of an instinct rooted in our Pleistocene past as tribal creatures, whose success depended on group cohesion and navigable hierarchies – this is a *ritual of exclusion* which creates new tribal circles, purges the social context of outliers and threats to cohesive action, and in general acts as a *prophylactic against abandonment* for those in danger of being left outside some other order.

In other words, independence of spirit, ethical character, and intellectual conscience are *not necessarily adaptive*: otherwise they would be more commonplace. On the contrary, anticipation of the vicissitudes of the group, moral posturing, social jockeying, shallow character, and the cognitive dissonance to keep those processes viscous and responsive *is the norm*: this is the harsh awakening COVID offers us, if we can stand to grasp the monstrous scale of what we're witnessing. What might have been a short episode of moral panic accompanied by a few violent expulsions of the independent loners and antisocial pirates on the fringes of the tribe 10,000 years ago, is now a global farce perpetrated by those clad in the garb of science, sanctioned biomedical crime, and the threat of police brutality. 21st century atrocities will not do us the favor of announcing themselves as such: they will sneak in the backdoor, they will wear a labcoat, they will be perpetrated by doctors, low-level bureaucratic technicians, and frustrated policemen seeking reprieve from their creeping realization of insignificance.

Mass aggressigenic hysteria is the tsunami emerging from deep fissures: only as it reaches the coastline of visibility do the incredible forces behind it become apparent. It requires a *mass* hysteria to overcome the resistance of *mass* repression: we have been telling ourselves and our children that we are already nonviolent, that "nonviolent life" is not a contradiction in terms, that the famous hypocrisies of morality are a thing of the past, that our political programs are rational and achievable – despite targeting and contradicting not only the entirety of human past but biology itself. From this perspective, does COVID hysteria look *more sane*? Indeed what COVID hysteria achieves is a very rational outcome: the creation of outlets for aggression, the creation of enemies, the drawing of distinct political lines, a justified war. One way or another our Pleistocene nature will find expression: monstrosities bred in the darkness of moralized denial, the twisted limbs of a generation caught between the increasingly impossible demands of a hypercivilized urban supercolony and the maladaptive torments of a body bred 10,000 years ago - for now these are the most visible expressions of our old nature. But the horrors of the early 20th century are seeking another backdoor, and it seems they will find one eventually.

THE WITCH-HUNT
BELONGS TO MODERNITY

W e just termed COVID "a one-size-fits-all politically correct mask for the exercise of morally justified witch-hunting" – but what's a "witch-hunt"?

In regard to COVID vaccination status, employing the term "witch-hunt" is neither sloppy historical analogue nor mere poetic license. Yet again I find that the term is used by those who sense an important connection but are unable to explain the relevant psychology.

The first fact to internalize concerning the history of witch-hunting in Europe, is that it peaked many centuries *after* the pagan world had truly expired. Any genuinely native European pagan sorcery was probably fully extinguished by 1200 AD, and yet the ostensible fear of witches rose to fever pitch in the late 16th century.

Generally everyone already understands that a *scapegoat* function was at work: or what decent psychologists used to term *projection*. But what precisely was projected? And what was the function of this projection? The difference between the perspective I'm outlining here and the usual psychologizing, is that I refuse all explanations which are satisfied with a demonstration of the uselessly irrational in neurotic behavior: I see *functional adaptive behavior* in these ceremonies of histrionic fear. I see the tribal human animal reasserting its dominion – I see the solenoid of the Pleistocene way of life struggling to clack shut... Mass aggressigenic hysteria *creates enemies* out of an ill-defined mass of social mobility; mass aggressigenic hysteria *creates moral certainties* out of a tangled morass of uncertainty...

To understand 16th century Europe and thus a little of our own time, let's enumerate what had recently changed:

→ The New World: the discovery and colonization of the New World threatened the Eurocentric worldview in a way comparable to the increasing weakening of locality in our age of globalization.

→ The Protestant Reformation and the weakening church: Luther's religious revolt expressed the need for a more private and personalized inner life. Not only the increasingly normative atheism of our time lies parallel, but the palpable wandering ramification of spiritual tourism among the younger generations... Soon nothing will be exotic enough to satisfy, just as yoga has long been trite and subsumed into suburban monotony.

→ Heliocentrism and the dawn of modern science: as the Copernican revolution slowly gained a foothold, the heliocentric model served as effigy and rallying point for a much deeper and unquantifiable change in *épistémè*, as Foucault would say. This encroachment of science into the everyday, parallels the increasingly ridiculous attitudes of *cargo cult scientificality* which one finds everywhere: one is as likely to find oneself arguing epidemiological protocol with the gas station clerk, because one refuses to wear a facemask-talisman, as in previous ages obscure religious debates sometimes served as an excuse to spill blood in the streets.

→ The emerging bourgeois and incipient corporate power: the rapid rise of the Dutch East India company and its ilk could easily be compared to Silicon Valley powermongering, alongside the threatened and weakening nationstate.

→ But the most important parallel might be this: the printing press and the rise of literacy. An explosion of books and a new relationship to knowledge suddenly flooded this emergent bourgeois world. But just as the almighty Internet is largely used for porn, spam, plagiarism, and gossip, so the printing press largely instituted a new Misinformation Age.

What were the top two bestsellers for the first 200 years of the printing press? The Bible – arguably the most spectacular compendium of misinformation to date – and a spiteful little book called the *Malleus Maleficarum*: "the Hammer of Witches", a legal manual and propaganda piece advocating the extermination of witches. Oddly enough, the timing is even similar: 30 years after the invention of the press, the *Malleus* gained a massive following – just as 30 years after the rise of the Internet in the 1990s, the COVID fiction gained its unassailable fanbase.

Who was its author, this Heinrich Kramer? Predictably enough, a sexual predator and a church inquisitor, who was even a little too unhinged for the church of his day: analyzing his personal motives would be a disgusting exercise we can thankfully forego. We need only mention that repressed sexuality and its consequent perversions obviously played a role in the fascination with witches. But male targets of persecution were at times just as likely. I don't believe that sexuality nor misogyny is the determinative factor in the broader appeal of the witch-hunt: the need to *discover enemies from within* is far more powerful. Therefore we must ask again: why was this stupid hateful book so wildly popular in an age that lacked any real witches? Put another way, why would histrionic fear of an obviously nondeadly virus be so wildly popular in another age?

The enigmatic answer which we will unravel, runs thusly: *the reciprocal of anxiety is persecution.*

- 23 -

What we must understand is that when anxiety proliferates in a population, a set of instinctual responses is initiated which reveal our indelible tribal nature. The *Malleus Maleficarum* and the witch-hunt fever addressed and becalmed the uncertainties of the time: the surprising corollary is that the witch-hunt is not "medieval", it is *essentially modern.*

The medieval mindset was actually *less anxious* and thus less susceptible to moral panic. The medieval worldview was confident, pyramidical, and as redundantly buttressed against visible contradiction as a Gothic church. The "Age of Sail", on the other hand, frightened and overwhelmed the average newly literate bourgeois man: Francis Bacon and Galileo represented a tiny minority of those capable of being *inspired* by the New World and incipient science rather than terrified of it. Heinrich Kramer, Girolamo Savonarola, and Ignatius of Loyola represent the much more prevalent attitudes of bigoted outrage.

When Goya said, "El sueño de la razón produce monstruos", he expressed the same assumption I see in almost every analysis of the COVID panic: that if only the general populace were *more rational*, if only the scientific attitude were more widespread, our monsters would remain safely trapped within forgettable dreams. But this is false.

It is precisely the encroachment of the *unrelenting uncertainty* which true science demands, the gradual undermining of religious harmonies and their prettily painted and nested *matryoshki*, the weakening of moral categorical imperative, the increasingly urgent "whereto" of the common man lost in the bewildering infinitude of the Information Age like a monumental chip aisle stretching to the vanishing point, with more choices than anyone could ever need or desire – to be *crushed by choice*, suffocated by a freedom of mind which only grows more parodic the more it is hastily buried beneath a frantic moral posturing and political mimicry – it is this uncertainty and the frustration of the innocent human animal to live a simple life with definite horizons, which *produces monsters*.

But Goya was perhaps subtle enough to have understood me, and meant not "the sleep of reason" but the *dream* of reason: the monstrosities of modernity, the atrocities which we regenerate, the history we seem doomed to repeat, is *always* disguised and perpetrated and *justified* by precisely that same "rationality". No word was tossed around more enthusiastically circa 1933 than "wissenschaftlich": the witch-hunts of modernity are conducted in a labcoat, in sterile conditions, draped with opaque bureaucratic filigree and every conceivable humanitarian posture... Make no mistake, should this path we're treading turn out to be the first steps toward a 21st century story of mass criminality, it will be conducted with the most assured and arrogant air of this same "rationality".

Haven't you noticed how the ostensible fear of COVID disappears so rapidly when in the presence of a justified outcast? How suddenly masks and infection vectors matter so much less than the opportunity to shame, blame, and police each other? Haven't we all noticed how the tone of this affair gradually became less about a pretense of cowering fear before a respiratory nuisance, and more about *hunting down the unvaccinated*?

We are now in a better position to ask *what repression is,* and discover its relationship to the untethered homeless anxiety our age is saturated with. We must first distinguish between complete successful repression and partial botched repression:

⇁ *Complete repression* halts the instinctual discharge before the associated affect has a chance to proliferate and seek energetic investments: the feeling remains virtual, merely as-if, like a thoroughly forgotten dream. Successful repression generates the kind of ominous suffocating atmosphere of your Midwestern grandparents, that old-fashioned New England stoicism, or the British "stiff upper lip". Anyone familiar with the robust rigidity and hermetic seal of the life of a true obsessive, would also have a clue what "successful" repression looks like.

⇁ *Partial repression* occurs when the initial energetic investment is repressed, but the displacing substitute is not fully integrated into the semantic network that is the unconscious mind – like a half-dead fly in a web it shakes and rends the whole psyche. This is the case with most neurotics one meets today – and thus almost everyone: that like the rest of their lives, their neurosis itself is uncommitted, ambivalent, and full of caveats and prevarication. They are usually partially aware of their problem: just enough to dislodge and disrupt the mechanism of repression, but not half enough to be free of it. Stuck halfway between the high-functioning repression of traditional life and the imagined freedom of a conscious convalescent: such is the modern wretch.

This pitiable individual suffers from partially lifted repression, a shallow psychological education and the lingua franca of therapeutic vocabulary, damaged half-functional societal institutions of previously coherent repressive schemata, and the abandonment by the community to their own "self-help" in the midst of unthinkable contradiction: partial sexual liberation alongside more repression of aggression than ever; "celebration" of individuality alongside more moral censure of dissent than ever...

Therefore the proliferation of anxiety in modernity is not due to any decline in the capacity for discerning danger, it is due to the almost exponential growth of *instinctual frustration*: but this frustration itself *is* a danger. I insist that anxiety is adaptive: it is social leverage, it encourages group restlessness and destabilization of priorities, it prepares the way for

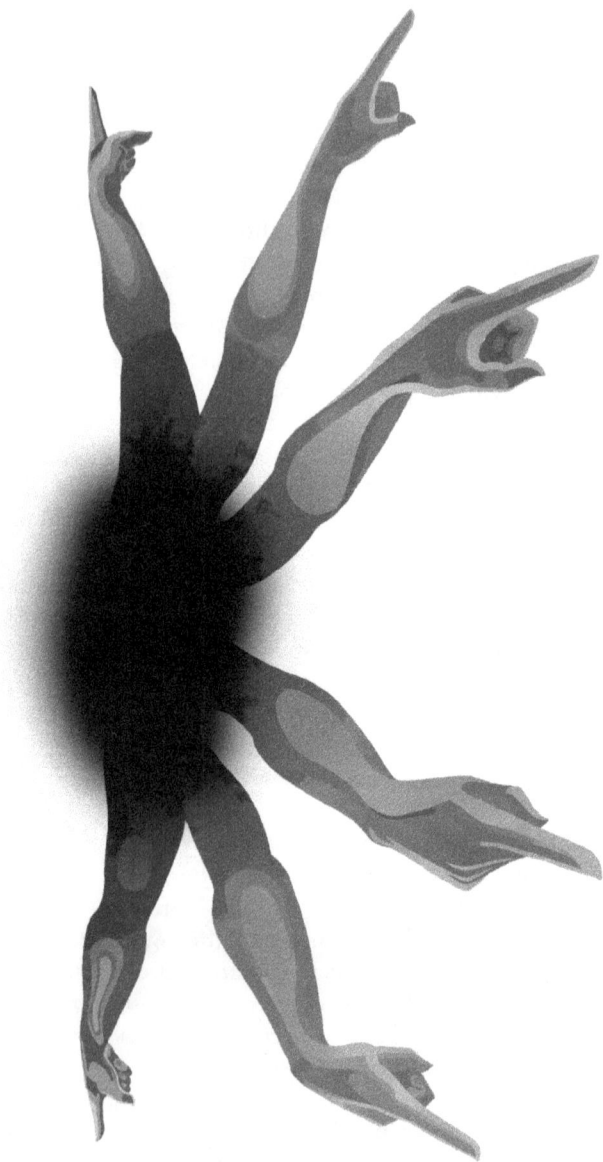

"acting out". Something is wrong, someone must be blamed, something must give.

- 25 -

There is a common confusion of the term "hysteria", as applied in two cases:

1. Those who are truly subject to their fears, as in paralyzing phobia.
2. The bad-faith histrionics of the social maneuverer.

21st century psychology is comfortable enough diagnosing the crippling anxieties of modernity – or at least in herding them into pharmaceutical dependence – but ignores and denies all signs that *anxiety has a social purpose*. What could the nail-biting agoraphobic, the evangelical preacher of doom, and the COVID-unvaccinated witch-hunt have to do with each other?

But the truth is that these types are deeply related and lie along a spectrum, in which the saturation of subjective anxiety dissipates proportionally to the degree of complicity in ritual exclusion and disguised mass violence: like unexpected origami, *paralyzing anxiety is inverted into persecution*. Personal anxiety on the one hand, and emboldened group persecution on the other, are merely the embryonic and full-fledged forms of the same adaptive response to frustration: to achieve social advantage through the rituals of fear, emergency, and even heroism. If you don't believe me, see the history of the mob violence of early Christian monks against pagans and Jews, the destruction of the Serapeum, and the French Revolution. It should serve as sufficient parable to learn that the paramilitary *Parabalani*, who were originally uneducated nurses recruited to handle local epidemics, were eventually lawless bodyguards to belligerent bishops seeking to forcefully subdue unbelievers in the 5th century: how long until a "Public Health Task Force" is given perpetual emergency powers in your jurisdiction? Will the next pandemic seal the deal?

Where Freudian theory falls short is when it fails to see *the aggression within ceremonies of fear*: rather than maladaptive and uselessly neurotic, I see modern anxiety as just another sneaky vector to advantage within sociality. The more permissive toward manipulative hysteria and histrionic victimhood, and simultaneously intolerant of *overt* aggression our age becomes, the more anxiety proliferates as a profitable strategy. One may be paralyzed and overwhelmed by the symptoms, but the initial phases of the anxiety response may eventually have a chance to develop into their evil twin sister: mass persecution, the witch-hunt, the reign of terror.

- 26 -

If the illustration accompanying this piece does not make you shudder a little in recognition, you have not been paying attention to these last two years. Notice how the center is dark. Radial blame bristling from an anonymous core: that is what I mean by the ancient force of "ritual exclusion". This is a ceremony all of us already understand: we merely take up our places within or without the circle – there are no other loci. One of the most valuable and surprisingly joyful aspects of the COVID debacle, is the way it's brought together disparate scattered loners and the invisibly ethical: we did not know where we stood until we were tested. Like a broken down subway car or a stuck elevator, suddenly it seems worthwhile to communicate with strangers – suddenly I share a political alignment with people I would never otherwise associate with. COVID is a darkness which reveals autonomous lights: may we never lose sight of this.

THE WITCH-HUNT BELONGS TO MODERNITY

MUTUALLY DEPENDENT FICTIONS

- 27 -

So much for mass hysteria and the witch-hunt. In this postscript, I turn the laserbeam around: how has fighting the COVID monstrosity been gratifying for us? Do some of us crave that transient relevance and are we sorry to see the ceremony die away?

- 28 -

The mechanics of hysteria can help us understand yet another curious fact about the COVID debacle: how the histrionic fear of a nondeadly respiratory nuisance has managed to distract and defer reckoning with one of the few serious ethical questions at the heart of the problem: should we allow the virologists who almost certainly engineered this disease to go unpunished? Why shouldn't "gain-of-function" research be considered *more dangerous than nuclear weaponry*? Despite a long history of lab leaks, virologists openly boast of hybridizing smallpox and synthesizing polio as though they were doing the world a favor. There is an extremely plausible reason the COVID virus has curious properties and seems especially virulent: it was *engineered* to adhere to human lung tissue, tested against one of the more monstrous attractions of the increasingly macabre menagerie of 21st century science – human-hybrid mice with a humanized immune system and human lung tissue. Here a little panic might do us some good: yet in a slow moving mass crime, the perpetrators are both absconded and applauded. Why?

Because hysterical dynamics demand that any unritualized danger be avoided: else the displacing substitute will lose ground and the whole farcical ceremony of fear will dissolve into rational action. The unexciting sobriety of rational action is therefore not something we can expect within the large fallout radius COVID commands. A *fictional pandemic* is highly desirable for the expression of repressed needs - a real emergency must therefore be suppressed and ignored: that's the mindjob of COVID.

- 29 -

In COVID a conspiracy is afoot, but not the kind everyone assumes: there is no grand governmental conspiracy, no "Great Reset". All such theories are wishful thinking and betray the inability to let go of the comforting notion that someone, somewhere, is in control: the truth is that *no one is driving the bus.* If only humankind were wicked and motivated enough for a grand conspiracy! ...rather than merely clumsy, unconsciously suicidal, and running from its own reflection. The forces of global capitalism do not strictly benefit from lockdown: there was no need for a "Great Reset" because things were already befitting the ruling classes. Accelerating wealth inequality was already an avalanche toppling the 20th century into the 21st.

We desire oppression because we desire *relief from the anxiety of individuation*: that is the "grand conspiracy" governmental forces are scrambling to keep up with like a Ben and Jerry's factory in the 90s. That a crowd of political opportunists and the hyenas of global capitalism are circling the bloody scene is hardly surprising – but temple-moneychangers, scalpers, and desperate demagogues should not be confused with masterminds.

- 30 -

I must concede that the awkward facts of sly cooperation between a Chinese lab and the US National Institutes of Health, for whom gain-of-function research had been previously forbidden, obviously motivated the initial coverup and indeed constitutes a *minor* conspiracy. But there are always minor conspiracies at play at any given time in human history: such is politics and the cleverness of apes. In other words, even if we eventually discover many more conspiratorial forces orbiting this maelstrom of power and deception, *it's irrelevant.* It's much more important to ask: why was the general public so deeply and immediately attached to the pandemic narrative? Why was your neighbor, your friends, your family, your spouse so attached to it? Why did everyone seem so eager to participate in a decentralized, silently scripted, and *unconscious* conspiracy? Try on this hypothesis: the media *sell what sells*, not what they are "told" to sell. Despite the appearance of uniformity, there is no smoke-filled backroom where the "elites" plan our future with deep cackling laughter: as though Bill Gates, Joe Biden, Oprah, a Pfizer executive, the editors of the Lancet, and Xi Jinping meet in an underground cavern and deliver speeches to a roaring crowd of torch-bearing and hooded billionaires. The human world is not this well-organized: it's greedy, opportunistic, mendacious, and fearfully conformist, not devilishly determined. The most well-funded military in the world, the American armed forces, can hardly keep from shooting itself in the foot... But an *unconscious* agenda spreading through the most homogeneous elements of the absurdly miserable first-world – that's possible.

Therefore despite all the sloppy mishandling, the improvised diversion-ary tactic of overstating the danger of COVID succeeded beyond anyone's expectations: like a delusional alchemist accidentally discovering gun-powder, with this fictionally deadly pandemic Anthony Fauci and company stumbled upon the right formula for releasing the accumulated frustrations of firstworld misery. They lit a match in the dark without knowing what that funny smell was...

- 31 -

It seems almost no one has the intellectual conscience to stand these two statements side by side:

1. The virus is not deadly and therefore does not constitute a pandemic.

2. The virus was engineered and for that reason alone should be taken seriously.

In the case of many of my present readers, who have admitted that the virus is not deadly and who are unspeakably nauseated by COVID hyster-ics, there is reason enough to ignore statement #2: because if it was indeed engineered, it would seem to contribute to the fearful aura – some would rather deny the virus exists, than acknowledge that it is a very dangerous precedent and could indeed have curious properties – such as an immunosuppressant function. "Long COVID" is all too real. The truth is that we were merely lucky it wasn't something much worse – although forcing experimental mRNA gene therapy on half the world might in the end be *much worse*...

It would be easy to imagine that among those who lap up COVID hysteria as though it were a steamy bowl of amphetamines, the lab-leak story would be enthusiastically adopted and put to work. But I only see the most entrenched conspiracy theorists taking this route: those who want to believe that the virus was meant to depopulate the globe. There's no reason to accept the explanation that "the media" is reporting what it's told to report. Look more carefully at your neighbor's attachment to the pandemic narrative and you will discover something else: an *entirely fictional* pandemic is desired by *both* the conformist, *and* the conspiracy theorist... Do not be deceived: the actor knows the play is false. Its falsehood is necessary for ritual efficacy: unconscious stewardship of a fiction is one of the prerequisites to magical thinking.

The bad news, my friends, is that the conspiracy theorist is also subject to hysterical mechanics: in place of a fictional pandemic he has substituted a fictional grand conspiracy... The result is the same: *vicarious identification with the perpetrators*, victimhood and justified powerlessness, and the continued belief in a guiding authority. Neither has the capacity to acknowledge what COVID teaches, what COVID forces upon our closed eyes: the human world is *largely unconscious*, largely flailing, largely afraid of its own reflection.

- 32 -

Who is the conspiracy theorist? A powerless nobody, an outsider, someone with surplus intelligence to burn, someone who'd like to prove to themselves and anyone their *eligibility for power*. A conspiracy theory is a fantasy of power, a steamy novella of intrigue sold to oneself and anyone who will listen. Haven't you noticed how eager he is to spread his secret knowledge? How *being witnessed as knowledgeable* is central to the whole formation? Moreover, haven't you noticed how much these types seem to *want* a "Great Reset"?

Who's the mirror image of the conspiracy theorist? They would have us believe they stand opposite the "conformist": the great majority who merely seek to get by, wincing and grimacing and seeking to escape notice. Most conformists have their quiet questions, and many have already admitted what's true and what isn't: but talking themselves out of their better judgment is their specialty – one glance at a life drenched in regret and half-hearted choices should tell us how easy it might be for someone like this to stack merely one more lie atop the pile. The Asch Conformity Experiment should tell us, that the great majority of the human race will betray its own judgment for the sake of belonging, even when *almost nothing is at stake*, other than *one moment* of standing outside group consensus. So great is ritual exclusion and our tribal ancestry.

But the twin brother of the conspiracy theorist is the *evangelist*: he who mines the narrative for all the power it can offer, he who is is wedded to the narrative for the sake of the dowry alone, he who has found in the histrionics of COVID the motherlode of moral-political charade.

But how are these two mutually dependent? Because every evangelist needs his demons: the best enemy of a glaring monumental fiction, is a frightening exaggerated fiction. It's not that a lie cannot defeat a truth: truth is weak, multivalent, subtle, fragile – almost nothing is easier than displacing truth. A monstrous lie feeds upon truth like merely breathing – it gains no glory from pushing aside this weakling. A monster needs heroes to devour, to stage battles in the sky... In the midst of the monstrosity of COVID on the one hand, and the blustering frantic conspiracy theorizing on the other, haven't we sometimes felt ourselves slipping into the cracks, into an abyss of the loneliness of quiet and complicated truth?

And does the conspiracy theorist need his voracious evangelist? Absolutely: the alternative is retreat into a loneliness and irrelevance. Trailerpark all-caps raving about the "Great Reset", and sanctimonious upper-middle class hand-clasping about the necessity of vaccinating children into oblivion: one has a fugitive sense of rugged independence to comfort him, the other has his money and moralizing mien to hide his desperation – but they are not so different.

- 33 -

So what are we? Our critics would like to dismiss us as conspiracy theorists: untangling the Gordian knot of COVID neuroses requires far more psychological acumen and intellectual discipline than is commonly available, so it is hardly any wonder that my wouldbe comrades so often resort to paranoid speculations about what "they" intend and why. Where others cannot help but see agency, I see nonlinear emergent dynamics: all psychology begins as animism, and it requires many years to unlearn the habit.

And wouldn't it be an immense relief if a grand conspiracy were really at play? If something real and grandiose happened in our lifetime - if something could break the spell of meaningless anxiety and petty bickering? If an unambiguous enemy could for once be identified? As a 21st century American man undergoing the remedial education of offgrid living and incremental independence, I am all too aware of the pleasures of "prepping". We must also admit that the fantasies of global depopulation which have become so popular, appeal to us all at a deep level – and for us avowed misanthropes, this appeal is not nearly so unconscious as with the rest.

We too have indulged our moral outrage, haven't we? When I think of the countless millions of children tossed into the pit of COVID, their blood repeatedly polluted with biomedical profiteering schemes, their faces covered *as though youth were the problem* – my heart aches and I cannot help but want blood in exchange for blood. That this is just another slow-moving mass crime among so many, is too cynical for that moment of genuine recognition: what response do we have but anger? But what recourse do we have but indignant pride? The question is: can we walk the knife-edge of merciless truth? The path wherein no redemption, no solution, no justice is guaranteed nor likely, without losing our courage and cheer and determination?

MUTUALLY DEPENDENT FICTIONS

WE DID IT, NOT "NUDGE"

Chez eux, la faveur publique semble aussi nécessaire que l'air que l'on respire, et c'est, pour ainsi dire, ne pas vivre que d'être en désaccord avec la masse. Celle-ci n'a pas besoin d'employer les lois pour plier ceux qui ne pensent pas comme elle. Il lui suffit de les désapprouver. Le sentiment de leur isolement et de leur impuissance les accable aussitôt et les désespère.

Among them public favor seems as necessary as the air we breathe, and to live at variance with the multitude is, as it were, not to live. The masses do not need laws to coerce those who think differently. Public disapproval suffices. The feeling of their loneliness and impotence soon overwhelms them and drives them to despair.

de Toqueville, *De la Démocratie en Amérique*, §4.XXI

- 34 -

Some of us have recently become aware of something called "nudge theory": essentially a morsel of cognitive behavioral psychology applied to regulatory questions with an immense découpage of rhetoric and the right sort of corporate-compatible scientificality sufficient to impress the politicians who mete out budget – the kind of HR-friendly "science" that fits into a 15-minute presentation.

Laura Dodsworth, a British journalist, has become a bit famous for exposing the role this theory supposedly played in the COVID panic – at least in the U.K. and probably a few other European governments.

As gripping as this tale of gossip might be, this is definitely the *wrong direction* for any genuine inquiry into the etiology of COVID mass hysteria. Our governments – as duplicitous, as pernicious, and paternalistic as all bloated bureaucratic governments always are – are not to blame for the panic. *We* created it. The people wanted it: that any politician or governmental agency would like to take credit for it, is only a sign of how deeply motivated the whole ceremony was.

Therefore Dodsworth is just another aspect of the ritual: to *find someone to blame* was always the primary motive... There will no doubt continue to be many more exploits of investigative journalism: it's important not to lose sight of one's own intuition about what we saw in the faces of our neighbors and friends in those years – was it or wasn't it bloodlust, delight in having found a victim, the excitement of anonymous violence?

- 35 -

The perspective represented by Dodsworth says: "Everything important happens in government; the government is in control." Which is itself a very pampered and insufferably European point of view, isn't it?

Blaming the manifold mass crimes of COVID on some adorably ambitious government department and mere "policy error", is the *most politically correct means of securing a contrarian stance* – and therefore will be the majority view eventually. Dodsworth has merely anticipated and prepared the politically safe way to shunt blame for the collateral damage of the rituals of mass hysteria.

A grasp of the principles and predominance of mass psychology seems lacking: but this is only an illusion. It's already a tired truism to say, "a person is smart, people are stupid and dangerous." What's particularly difficult to grok, is that almost everyone already understands group psychology extremely well: what they seek is to be on the right side at the right time, and therefore feigned ignorance is essential – feigned ignorance of your own calculations, feigned ignorance of your trajectory mapping of group consensus, feigned ignorance of how often and adeptly we sample group consensus... Of course this dance of ignorance must itself be disguised, lest the pretense become conscious – make no mistake, *becoming conscious* in the midst of any of these commonplace cognitive distortions is guarded against at all costs: but how do we hide a feigned ignorance from ourselves? With "virtue": all too often, feigned ignorance is called humility, or prudence, or "maturity", or "social responsibility"... With a loud lie a quiet lie is hidden: moral posturing is the convenient garish lie we are accustomed to, and we take its presence as a kind of *sign of social quorum* – where three or more are gathered in the name of morality, an unholy spirit will appear.

- 36 -

The essential question is: *why did the majority love a fictional pandemic?* What's to gain? Why do people seem to adore fascism? This is one of my formulae: no conspiracy, everyone a conspirator. How can that be?

If we look at the totalitarian regimes of the early 20th century, if we ask Hannah Arendt about it, what does she ultimately say was the deciding factor? Firstly a threshold of homogeneity in needs and frustration among the middle class. A sense of going nowhere, with nothing to gain but a marginal distance from poverty, with nothing to trust but the inevitability of anxiety: remember this was before the age of television, internet, Xanax, and corn syrup – there were only slower and cruder drugs such as alcohol, laudanum, and newspapers. Therefore it starts to look probable, that what's happening is that firstworld misery has merely exceeded the threshold which the old 20th century narcotics were able to hold back – the levee broke, and the flood spilled. What's the ooze? *Alienation, frustrated aggression, and moral hypocrisy.* Those are the seeds of fascism, those are the seeds which call forth a fascist regime from the otherwise tangled impotent mess that is mass governance – *not* conscious planning, *not* conscious conspiracy, but something much deeper and more difficult to perceive except at greater historical distance...

- 37 -

Unless I'm missing something, I don't see in any of these governmental responses to COVID, anything like *indirect suggestion* or hypnoid means of control. I see repetitive slogans, hamfisted insistence, and the same kind of smothering condescending tone that a spa takes towards its customers.

I've lived in Europe. The way a Western European government relates to its citizens feels like something between a dentist's waiting room and a "Living With Herpes" brochure. To acquiesce in a thousand ways to the life of a stupid child, an invalid, a prematurely geriatric superfluity – and at the last moment suddenly protest: could it really be that Dodsworth and her ilk have just now woken up into the world their upper middle class preferences created *a long time ago*?

- 38 -

The "nudge unit" is simply the logical conclusion to the kind of socialist-creep the European has been supporting for decades: but suddenly they've noticed how inconvenient it is, when a government infringes upon the upper middle class lifestyle in another form other than the guilt-laundering service of a high tax rate. Suddenly an increasingly socialist state begins to look a little bit fascist? That this surprises anyone, is only further evidence of how common is the preference for a tame benumbed life, how shallow and worthless the general education is, and how little anyone has managed to internalize the history of the 20th century: I am not yet tired of repeating, along with the scholar A. James Gregor, that fascist doctrine was first developed by socialists.

It's not that I don't think anyone can be held responsible – again I'd love to see *the virologists who created the virus held responsible* – but that indeed a much profounder reckoning is called for than this superficial hand-wringing about some very British "ministry of conformity"... A reckoning with the civilizational forces that brought us here is called for, a revaluation of the viability of the coexistence of privileged freedom and paternal interventionist technocracy is called for...

- 39 -

I cannot for the life of me find a single example of a genuine indirect suggestion related to COVID – at least nothing beyond the typical marketing savvy which the average 20-something business school dropout might possess. The example which "nudge theory" seems most proud of, is the printed image of the housefly on the public urinal, which is irresistible to the urges of men and serves to make us less errant in our duties. I've seen these in airports and I admit it's very clever and effective. But everything related to COVID was clumsy, repetitive, obsequious, and not at all subtle but *hyperbolic*. If they were taking credit for the unconscious effects induced by an *exaggerated and histrionic* demonstration of fear, I would be impressed: because false, histrionic fear is indeed a powerful social signal. It says: "there's another hidden agenda of which we will not speak, and the goals of which you must guess." But above all, it promises: "Go along and you'll get your chance to play persecutor."

- 40 -

Please don't be overawed by the fact that a committee bestowed upon this Richard Thaler the Nobel Prize in economics. Economics is almost as weak a science as psychology, and perhaps even more susceptible to political fashion. Moreover this is the same organization that gave Barack Obama the Nobel Peace Prize for being elected, as though he had earned the same honor as Nelson Mandela: more than a little political buffoonery is at work here...

- 41 -

Behavioral economics seems to have gotten about as far as Hobbes: they've caught up to the idea that *humanity can be irrational* – and decorate the realization with fashionable vocabulary borrowed from statistics and set theory. But they have no idea of *unconscious mechanics*: neither repression, nor displacement, nor projection, nor overdetermination, nor the ethology of symbolization, nor the proclivity to envy among primates... They have no anthropological education and no historical perspective whatever – a Foucaultian sense for the recursivity of historical domains is entirely too much to ask. I'd almost prefer a Marxist economist to these impossibly smug professors of the *dismal science*: at least "class consciousness" would be closer to the mark, since it at least traces *impersonal* forces and sees the individual as a node in a network, rather than this impeccably bourgeois prejudice that the individual "mind" is the indivisible atomic unit in which all decision occurs. As though all meaningful psychology can be reduced to "cognitive bias" and a list of typical fallacies – as though human nature were merely a faulty computer...

Moreover, *"irrational" is incorrect!* No animal is strictly irrational: only under the extreme pressures of post-agricultural civilization does humanity begin to look "irrational" – which would mean nothing else than that it *fails to meet its own needs*. The instincts are above all *rational* in their outcome. And even homo sapiens in the midst of civilizational maladaptation, still achieves largely rational outcomes: one only needs to understand *what needs* are being met, to understand their functionality. I insist that merely two forces suffice to explain the vast majority of seemingly irrational human behavior: *loneliness and envy*. "Am I in the group? And if so, what's my status?" These two questions ring like an incessant bell in the head of modern humanity. The student of psychology who keeps them in mind will avoid many detours and deadends.

Social conformity, avoidance of abandonment, and unconscious strategic positioning: everything else is largely a matter of elaboration and disguise. That's the introductory phase of *my* "böser Blick".

- 42 -

There is another important factor never to lose sight of, when dealing with transient pop science of this kind: *what's the gratification?* should always be the first question asked. Why is "behavioral psychology" popular? Because it says: "People are irrational, but we're not." And for the small price of applause, you are invited to this club. And with one stroke, the increasingly obvious prevalence of unconscious mass psychology in an age of overpopulation is explained, defused, and neutralized – so that one may return to that "illusion of control" they like to speak of, without ever considering whether their shallow theorizing does not also constitute an *illusion*.

- 43 -

Y'all are granting far too much power and sophistication to these cognitive behavioral psychologists: actually they are sloppy, uneducated, and forgettable. "Evidence-based" behavioral psychology is fundamentally the art of statistical fraud, political posturing, and shallow quantization methods: they seek to study the multivariate statespace of social behavior with blockheaded questionnaires and computer-administered multiple-choice. Their studies are a test of the subject's willingness *to anticipate the socially correct answer*. Among insiders, it's well known that no other field is so riddled with fraudulent wishful "evidence": in the case of Diederik Stapel, he was just a little too lazy about hiding it.

Moreover, modern psychology is largely the field which collects aimless academic nobodies too lazy and untalented for real science: thus the predominance of the lonely cat-lady, the simpering neckbeard, the soft-handed urban manchild seeking authority over those even more neurotic and impotent than himself. Who becomes a psychologist today? Desperate bescarfed women who begin their middle age in their late 20s, who collect patients like roadkill, who feed on a transient sense of superiority and sophistication only by gathering a following of true losers and keeping them ill. This is not godlike science, believe an insider: they have no power over anyone but the extremely weak and willing.

- 44 -

Leading a tangled morass of fully tamed, frustrated, anxious bores of the 21st century into almost any scheme is *easy*, as long as it appeals to funda-mental needs: distraction from personal failure, the illusion of meaningfulness, and social inclusion. Inducing histrionic fear in a popu-lation as cowering and feckless as the British have become, only requires a "nudge": but this fear is decidedly *not genuine* – it is a *simulacrum of fear* and moral prostration which everyone understood and already knew how to mime.

There is no nefarious psychological sophistication at work: merely endless repetition, intimidation, statistical fiddling, a serious mien, and various forms of inflating the hollow but brightly colored sack that is political clout. Have you ever attempted to impersonate an official in a vague context? Carry a clipboard, wear a pantsuit and an ID on a lanyard, frown and strut around and discover for yourself the power of undefined authority. Have you ever stood in line without knowing why? Have you ever felt a panic surge through a crowd? Manipulation of the civilized human race – the increasingly ill, increasingly alienated, increasingly bereft human race – requires no more psychological acuity than what an intelligent 15 year old girl is capable of crafting in her own tales of high school intrigue and betrayal, and since her enemies include the adept unconscious maneuvers of other high school girls, probably indeed much less.

- 45 -

Actually the hypnotic arts and the study of mass propaganda peaked in the early 20th century: Goebbels drew on a long line of scholars of propa-ganda, including some well-respected American and British thinkers in the mid-twenties – e.g., Edward L. Bernays, the "father of spin" and a nephew to none other than Sigmund Freud... In fact I might argue that the more religiously grounded, family-oriented, less neurotic, and slower-paced populations of the 1920s represented a *more difficult* populace upon which to work propaganda than the hapless, anxious, chronically ill, aesthetically hopeless mass of slobs that constitute the 21st century firstworld. We imagine that the Information Age and smartphones and plastic underwear add up somehow to proof of our intellectual superiority: but technological dependence and personal frailty increase proportionally – access to the sum of human knowledge does not make the average human creature "smarter", it makes it more desperate for a closed horizon of certainty.

- 46 -

The governmental use of propaganda is in no wise new: prewar Germany is not at all the only example, as both the UK and US used propaganda campaigns extensively before, during, and after WWII to great effect. At least the 1940s standard for graphic art was far superior to our own and their slogans much less sanctimonious. And I'd argue that repressive normalization, shame, and social pressure were employed more effectively during the hot and cold war efforts than at any time since: governmental paternalism is not new, mobilized shame is not new, subtle and unsubtle means of coercion are not new.

This show of outrage and cries of "anti-democratic" are just another strategic anticipation of political advantage, and in the final analysis just another stageplay by which the majority shall bury the embarrassing revelations under a flurry of noise.

- 47 -

Did you imagine that a life of meaningless drudgery – schlepping from an indifferently depressing apartment to a hopelessly vapid office to a monumentally monotonous grocery chain, only to repeat the same endlessly - was somehow rational, sane, and *volitional*? Did you imagine that Pepsi or Doritos or Toyota were somehow an objectively sane choice and not "nudged"?

Across the firstworld, these are the same people who are convinced year after year that the Oscars are important, that the World Cup and the Olympics are not a corporate orgy, that accruing carcinogens while sitting on your ass answering emails under fluorescent lights is "as good as one can hope for". These are all forms of *implicit and deferred violence* which the general population was already inured to.

That a government official here and there seized the chance to garner a promotion by seeming to have caused what was already happening, should not warrant our attention. COVID panic is not proof of some godlike power our governments have, it's proof of how weak, vicious, and thirsty the human race is for a form of sanctioned violence.

But the stupidity and gullibility of the civilized human being is *superficial* and only another disguise: actually it is constantly calculating its best advantage – that's what it means to be weak and vicious. It's only the strong who can afford to be stupid: they step out of line by walking in a straight line, they give the wrong answer when they believe it right, they lose their standing by standing their ground.

- 48 -

At first, in order to address the malformed heuristics of conspiracy theory and "policy error", I was going to write about paranoia and the persecution complex... I even picked up my old copy of Lacan's *Écrits* and was going to talk about the "paranoiac structure of knowledge" – which would be a fascinating navelgaze, I'm sure. And frankly it would be easy for me to waltz through the bespectacled latté-clutching crowd of urban trendsetters with Lacanian masturbatory aids like intricately crafted toys – and certainly I'd obtain more readers that way – but what I really have to say is not half so gratifying nor metapsychological: the induced paranoia among COVID skeptics is only another symptom, and *not* what prevents the dialogue from touching upon the truth. It's not paranoia, nor even lack of the psychological education sufficient to identify unconscious mechanics which guides this detour into a show of outrage at governmental schemes, – it's the unwillingness to face what COVID makes so painfully obvious: the overwhelming *hostility to youth, hostility to health, hostility to freedom*. It's an ugly underbelly, a revolting and somewhat surprisingly fierce hatred that bubbles there in the shadows – we didn't know how much resentment the firstworld had accumulated – so it is hardly any wonder that so few have the stomach for it. But perhaps the real answer is that so few of us are sufficiently free from this same resentment, such that we can afford to acknowledge it: our aggression has clearer lines of descent and ascent, and thus we have no need to hide the genealogy of our attitudes from ourselves.

- 49 -

The problem is that many of my potential readers have glimpsed for the first time, the *reality and power of the unconscious*. For the first time in our lifetimes, much of the human mass on this planet spasmed in unison, shared a nightmare, and began enacting its repressed urges. It's been known since at least Heraclitus and perhaps Democritus, that in large groups, the average human creature loses its inhibitions and finds its repressed impulses suddenly amplified – but many of you do not have the stomach for this vision, and would rather believe in vast conspiracies with vague objectives and even more vague means. Many of you would rather fantasize about global governmental control and "the elites", than face the fact that modern humanity requires no elaborate nefarious plot to obtain obedience from it, and that the world order has already been precisely what the elite class has wanted it to be, for a very long time.

Where others cannot help but see agency, I see nonlinear emergent dynamics.

- 50 -

And even those who would like to believe that the COVID panic was insti-gated by a program of subtle hypnosis, and thus give credit to the power of suggestibility and unconscious reasoning, are unaware of an important fact: the most powerful suggestion is *transmitted by an unconscious mind*. Conscious suggestion is nothing compared to the *ceaseless unconscious communication* the human species is born into. The most effective hypno-tist does not command nor scheme nor employ formulaic indirect suggestions, he trains his conscious mind to be quiet enough to allow his body to act effectively, and does not know precisely what he's going to do and cannot except in rare cases explain it precisely: these cute CBT methods of suggestion are nothing and indeed less than nothing – because they obstruct with smug shallow imitation and social shame more than they guide or heal – compared to the kind of Ericksonian mastery I'm speaking of.

- 51 -

We did it: but who do I mean by "we"? Everyone in the firstworld who has ever tried to be politically correct, whether left or right; everyone who employs repressive schemata to get what they want; everyone who navigates firstworld misery with the appropriate masks as though nothing were the matter; everyone who has ever compromised their better judgment for the sake of getting by; everyone who's ever swallowed a piece of petty aggression and lived to regret it; everyone who's ever indulged a shitty person because it was the "right" thing to do – in other words, *all of us*.

When I first heard of COVID, I noticed the glee and wishful bloodlust in the eyes of the informant. The next thing I did was to look up age statistics. Therefore on day one, I discovered the average age of death "from" COVID was around 80.

Those of us who never believed the histrionics, who like myself never capitulated and never wore a medical mask, who have fought it at every step – how could we be responsible? Because it's our world too, because we also made too many compromises with this same spirit in the past, because we were too complacent and indulgent of the strategies of moral posturing. If there is a "they" at work here, it is the swirling spirits of the worst of apenature: the mendacious moralist, the disguised bigot, the poisoncraft of lying-in-wait, the wannabe-fascist, the voracious bureaucrat, the bitter old hag and the avaricious old fart – the sick and geriatric of all ages.

- 52 -

The more government and policy and conscious conspiracy is blamed and suspected, the further recedes the revelation COVID offers us. The more that you, my dear skeptic, prefer to imagine government intention, international intrigue, or a plot of the "elites", the less likely it is that you will confront *the responsibility we all share*. This is not the first spasm of anonymous mass violence and it will not be the last: it's likely to be only the beginning of an age of ideological purgings, of dogmatic wars, of fictional enemies and very real consequences.

Yet I don't primarily feel afraid and I want above all to inspire courage: let's be grateful that the monster has finally surfaced from the deep! Let's be grateful that we have lived to see the plotting and envious bigots we previously suspected, finally play their hand. There is a sense in which many prematurely exposed their nastiness and *misplayed* their cards, so eager were they to see the independent and disobedient punished... It's our task therefore to internalize the lesson, to grow up into our own strength of character, to become hard, unyielding, a guardian of precious and delicate things. Truth and beauty is a delicate and precious thing, my friends.

WE DID IT, NOT "NUDGE"

HOARDING INNER
POVERTY

It seems many of those who would like to trace a causal line from the COVID affair to wealth inequality, are out of their depth when discussing "the elites". While we're partly sympathetic to the impulse, we also cannot help but suspect a combination of limited life experience and – once again – the urge to *find someone to blame*. Someone who is not your neighbor, not your mother-in-law, not your coworker, not the mailman, not your own grimy reflection.

Be not deceived: while there is immense and accelerating wealth inequality in our world, the extremes do not directly correlate to a *competence* inequality – nor an inequality of willpower, nor an inequality in the ability and willingness to take responsibility for human affairs. The rich are adept at becoming richer: everything else they do is largely just as short-sighted and emotionally limited as the rest of humanity – and with the additional means of avoidance and displacement, often much more emotionally truncated.

I once worked as a "building superintendent" – a sort of glorified janitor – for a Wall Street broker with some Manhattan real estate. He had made his money in derivatives before the 2007 crash, and was proud of having thieved hundreds of millions from the world. But he was paranoid, fragile, pathetically grandiose, and personally impotent – most of his joys came from harassing his tenants and kvetching about minor expenses.

A billionaire is much more likely to obsess about the leaves in the pool he never swims in, than the course of world affairs: he simply does not have the ego strength for anything else. The reality of the life of an obscenely rich man is generally not one of mighty conquest, farsighted ambition, and actualized powerlust: those are extremely rare qualities, limited perhaps to a few political monsters here and there, a gifted corporate climber, and probably just as often occurs in those whose ambitions have less to do with money. And even in the case of an exceptional rags-to-riches Horatio Alger type, the success usually undermines precisely their strengths and draws out their latent weakness: the biography of any compelling rockstar demonstrates this amply – Elvis died on the toilet.

- 54 -

A billionaire or a powerful celebrity is typically *regressed*, childish, impossibly vain and fragile. He lives in a gilded cage of yesmen, chauffeurs, and goosedown buffers between himself and everything uncomfortable. The rich usually don't manage their own money, much less want to bother with our collective fate. They're not tough-minded, realistic, nor even really prepared to think in the long-term: they *avoid* reality because they avoid confrontation with who and what they really are. Upon realizing a high degree of wealth, most will immediately begin a program of *regression, indulgence, and denial*. Everything else is merely the gilded showmanship and guilt-laundering of "charity". At most, among the older money you find a practiced cynicism, apathy, and class hatred that borders on realism, but not much more.

- 55 -

Most of "the elites" obtained their position through *dumb luck*. Many of them are vaguely aware of this – especially the newer Silicon Valley type – and seek to hide it from themselves through many distractions and pretenses to mastery: actually confronting the unthinkable complexity of our world and the manifold difficulties of accomplishing anything that money cannot buy, would be far too much to ask.

- 56 -

A billionaire hoards *inner poverty*. He carries shantytowns of poverty, a bottomless pit of poverty, an endless hunger of poverty.

- 57 -

Or did you imagine that our squelched life of obedience and drudgery is somehow inconvenient to the superrich? Do you imagine that if and when peak oil drives food price inflation, that it will be the billionaires who suffer? If a cheeseburger cost $1000 tomorrow, it would only taste all the more delicious.

They don't need you to stop traveling to beautiful places: they loiter on islands you've never heard of, they linger on yachts in international waters, they step on your heads as you line up like cattle for products you don't need... In fact, they *revel* in the grotesque numbers of humanity, because it makes them feel that much more important. Without your squirming numbers and your desperate faces glimpsed from tinted windows, they might begin to feel their spiritual poverty.

The elites have no need of depopulation – in fact most of them are so lonely that this secret alone would be enough to forbid any such plan... It is *we* suckers near the bottom of the firstworld who would benefit from depopulation! Thus our fixation on the problem...

- 58 -

Only a few very sharp characters deep in the NSA or MI6 or whatnot, would have the kind of willpower and patience necessary to have done anything significant relative to the COVID affair: and I don't rule this out. I'm quite sure that more than one covert operation took the opportunity to test out a few pandemic scenarios, and probably more than one CIA analyst feels very gratified to see his predictions play out... And probably there have been many coverups, many *competing agendas*, many silent wars of intrigue going on in the background – as is always the case in politics. And perhaps after all, this virus was leaked intentionally. And perhaps the Wuhan laboratory was only framed. And perhaps someone did have a depopulation scheme in mind when COVID was engineered. There's not much point in these speculations, and the important thing is not to indulge them, but to observe in oneself how much *you want it to be true*: you wanted a deadly pandemic, you wanted to see the world burn, you wanted something vital and serious to snap the monotony and diseased ease of your stunted life in half, so that you may set yourself free to become something worthy of the human ancestry – a survivor, a warrior, a real woman with a fearless heart and a real man who can shape his spirit into a quivering blade.

- 59 -

Let's pause here and note something I just said about the likelihood of *competing agendas*: no doubt, within the belly of most intelligence agencies there are covert groups which compete with one another – *without knowing it*. I can imagine a CIA legend about the two agents with adjoining offices battling each other for years without ever realizing who the enemy was. And what's probably even more likely, given apenature, is that they know very well and are all the more rivalrous. The *comedy of errors* did not achieve its place among the arts for no reason...

- 60 -

Of course, a deep appreciation of accelerating wealth inequality is all part of the healthy breakfast of our 21st century philosophy – but such an appreciation should not devolve into magical thinking regarding an Illuminati pantheon. The human world is greedy, opportunistic, extremely efficient in its exploitation of power niche: what Foucault names "une microphysique du pouvoir"... Like most complexities, it operates most efficiently through emergent bottomup dynamics, not topdown guidance: attractors exist as inevitable expressions of underlying constants, but imagining that the conscious plans and conspiracies of any one human agency do anything more than *exploit opportunities* is to be hopelessly ignorant of the history of war, intrigue, and politics.

The sobering truth about the presently increasing wealth inequality on this planet, is that it most likely represents a *course correction* from the brief aberration of 20th century wealth distribution: in other words, the socioeconomic consequences of *cheap fossil fuels*. The period between 1945 and 1970 was probably the easiest time to thrive in the firstworld – thus the insufferable babyboomer attitude. The only graph you really need from economics, is the one which maps wage against inflation: it flattens sometime in the 70s – but somehow the American underclass has been cajoled into believing they are still the middle class, and that $35k/year is still a living wage, despite the fact that a house costs an order of magnitude more than it did 40 years ago.

- 61 -

When I speak of "firstworld misery" and pampered passivity, some of my readers may not understand me. We are surrounded by forms of wealth it's effortless to overlook: serviced roads, a reliable electric grid, sufficiently safe cities, a stable currency, and access to clean water. Most of the firstworld *shits in potable water* – something once considered a capital offense in some places.

Not to instigate more guilt – but to be *unashamedly grateful* for this wealth and take responsibility for navigating this world to the best of your ability and advantage:

> ... die Ungleichheit der Rechte ist erst die Bedingung dafür, dass es überhaupt Rechte gibt. — Ein Recht ist ein Vorrecht.
>
> ... the inequality of rights is the prerequisite to the existence of rights. Every right is a privilege.
>
> Nietzsche, *Der Antichrist*, §57

Can you internalize this insight, without resorting either to a pretense of moral outrage nor a disingenuous belligerence? Our birthright is also a burden. In other words, *we are the elites*.

- 62 -

As I keep laboring to point out, indulging in conspiracy theory, blaming governmental manipulation, or worst of all to shrug about "policy error", defers confrontation: the small sphere of your life, the tiny circle of influence, *where you put your body in space and time*. Indulging in theories about which you can do nothing, and which even if true are not harmed by your wild speculations but largely helped – nothing helps a real conspiracy like a crowd of wild-eyed morons missing the point and generating red herrings – is all trivial compared to confronting what you *can* do today. And what's unjustly overlooked amidst all this noise, are the quiet stories of that kind of confrontation: there are many who chose to forfeit a job, uprooted a life, ended a relationship, and resolved to live a better life... To confront the reality of who and what people are around you – who can and cannot be trusted, how precarious our freedoms are – that is our task.

WHAT IS LONG COVID?

- 63 -

This is the point where the Möbius strip makes its fateful twist. This is the point where the autotrophic Klein bottle cannot resist. This is where we separate those who want to tell the whole truth, from those who only want another ideological *cause célèbre*.

- 64 -

We must grow into the intellectual conscience and *emotional maturity* required to tolerate these two statements side by side, without allowing either to neutralize the force of the other:

1. SARS-CoV-2 is *not at all deadly* and therefore does not qualify as a pandemic. The COVID affair was a case of what I call mass aggressigenic hysteria.

2. SARS-CoV-2 was *engineered* in a laboratory and for that reason alone should be taken seriously. Long COVID is probably a consequence of this engineering[1].

- 65 -

Truth is n-dimensional, and takes no leave from our narrow expectations nor gives any quarter to our hopes. Despite what we skeptics might wish, long COVID is all too real.

I have sought to be unyielding in my insistence that the COVID affair gained the traction and prominence it has, because it lit a match under the gunpowder of firstworld frustration: for at least 2 years, COVID was a case of mass hysteria on an unprecedented scale. But there is so much happening at once in all this, that the whole story could never possibly be simple, nor convenient, nor ideologically aligned. The SARS-CoV-2 virus is not a scam, nor was the entire panic somehow orchestrated by an unimaginable global conspiracy, and unfortunately, while *not at all deadly* by itself, the virus does have curious properties which should be taken seriously.

I'm proud that I never sought to hide this from myself, and published it as early as the spring of 2021. Since then, I've done more research concerning the mechanism of long COVID and most importantly, I have personal experience which has convinced me all the more of my initial intuition: *the whole thing stinks*. Everything about this is upside down:

¬ **We're told the virus is deadly:** it's not remotely deadly, which a glance at the "infection fatality rate" across ages tells us.

¬ **We're told the virus was not engineered** and did not come from the Wuhan Institute of Virology: its extraordinary ability to invade human epithelial tissue says otherwise, as does its origin[2] next door to the most advanced virology laboratory in China where they had previously declared their success[3] in mutating the original bat virus known as "SHC014" – as does common sense, and the *merest familiarity with human hubris*.

¬ **We're told endlessly about "new cases":** yet the virus is known to be so extremely virulent and largely asymptomatic that in all likelihood, every human being on planet earth has had the disease at least once by now, and the majority of urban dwellers have probably never been rid of it since first exposure in early 2020.

¬ **All attention has been on the sick and dying:** while *comorbidity* has been conflated with conspiracy theory, and almost no one has studied the effect on the young and healthy – yet in my opinion this is all that matters and has ever mattered. The young and healthy are the future and keystone of the human race, not the moaning geriatric sea of avarice and waste.

Therefore only now, years later, is general attention finally turning to what I noticed the very first time I acquired this nasty little bug: *an unsettling power of immunoevasion*. Only now that the ceremony of histrionic and demonstrative fear has waned, now that the gratifications of moral posturing have paled, has the general populace begun to reluctantly admit what's been obvious: it doesn't make you sick, it makes you *unsick*.

- 66 -

Here's a confirmed finding[4] worth internalizing: Post-Acute Sequelae of COVID-19 (PASC), commonly referred to as "long COVID", are observed in 30–70% of individuals post SARS-CoV-2 infection. My guess is that this number is actually much closer to 100%, and that the symptoms are only masked by *other chronic illnesses*: it's already a very crowded and depressing elevator ride, here in the overburdened and underutilized modern body...

- 67 -

A word to those readers who refuse to believe anything "the Science" says anymore, and have learned to doubt not only the seriousness the virus but the existence of "long COVID" itself: how could someone like myself, who strives to be unyielding and more accurate than anyone else in diagnosing the COVID affair as mass hysteria, consider recent COVID research anything but collective lies and posturing? I say as much freely, when it comes to social psychology. I am only too glad to swaggeringly dismiss whole fields devoted to topics such the history of morals, consciousness, and the origins of religion.

What we must learn is that the human creature tends to tell the truth in the *minute details*, while happily propagating a monstrous lie as long as it spans further than individual responsibility. We prefer the big lie to the petty lie. The modern human being will not cheat his taxes, will not cut in line, will present his resumé truthfully – but he will also gladly *live a lie* and participate in obscene falsehoods as long as they are socially advantageous. For example, the explicitly religious may profess absurd things which no one actually believes, but they drive their cars sensibly enough, they bake cakes and write books and ride bicycles without a trace of absurd belief; they make good chemists and mechanics and computer scientists – in some ways they are in fact *more sane*, because their anxieties and absurdities have a terminus and a harmless sphere of activity...

These biologists are therefore to be trusted when they speak of the *details* of their science. When they talk about "ACE2 receptors", "Type I Interferons", and "STAT1 transcription factors", they are telling the truth. When they go along with the *peasant-superstition of ignoring comorbidity*, they are telling lies. When they interpret and advise, they are clowns. As soon as

THE SEEDS OF FASCISM

they speak of the "social good", as soon as they put on their moral costume, as soon as they appear "concerned" and correct – it's best to laugh and move on.

- 68 -

It's one thing to study infection fatality rates, age distribution charts, and comorbidity data: almost anyone can do that much and it required therefore only the merest intellectual conscience to realize how much everyone was lying to each other about the deadliness of COVID. But studying the possible mechanism and implications of long COVID is an entirely different matter requiring an education in immunology, genomics, transcription factors, and cell signaling: fields which are brimming with impressive findings and complicated nomenclature which add up to *almost more ignorance* than we started with, because this fundamental ignorance of the bewildering complexity of vertebrate life gets gussied up in *arrogant but still shallow* science which lacks respect and awe before biological reality... Probably a contributing factor in how and why we ended up in this mess, yes?

Therefore, I don't want to pretend that I'm fully qualified to interpret the mountain of research concerning COVID's effect on the immune system. However, due to the way COVID has polarized us, there is a serious dearth of sane interpretation and so I feel forced to research primary sources for myself – as is almost always the case. One finds generally only three approaches:

1. *Opportunistic fearmongering*: most talk about long COVID is so overdetermined by the manifold delights of hysterical displacement, that it amounts to intolerable nonsense.

2. *Myopic tinkering and cowardice*: the biologists qualified to summarize and interpret the data, are so absorbed by the minutiae of their findings and their own petty rivalries in the burgeoning fields of cell signaling and epigenetics, that they almost unfailingly cannot see nor speak articulately of the bigger picture. A certain professorial myopia is to be expected, but this factor combines with the atmosphere of political terror to produce scientists who *hide behind the details* – and anyone who steps out of line to say the obvious seems to be simply ignored and cannot get published.

3. Rabid cynicism of the bystander: there is a small but vocal minority of skeptics who have become so nauseated by the moral fraud and cognitive dissonance at work in the last few years, that they will tolerate absolutely no talk of any danger relative to COVID. Many of them believe long COVID is merely hypochondria – and no doubt *much of it is.*

- 69 -

Let's get something straight. "Severe Acute Respiratory Syndrome" (SARS) is a *syndrome*; it is not a *cause* of disease. Both CoV-1 and CoV-2 cause SARS. Somehow in the midst of all this noise, most of the bystanders seem to have never fully understood that what we're dealing with is a novel virus in a family of viruses which causes a *well documented syndrome* – namely both SARS and MERS.

- 70 -

> The SARS coronaviruses use various mechanisms to hamper IFN production and response. Consequently, target cells proximal to the site of the initial infection fail to receive critical and protective IFN signals, allowing the virus to spread and replicate without hindrance. A hallmark of SARS-CoV-2 infection is impaired IFN-I and III production and responses, which masks the IFN-related fever symptoms and leads to naive spreading of the virus.
>
> "An aberrant STAT pathway is central to COVID-19"[5]

Long COVID both is and is not a mystery.

⌐ It's been known for many years that SARS-CoV-1 suppresses interferon signaling (IFN) and demonstrates post-infection sequelae that may last 6 months. SARS-CoV-2 follows the same pattern: therefore long COVID is no mystery.

⌐ While the cluster of symptoms known as "Severe Acute Respiratory Syndrome" is well documented, and many of the mechanisms which cause it are fairly well understood, the reasons behind the post-infection sequelae of the SARS coronaviruses are not fully known. In addition,

SARS-CoV-2 shows key differences from its predecessor which may contribute to its longevity in the body.

Therefore long COVID is a minor mystery: although one which I believe is relatively unimportant to solve in theory – much more important is to solve it *in your body*, which most of us are already working on, whether we know it or not.

- 71 -

Even without any special intervention, I believe any healthy immune system can defeat long COVID. I am not in the business of handing out concrete medical advice, therefore I will remain silent about my own tactics: but finding this information is relatively easy, and requires careful personal experimentation in any case – anyway personal experimentation is always the *healthy* attitude towards health, not the one-size-fits-all barbaric reductionism of biomedical modernity, in which healthy bodies represent a *threat* to the thriving industry of shuffling doomed cases around an unthinkably expensive junk drawer of savage interventions... One day our age will be considered medieval and barbaric, because of the arrogant brutality of our attitude toward the human body.

- 72 -

What I can tell you, is that no one knows for sure what long COVID is. My best guess at the convergent mechanisms are:

1.   Extremely effective mACE2 binding. SARS-CoV-2 is *many times more virulent* than CoV-1 and seems to invade various tissues of the body with a ferocity that's difficult to account for, other than the efficiency with which it binds to the cellular transmembrane protein site known as "(membrane) angiotensin-converting enzyme 2", or mACE2. Every virus has to sneak through the cell wall somehow, and this one does so by presenting a key for opening one of the trapdoors along that wall. This efficiency seems to be driven by the infamous *furin cleavage site*: otherwise known as the "virologist's smoking gun". It's known that CoV-2 binds about 20 times more effectively to target cells than CoV-1: which means it infects new hosts more readily, and invades tissues more fiercely.

2. *Immunoevasion*. SARS-CoV-2 suppresses interferon signaling in a way similar to CoV-1, but due either to the mACE2 binding efficiency which might create *viral reservoirs* deep in various tissues, or some other as yet unexplained immunoevasive pathway which CoV-1 did not have, CoV-2 seems to either match or exceed the ability of the first version to persist.

3. *Reverse transcription*. There are some highly qualified researchers[6] who are convinced that CoV-2 has the ability to reverse transcribe itself into the human genome: so far they've discovered sufficient evidence to claim that CoV-2 chimera found long after viral clearance are likely due to partial reverse transcription. This does *not* mean CoV-2 qualifies as a "retrovirus" in the same sense that HIV does, because these fragments seem not to be viable. However, the theory does account for persistent positive tests in patients who are clearly not ill. And most importantly, the theory could help account for long COVID: it's possible that the strange persistent mild symptoms in healthy individuals, are due to a kind of autoimmunity. Infected cells whose genetic material now contain fragments of the virus via "retrotransposon mediation", are theoretically expressing these viral chimera and thereby triggering sporadic immune response, although the virus is actually largely cleared.

In other words, it's very easy to catch, and very hard to eliminate. And even once technically dead, it may have coded itself into infected cells such that the immune system reacts as if it were still present.

- 73 -

All this accounts for my own personal experience with long COVID. I hesitate to resort to anecdote and reveal anything personal – but on the other hand, this entire affair is precisely defined by a profound *invasion of the personal* by very impersonal forces: what power do we have when some blithering virologist anywhere on the globe arrogates himself to endanger the collective health of the human race, but to *take it personally*?

What's funny about my case, is that despite my conviction that lockdowns were entirely ineffective and a function of some of the ugliest moral hypocrisy imaginable, I myself have been living in a self-imposed "lockdown" for years. Therefore I represent in several ways an ideal case study:

⇁   I live many miles from any outside human presence.

⌐ During 2020-2021, the span between my visits to civilization ranged as high as 2 months.

⌐ I am very healthy. Every day, I hike several miles through my desert backcountry.

⌐ I have an extremely reactive immune system: when I caught swine flu in 2010, I was briefly in mortal danger due to a raging "cytokine storm".

⌐ Because I have traveled and lived in the developing world, I'm familiar with a few serious diseases. For example, I've had *dengue fever*: the lingering symptoms of long COVID remind me of dengue, which required about 3 months to fully dissipate.

But even dengue and the resulting fatigue eventually cleared: I've never experienced anything like long COVID. What I believe has been happening is this:

⌐ For most of 2020-2021, during every trip to the outside world, I was catching COVID again. This is due to its extreme virulence and the laughable ineffectiveness of lockdowns and the masking policy.

⌐ During the weeks of isolation that followed each exposure, I was fighting off a new infection and possibly variant strains. This leads to a slowly accumulating overload of an immune system which is nonetheless being evaded, due to interferon suppression.

⌐ Most of the infections were *asymptomatic* – at least they would be considered so in most modern human subjects of the firstworld. What my lifestyle helps reveal, is that this asymptomatic quality is actually an illusion: *I could tell*, because I exercise vigorously, because I expose myself to extremes of temperature, and because I am otherwise much healthier than is common among firstworld adults. For more than 2 years, there was low-level chronic inflammation in my upper throat and nasal passages, which only becomes noticeable in a *harsh cold wind*. My supposition, is that nearly *everyone has similar symptoms*, but they are masked by other problems: lack of strenuous exercise, reliance on sugar and caffeine for energetic input, unfamiliarity with the subtle variances of microbiotic health, dependence on profoundly mood-altering pharmacological weaponry such as SSRIs, and so on.

In other words, most of the firstworld is already so mildly ill with a large variety of systemic problems, that they simply do not have the kind of health which would be discernibly impacted by the disease. Everyone has had it many times over, and likely almost every child on the planet has already developed sufficient natural immunity, despite all the perverse unconscious attempts to sabotage their future.

- 74 -

We're all going to be fighting SARS for the rest of our lives: true. But please remember with all due sobriety, that we have all been fighting an enormous variety of endemic diseases up to now – including some coronaviruses which cause the syndrome we call the "common cold": the reason young children are sick so often is due to the accumulated backlog of endemic diseases which civilization has been collecting since roughly the agricultural revolution of 8000 BC.

- 75 -

To reiterate:

→ SARS-CoV-2 is extremely virulent, because it was engineered to adhere to mACE2 cellular receptors in human tissue. This accounts for *both* its virulence and probably contributes to long COVID.

→ Infection is largely asymptomatic.

→ It evades immune function, namely via suppression of interferon signaling. This is the same kind of interferon antagonism of CoV-1, which accounts for the asymptomatic presentation and contributes to long COVID.

→ The moment it leaked, it was with us forever and all efforts to stop its spread have been futile and more motivated by the desire to express Foucaultian civilizational brutalities, than "save lives".

So what's "long COVID"? The consequences of engineering a virus which already possessed immunoevasive powers, with the perfect mechanism for binding to human lung tissue.

Fortunately, the vertebrate immune system is an awesome power, with multiple redundancies and backups. Defeating one of its primary mechanisms in a very targeted way, as these viruses do, may lead to viral longevity but ultimately a healthy immune system will win via alternate channels. It's a war of attrition: what the research seems to indicate, and what my own experience says, is that the immune system may only be operating at 5% capacity, and thus what could take a healthy system only a few days to overwhelm and destroy, requires months.

- 76 -

Hidden in the COVID research, are hints[7] of a possible *longterm autoimmune syndrome*. This is the point at which the COVID affair becomes serious again.

Here we should exercise extreme caution in speculation. We should avoid the gratifications of hysteria: dreaming up worst-case scenarios affords a fleeting sense of importance; but more vitally it displaces anxieties into a visible target...

Nevertheless, it's crossed my mind often enough that I believe it's worth saying in a very quiet voice: it's possible that continued reinfection, the gradual establishment of viral reservoirs in the many tissues which express mACE2, and the hypothetical potential for reverse transcription in infected cells, will lead to an AIDS-like syndrome. It's known that a single HIV infection is generally not sufficient to induce AIDS: multiple infections with variant viruses are required to overwhelm the immune system sufficiently, such that AIDS sets in over many years.

But, perhaps this is only likely in the unhealthy: a beta-coronavirus is not HIV. What's most likely, is that SARS-CoV-2 will continue to circulate endemically like any other virus, becoming less virulent with increasing herd immunity, and despite all its special abilities only represent *another single notch down* in the collective human health. Civilized humanity has dealt with many diseases much more serious than this for the last 3000 years: smallpox, typhoid, cholera, tuberculosis... Only another step down the ladder from Pleistocene health, only another dent in the door of this jalopy, only another bean to count.

Therefore, although COVID *represents* something extremely dangerous from at least two angles:

→ Emotionally stunted virologists fucking with biological timebombs without adult supervision.
→ The potential for mass hysteria in a globally united humanity thirsty for anonymous mass violence.

My guess is that in the final analysis, the virus called SARS-CoV-2 is actually trivial next to several other factors impacting human health: for example, the *sugar epidemic*. An *annihilated microbiome* due to the uncontrolled consumption of sucrose next to the uncontrolled consumption of antibiotics is probably orders of magnitude more serious to the future of the human race than SARS ever could be. The *obesity syndrome* and its associated endocrine imbalance is probably many times more urgent to address... But those are real problems, and real problems require mature adults – and emotional maturity grows scarce in an atmosphere of pampered anxieties and emboldened hysterical displacement.

1. https://doi.org/10.1021/acsmedchemlett.1c00274
2. https://doi.org/10.37282/991819.22.13
3. https://doi.org/10.1038/nm.3985
4. https://doi.org/10.1016/j.cell.2022.01.014
5. https://doi.org/10.1038/s41418-020-00633-7
6. https://doi.org/10.1073/pnas.2105968118
7. https://doi.org/10.1038/s41590-021-01104-y

OUR BODIES RESONATE WITH MALADAPTATIVE FRICTION

Rumour is a pipe
Blown by surmises, jealousies, conjectures,
And of so easy and so plain a stop
That the blunt monster with uncounted heads,
The still-discordant wav'ring multitude,
Can play upon it.

Henry IV Part II

- 77 -

It's no longer cool to talk about COVID. The central mass has moved on and the distractions multiply. There are and have been already many trajectories of denial, forgetfulness, and the redirection of blame. There was from the beginning, a barely concealed sense of embarrassment which only vanished in the midst of the most frenzied histrionics: much of it found concealment in blank-eyed obedience – the same kind which most of the population employs in its daily contortions of humiliation and drudgery. Many quietly enjoyed the irony: at least everyone finally seemed closer to an equality of punitive absurdity. This is the consolation of a traffic jam, a brutal commute, a stalled bus: everyone's in the same fix.

Why is it so important for us to fully analyze this mess? Not because we are naïve enough to believe in the machinations of justice, and not because we believe we can prevent its recurrence, but because we can prepare ourselves. The COVID affair was not isolated: it represents an emergent pattern of civilizational maladaptation which has occurred before and *will again*.

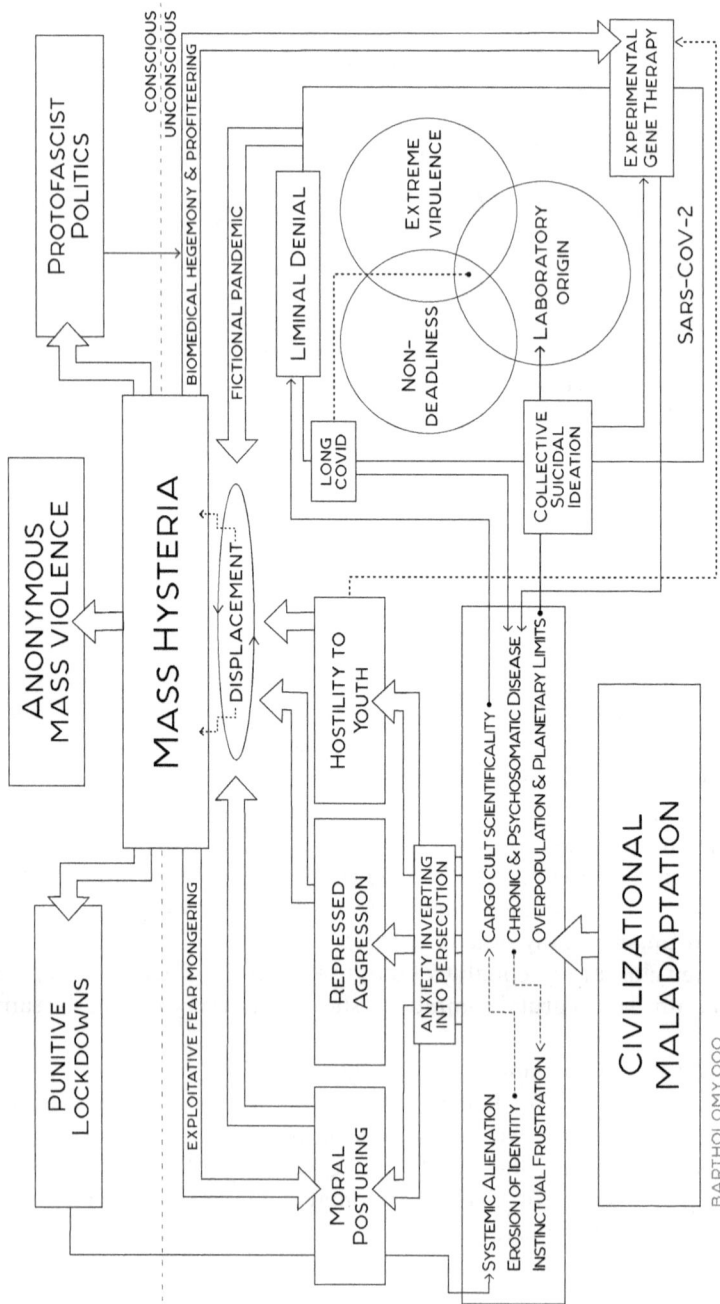

BARTHOLOMY.OOO

In order to model mass psychology as a dynamic system, we must take seriously the idea of *feedback*. What causes feedback? Primarily, responsive limitation: friction, orbital constraint, limited dissipative capacity. There are only so many modes of dissipation in any one system, and only so much energy any one mode can dissipate. But there is also systemic response to output: the system changes ambient environment which modulates energetic input – "self-oscillation" or negative damping.

As far as I know, no one outside the very limited sphere of the "synergetics" enthusiasm of the 80s and 90s has yet taken this idea terribly seriously in the realm of psychology. Yet in economics it's a commonplace: hence bubbles, crashes, and their cycles. Worried talk about the "echo chambers" of the internet is also common enough.

Yet I seem to be alone in focusing attention on *bodily misery* as a causative factor – in conceiving of the human body and our *collective health* as a resonance chamber and a form of cultural memory, in which what we *feel* determines what we *do* which determines what we *feel*: I will not participate in the farcical quest for some noumenal ether in which psychology is supposed to take place, as though "the mind" were the only entity at play in mass psychology or cultural history or sociological institution – the *body* is at stake. *What we do with our bodies in space and time*: we must constantly attenuate all thinking and dreaming which does not return to this formula, and remind ourselves of what finally matters. Our intellectual life is not an end in itself, but a weapon and a weaponizing.

Firstworld misery caused the COVID affair, which amplified firstworld misery, which prepared the way for a more efficient manifestation of whatever the COVID affair was becoming before it lost coherence. The path of the tornado is still quite visible however, and the winds still swirling: the substrate is more homogeneous and prepared than previously.

> Par leur puissance uniquement destructive, elles agissent comme ces microbes qui activent la dissolution des corps débilités ou des cadavres. Quand l'édifice d'une civilisation est vermoulu, ce sont toujours les foules qui en amènent l'écroulement.

In consequence of the purely destructive nature of their power, crowds act like those microbes which hasten the dissolution of enfeebled or dead bodies. When the structure of a civilisation is rotten, it is always the masses that bring about its downfall.

Gustave Le Bon, *Psychologie des Foules*, Introduction

- 79 -

Please take a close look at the diagram accompanying this chapter: it's the result of years of reflection and many productive conversations with a student of mine. Every path and grouping is well considered. I'll elucidate a few special points:

⇀ The first thing to notice about the diagram is that nearly all vectors reside in the *unconscious field*: "unconscious" means unknown, unseen, and gains special significance through an understanding of the traceable marks of repression. And yet all these vectors are visible via their displaced representatives: the reason I know about these factors and have come to name them, is because I've learned to trace backward the paths of displacement along semantic lines. However what becomes most visible at the top of the conscious field – namely lockdowns, protofascist politics, and especially anonymous mass violence - due to their genealogy deep within the unconscious field and a long history of displacing substitution, take on an uncanny aspect in the light of day. They are never precisely what they seem to be, never what they name themselves, and always imply much more than they are ready to proclaim: "aménagements subtils d'apparence innocente". Anonymous mass violence never announces itself as such: it is always justified, rational, fair, and – most dangerous of all – *compassionate*.

⇀ *Mass hysteria*: see the previous chapters to understand the scope of what I mean by this term. We must not allow the richness of our best psychological insight to be buried underneath the renewed effort to conceal our nature from ourselves: in other words, "hysteria" remains very much a relevant syndrome.

⇀ *Exploitative fearmongering*: by this phrase, we mean both media exploitation, and the many political and industrial agencies which found advantage in stoking the flames of panic. Notice that it feeds back into *moral posturing*, which then feeds into the swirl of displacement powering *mass hysteria*: a histrionic atmosphere of false postures encourages the many actors who thrive under conditions of hysteria, which further repulses and disqualifies honesty and rationality, such that those traits in the mediocre majority are suppressed. Most of humanity is not dominated by either truthfulness nor pure deception, but adapts itself to the time and place according to minimal risk. Much of the "panic" was merely *mimicry*: just as most belief is.

⌐ *Liminal denial*: this is a region of partly obscured denial. We may think of it as "preconscious" falsehood: something very like the pretense involved in religious ceremony. What's involved in "belief"? A will to *ignorance* accommodated to a will to *power*: we make many things true by collectively behaving as though they are. Therefore, none of the facts shown within this region are "repressed" in the strict sense: everyone knows, as well as I do, that the virus is not deadly. What everyone does not know, are the *social consequences* of acknowledging what they know – but they can guess well enough.

⌐ *Long COVID*: notice that it emerges as a confluence of these denied factors, and yet stands slightly outside the realm of denial. But only now that the ritual coherence is dying away, is group attention turning to this reality: because a reality cannot by definition fuel a hysteria without distortion, but it does retroactively seem to confirm the seriousness of the virus and thus provide shelter from repercussion.

- 80 -

The effort to blur the mirror of COVID, extends from those who want to hold government manipulation responsible, to those less clever who would like to blame "the elites", to those nearest to our camp of psychological interpretation who nonetheless miss the mark by a wide margin – *on purpose.*

I'm aware that the newly coined "mass formation psychosis" has gained a certain popularity. However I find in this term yet another evasive maneuver, and more symptomatic of the manifold efforts to disguise what COVID reveals than descriptive of what happened. *COVID had nothing to do with psychosis.* Once we understand the full implications, the inherited term "mass hysteria" is a much more fruitful and accurate place to begin a diagnosis.

It is by definition impossible for a psychosis to be shared: psychotic phenomena are characterized by a *severance of social function* and a reversion to idiosyncratic and novel forms of hallucination. Cases of so-called *folie à deux* are rare, and arise only in the context of a very intimate and dependent relationship, such as the mother-child dyad: the delusional contagion is largely just mimicry.

The psychotic *stops performing* socially, and instead generates novel symbolic relationships to his world, in response to an overwhelming disturbance of previous egoic structures which could no longer withstand the tension. *Psychosis cannot be shared*: this is the original sense of the term "idiot" – one who cannot be reached. *Hysteria* however, and its fundamental mechanism *displacement*, integrates almost seamlessly with social function in the tribal animal, which has a constant need to reassign blame and manage the delicate economy of frustrated instinct within the demands of communal living. When these frustrations reach a critical threshold, they generate an order parameter I call "ritual exclusion": enemies must be found within the tribe, because the tribe has ceased to function efficiently. I insist that all of this makes sense in a Pleistocene epoch amongst a band of 50 to 100 hominidae. It only appears monstrous, alien, and otherwise impossible to explain, in the context of an overpopulated civilization. Therefore framing the emergent COVID dynamic as "psychosis", is a symptom of *not wanting to understand* – to dismiss everything that happened as merely a case of contagious crazies powered by social media, and having no discernible etiology within the reality of *the way we live*, with our bodies, day to day.

- 81 -

In defining psychosis, the case of one Herr Daniel Schreber is considered canonical: if you want to know what psychosis looks and feels like, read his memoirs. In a sense, what COVID exhibits is the antipode: *maximum sociality* at the expense of authentic subjectivity – psychosis is nothing if not authentic and subjective. Hysteria, protofascism, and the extensible canalizations of blame share a common origin in the previously adaptive package by which the baboon-like primate troop became the cooperative hunting tribe: displacement of aggression along symbolic vectors lies right at the heart of what has made us so successful.

Either you get used to this idea, or you don't: I feel that all of this is written out in the history of the early 20th century. Rabid nationalism, scientific racism, and warmongering were at the time the shape these same forces took, in a more potently postcolonial and peak capitalistic world. Our 21st century bodies and spirits are not robust enough for these more explicitly violent eruptions: therefore *displacement of aggression* is more needful and salient. More hand-wringing and moral posturing is required: this is why a fictional pandemic, with all its ostensible and *deeply suspicious* humanitarian concern, was uniquely capable of initiating the requisite catharsis toward the final aim of *anonymous mass violence*.

Ultimately what we've witnessed is only a minor spasm. I only continue to bring it up because *at last I understand* – a great deal of what I almost refused to think about, suddenly becomes not only possible to think through but wholly necessary.

A LOVE LETTER TO THE NEWLY DISILLUSIONED

- 82 -

S ome of my readers are suffering from a new sudden clarity, from the now irresolvable difference in values between themselves and almost everyone they know, from the burden of wondering whether the sense of isolation and loss will ever fade. I feel confident enough to say: it *will* fade. Keep on the path your virtue has led you to, and one day that sadness will be replaced with quiet certainty, the loneliness with pride, and the loss with a freedom you will learn to savor like blue sky.

I feel that I've suddenly gained access to a perhaps temporary and very special portal, in which a tiny cross-section of the global first world has been carved out for us: this is a precious moment in which to discover *who* can think for themselves, who will stand alone, who will sacrifice certainty for the sake of an integrity that promises no reward but itself.

We have been forced to *grow up* into the full possession of our integrity: we can no longer merely flirt with ethics, no longer play hipster and self-pitying loner, no longer hide behind a vague wishful benevolence – we have to graduate into the seriousness of a Yes and a No. It's rejuvenated some of us already: this hardship may prove to be the most important gift of our previously all-too-comfortable, ill-defined lives of restless recreation and protracted procrastination. Be glad the test didn't come too late!

You see, COVID has blessed me. I have been a misanthrope, but with COVID I was forced to actualize it: to stop imagining that around the next corner of growth I would find tolerance for the intolerable. This episode has served to tip the scales and confirm for me finally: trust the mistrust. For many of us, the most neurotic aspect of our relationships was not our recurrent antipathy, but the way we've tried to *silence our mistrust*.

Your instincts are not something you should seek to overcome or annihilate with any self-flagellating compassion: your instincts of repulsion are to be refined into a shield and a watchful guardian of the truth – we des-

83

perately need *your* ability to tell the truth. The moment you resolve not to tolerate the gratifications of moral posturing and the complicity of anonymous violence, is the moment that signal will propagate through the unconscious matrix of human community we are all reading at all times: in other words, folks can tell when you will eat shit as though it were caviar, and when you won't.

A LOVE LETTER TO THE NEWLY DISILLUSIONED

I.2

PSYCHOLOGY IS NOT YET BORN

REPRESSION AND THE
UNCANNY

There is a Chinese myth about the origin of writing, the antiquity and significance of which one should be able to intuit. In this story, the inventor of Chinese characters was one Cangjie 倉頡, a man with four eyes. In one version, it was the tracks of animals which inspired him: to an informed hunter, every animal leaves a distinct track – and although only representing a fraction of the whole, each trace is distinct. Cangjie was thus inspired to discover the *minimally distinct trace* for every word, and thus generate a maximally efficient medium of communication with minimal redundancy. Ancient Chinese is one of the most terse and informatively dense human languages I know of: it was possible to say with a four character string what no modern language could match in richness and implication.

But why does Cangjie have four eyes? To begin to answer this, we turn to another version of the myth which I believe is of greater antiquity: in this story, it's said he discovered the signs in the cracks of a turtle shell. The practice of divination among at least some of the Neolithic Chinese seemed to focus almost exclusively on the art of reading cracks in the turtle plastron. First, small divots were bored into the underside, the bone was then heated over a fire, and the resulting cracks were read by the oracle and a prognostication generated from them. As far as I know, no one has yet made a guess at what seems obvious to me: that the art in question here, was originally to *hallucinate characters* in these cracks, to perceive signs emergent in the world.

It's also my guess that both the extant Shang dynasty oracle bones circa 1200 BC and the Zhou dynasty Yijing text circa 600 BC were formulated as a quick-and-dirty shorthand long after this kind of practice had ceased to be genuine and improvisational, much as the Delphic oracle ceased to function by the time of Plutarch. In its most evocative and ancient form, divination is the art of *creating useful messages out of a contained entropic space* – seeing what one needs to see, discovering the writing of the world.

The Xici 繫辭 commentary of the Yijing preserves a clue:

卬以觀于天文
頫以觀于地理

Gaze upward and discern the writing in the sky.
Bow your head and discern the logic of the earth.

- 84 -

Why is this important to us, we who fancy ourselves fully rational and cured of everything unscientific, we who pose in front of our many distorted digital mirrors like a hungover clown with running makeup lost in his own funhouse, we who imagine ourselves fully conscious, we who despite the raging incessant auditory hallucination of voices we call "thinking", imagine that we have no need of divination.

Since the early 20th century, whenever some ambitious thinker attempts a formulaic distillation of the proper practice of science, he concludes with the same wishful theory of Karl Popper: that science proceeds solely via *falsifiable hypotheses*. Rather than what really happens: intuitive theoretical saltations followed by a long tail of mostly tautological confirmation, entrenchment, and an increasingly erroneous certainty as we chase down persistent demons of inaccuracy into the distant decimals where so much of 21st century science now takes place. As neatly logical as the Popperian falsification model is, it fails to account for the importance of *guessing* – or "inductive inference" in a more elaborate dialect. The physicists talk of the three B's: "bed, bath, and bus" is where the eurekas come from, when the conscious mind wanders off, and the unconscious mind is allowed to do its work.

This is such common knowledge, that it's *shameful* to have to spell it out. Moreover it's shameful that my own field, psychology, which should be more aware of this process than any other, is more foreclosed and hostile to the process of intuitive divinatory knowledge than say, physics and mathematics, where intuition is still granted a place among the powers any practitioner must develop – and ultimately even the most trenchantly classical mathematicians have to occasionally concede that iconoclasts like L. E. J. Brouwer and Wittgenstein may have been seeking a *more rigorous* definition of truth than their own.

But why? Why is 21st century psychology so frightened of its own shadow and overeager to dress itself in scientific accoutrements? Is it because we know better? Is it because we've been burned by too many charlatans at too many distinct locales, and have learned to guard against quackery with rigorous method? Or is something more nefarious at work? 21st century psychology not only fails as psychology, it seeks to erase and undermine native intuitive psychological understanding, which in primates is no small charge. It's a science that makes you *stupider* than you really are.

I can grant that current academic psychology successfully keeps overt and obvious charlatanism at bay. What it does not do, is remain relevant - nor does it guard against the kind of *systemic and implicit* charlatanism which makes the entire project of psychology seem so worthless and dull.

- 85 -

As a rogue and apostate psychologist, it will noticed I am not kind to my wouldbe colleagues. Some would ascribe this to bitterness and no more – at least I can hardly pretend that rivalry plays no role. But I prefer to believe that I'm so unforgiving of contemporary psychology because I understand it: because I have walked those halls, have been among them, and because therefore I see nothing but their faults. I dismiss their compassion and well-meaning towards humanity as impotent at best, and repulsive hypocrisy in most cases. I dismiss their scientific efforts as desperate mimicry at best, and Foucaultian collaborative disciplines of social control in most cases. We critique most harshly what we do not wish to take for granted: I would much rather be judged maniacal and unfair than timid and complicit.

- 86 -

I'm unfair to their scientific rigor; I'm unfair to their attempts to ground psychology in physiology and neurology; I'm unfair to their earnest attempts to quantize and generate computational models of social behavior. Why? Because it's *all premature*. Premature scientificality does more than waste time – it even does more than hinder progress: it *regresses* the field. The field of psychology is much worse in the 21st century than the early 20th: unrelenting scientific posturing is part of why. This is an old battle: Kraepelin versus Freud, Skinner versus Erickson.

The premature Aristotelian scientificality defined nearly a millennium of learned discourse in both Christendom and the Islamosphere: the result was to encourage unreadable tomes of meticulously logical nonsense, from Avicenna to Maimonides to Aquinas. Premature systemization stultified Chinese medicine as early as the Huainanzi in 200 BC, and while excellent at the preservation of herbal lore and the factorization of the psychosomatic, the Chinese style also generated countless systemized deadends and alluring premature lattices of half-knowledge, from which the contemporary student of acupuncture still suffers.

Language is the urform of the system of knowledge: Lévi-Strauss is correct thus far. And I have always been extremely indulgent of the systemizations of language: ancient Chinese fascinates me more than almost anything... But why indulge these urges? Why should the Mayan logography be handled like a priceless scrying obsidian mirror? Because we are looking into the soulworld of reason. Because *this* is the neurological topology our scientific fools are seeking – if only they had the patience, humility, and imagination to understand what they're looking at. But scrying requires the ability to dream with the eyes open: logography in particular – the early Sumerian, the Egyptian, the Mayan, the Chinese – is an uncanny bridge between the concrete and the abstract. *Here* is the function of unconscious structuring at work, here are unconscious topological transformations revealed, with their invariant vertices, their reflexive spirals, their marriage of the phonological and the logical, their excursions to the limit of the dialectic of the particular within the matrix of the universal, or what we may provisionally term "deictic singularity"...

- 87 -

Dreaming with the eyes open: that means aim-directed hallucination, that means seeing what one needs to see, that means discovering latent knowledge by encouraging the redundancy of conscious formation – becoming-conscious is largely nothing but redundant marking. "We dream, we undream": it's often easier to understand what dreaming is, if we understand what I term "undreaming". Undreaming is redundant, saturated signification bounded by repression: what's vital to internalize, is that there is no hard line between conscious and unconscious, only a difference of degree. What we are conscious of, is what we are "uncon-scious of" many times over. Undreaming is to erase lines of descent, to erase the manifold traces of signification, to repress everything but the overwritten and overdetermined: this is why the conversation of most "normal" people is so bewilderingly monotonous, repetitive, colorless, and yet *brimming with the uncanny*. Spiritual monotony, the *école normale* of bourgeois modernity, is also an unsettling, slow, shuffling dance of masks: that there is a surface, implies a depth. That there is a certain something, so desperately grasped and grafted, implies an uncertain something else. This is the kind of "drama of the gifted child" which you and I have lived through: to have watched this maskdance many times over, knowing instinctively that it meant something drastically other than the explicit symbols, but not knowing what or why. A recovery from deep, abiding childhood paranoia is probably one of the prerequisites to under-standing my work: "The Truman Show" demonstrates, I suspect, a common spontaneous fantasy among bright little boys of the television age.

- 88 -

What is "uncanny"? The English word has a Germanic root, which ulti-mately leads back to a Proto-Indo-European stratum which ramifies into "ken", "can", "know", German "kennen", Greek γνῶσίς, and so on. There-fore uncanny means simply the "unknown". But there's a little more here: the German negation prefix "un-" has special qualities: sometimes it can be considered a simple inversion, and sometimes it seems to mean "worse, bad, terrifying". Such as the German "Untier", which is literally "un-animal", but means "monster"; or "Unfall", which is literally "non-event", but means "accident". There is even an old English word, "unweather" which means "storm".

In fact, agglutinate negation in many languages reveals something very important and ancient: in their deep core, many adjectival morphemes can be shown to denote an *axis of value*, rather than any one pole. Any sig-nifier pushed too far in one direction, eventually begins to acquire implications of its opposite: *ambivalence* is the only stable signifying locus, oddly enough. Freud first discovered this for himself in his analysis of dreams, and only much later became aware of the linguistic evidence.

...das »Nein« scheint für den Traum nicht zu existieren.

93

..."No" seems not to exist in the dream.

Die Traumdeutung, VI.C

There is much for the contemporary philologist to dispute here, but I'll point out an incontrovertible example from Freud's essay, "Über den Gegensinn der Urworte": the English word "with" was originally constructed from the Proto-Indo-European root u̯i-, meaning "separate, apart", and is also the root of the word "wide", originally meaning "sundered, distant". But as is so often the case with slippery semantics, "with" was formed by a reinforcing comparative to render u̯itero-, literally "even more separate". The history of language is the history of a crumbling shantytown built atop temple ruins built atop shantytowns...

In other words, "with" used to mean "without", and in some compounds like "withhold", still does.

- 89 -

What is uncanny? When something is what it is, but is also something else which is obscured by this first identity. It involves duplication, but is not quite synonymous with the Doppelgänger: it's not merely resemblance and twinning, but *repression* which imparts the uncanny effect. Freud says:

> Erstens, wenn die psychoanalytische Theorie in der Behauptung recht hat, daß jeder Affekt einer Gefühlsregung, gleichgültig von welcher Art, durch die Verdrängung in Angst verwandelt wird, so muß es unter den Fällen des Ängstlichen eine Gruppe geben, in der sich zeigen läßt, daß dies Ängstliche etwas wiederkehrendes Verdrängtes ist.

> If psychoanalytic theory is correct in maintaining that every affect of a feeling state, of whatever kind, is transformed by repression into anxiety, then among instances of the anxiety-inducing there must be one class in which this anxiety can be shown to be the return of something repressed.

Das Unheimliche, §II

Are you aware of the "uncanny valley" involved in the production of artificial life? The more closely an android resembles a human being, the worse the feeling of dread. Supposedly this disappears as the android becomes indistinguishable – but I'm not convinced that any emotionally intact creature would not feel deep alarm at this unholy camouflage: imagine the reaction of a healthy dog. Under what conditions does an animal ever encounter something pretending to be something it's not? The *predator-prey* relationship: when you are hiding from something that wants to eat you, or are hiding from something you want to eat. That this hasn't occurred to anyone, among all the endless excited chatter about artificial life, is only one more reason to keep a long hostile distance between ourselves and all the naïvely complicit, unconsciously malicious sycophantic flutter around "futurology": profound hostility to *organic life* surrounds this blinkered murder-suicide tinkering-in-the-dark with artificial life.

There is also something similar at work in plastic surgery: ever wondered why an aggressive nosejob is so unsettling?

- 91 -

It still remains to explain why Cangjie has four eyes.

If you'll forgive a liberal borrowing from information theory, we could assume that each eye produces one bit of information: the object either is, or is not perceived. This is the case with very simple eyes, for example the shadow-detecting eyes on the top of the heads of some lizards. Thus in an extremely reductionistic sense, two eyes produces four possible states: 00, 01, 10, 11: not, right, left, center. Following this exponentiation, four simple eyes would produce 16 possible states. As in the case of tetrachromatic women, the extra cone cell produces not $x*(n+1)$ colors, but x^{n+1}: each cone cell detects about 100 gradations, thus tetrachromacy yields an increase of two orders of magnitude, or about 100 million colors compared to 1 million. A better argument for the adaptive value of women as *herbalists* could hardly be found – and the medicinal value of common plants encountered everywhere you look once you know how to look, is also an exponentiation and overdetermination of the *Umwelt*, isn't it?

Thus if Cangjie's extra pair of eyes is the ability to read signs, he does not see merely double, he sees *logarithmically double*: in the sense that given $y = x^n$, if y is the exponentially increasing depth, x the possible states of any one eye, the exponent n is not only the number of eyes but the degree of apparent mastery over that complex field, since what we experience is never the total possible depth but *access* to complex perceptual results when we need it – our senses are inclined to produce gentle logarithmic responses which hide as much variance as reveal.

But this kind of power law relationship is one of the signatures of biological adaptation to nonlinearity: perceptual acuity is nonlinear, and attempts to map the "totality of subjective experience" always run up against the limitations of linear assumptions when dealing with complex manifolds – the topic gets away from you, the lattice disappears across some other horizon, prose falters, and poetical recoveries diminish into vacuity... This should sound an awful lot like most philosophy: if not, you either have not subjected yourself to its tortured paths, or are one of the perpetrators of the priestly banalization of the sacred.

In other words, a topological and statespace approach is called for: the persistent Platonic-Kantian assumptions about irreducible yet articulable categories of experience, which plague the Western tradition and make it so characteristically stupid, fail because they are essentially *a confusion of method with metaphysics*. Western thinking is typically brilliant in analytic method, and obtuse in synthetic speculation. But *speculum* means "mirror", and it was typical of the high middle ages, with its urge to summarize all knowledge into a bounded sphere, to produce literary *specula* – and by so doing approximate a long awkward journey back to preaxial mythological coherence, which said so much with densely packed details. But very little of the requisite *dreaminess* is present for these mirrors to function as divinatory aids: illuminated manuscripts are clearly such hypnoid divinatory aids, but despite their roots in sublime Celtic metallurgy, they speak largely of cloistered stink, rather than florid excursions.

- 92 -

All this becomes salient when comparing Western speculative philosophy with the Chinese tradition, which in my view more successfully preserved Neolithic means of cultivating and transmitting intuitive disciplines. The explicitly logographic nature of Chinese played no small part:

the core Chinese lexicon of radicals are all pictorial in origin and many are still recognizable. The logograph implies the likeness of the thing, the phonemic sequence, and the functional concept itself: signified, signifier, sign – in Peircian terminology, "object", "representamen", "interpretant". Unlike the more obscured semiosis of an alphabetic system, it is the *explicit compression* of the logograph that is uncanny: the logograph is not the thing it represents, and yet because the graph designates both the object and the phonemic sequence of the word, and the word designates the object, we cannot experience or demonstrate this object by any means which does not seem to invoke the same sequence in reverse. This is probably the reason for the southern Daoist tradition of "finger pointing" in transmitting intangible knowledge – along with occasional beatings for the especially obtuse... But pedantic "semiotics" always invokes a certain *need to be slapped*, doesn't it?

- 93 -

If this section seems more obscure and heady than I normally allow myself, let it be a testament to the influence of the topic and a witness to my method: what is discussed should percolate through the means, it should recurse and drive you a little mad, else you're not yet thinking to full capacity.

- 94 -

Discerning the writing in the world: why psychology devolves into conspiracy theory in the hands of the inept. Why psychology begins as animism. Why there is always an element of the superstitious in any psychological interpretation: every interpretation is properly considered a placeholder for a more complex experience. But the reduction of complexity and the suppression of implication, is precisely the function of consciousness: one must understand it as a useful falsification, else one has failed to understand one's own understanding - definition of postaxial technocratic arrogance.

Another point from information theory I should mention, is that the transmission of information depends upon uncertainty in the occurrence of signs: every meaningful communication requires a probabilistic head-room, a contained entropic space – otherwise it is merely formulaic redundancy. As I've hinted, "punitive normalcy" is this kind of redundancy: or rather, it is an attempt at the *erasure of meaning* through the expansion of the domain of redundancy. Freudian repression may not be just "pressing down" as the words *re-pression* and *Verdrängung* suggest, or defensive egoic "censure", or Kleinian "splitting": it may be more like an overwritten *palimpsest*, an erasure through repetitive redundancy – a kind of *antitrance*. It's noteworthy that the Ericksonian method of hypnotic induction often depends upon the frightfully unexpected – the man was capable of surprising bluntness, of an almost Daoist intensity: a healing trance, a desirable trance, requires first that an *antitrance* be disturbed... The slightest nudge in the right place, and what seemed like an immovable edifice of the uncanny – this overwritten, years-long trance of neurotic fixation, can move. Much of what is uncanny in human psychology is precisely this kind of doubling: everything is plainly said, plainly visible, the history of a person is written on the face – and yet everyone pretends not to know how to read.

Cangjie, as I understand the myth, is the critical juncture between divinatory seeing and *blind literacy*: a visionary made explicit what was implicit, and forever after those signs no longer function as magical invocations – or they do, but no one knows it. The history of most of the teachers of psychology I know of, follows a similar pattern: Freudians ruined the potency of Freudian concepts, the students of Erickson turned his art into a suspiciously "well-meaning" psychotherapeutic blandishment, the history of the influence of Heraklitus is one long misunderstanding and slander after another... As the Daoists say, one must return to the source, and be nourished by the wordless.

The careful reader will notice that there are at least two competing models of the uncanny in what I've said: that the uncanny is *invasive informative redundancy* as a result of Freudian repression, and that the uncanny arises from the *instability of signification*. But they are not so different: in both cases, something which means something explicitly, also implies something which its very meaning obscures. Every sign is written atop something else.

Unconscious phenomena are *compressed*: which in informational terms, means low redundancy in the message. I frequently speak of "overdetermination": nothing characterizes the dreamstate, like an object that is many things at once. The sign similarly, is many things at once. But it is the intrusion of unconscious repressive schemata into consciousness, which most visibly and daily gives us the experience of the uncanny: repression *compresses data* into the very means of obscuring it – namely redundancy. This is why brilliant psychoanalytic interpretation usually begins from some mundane neglected detail – often something the patient hesitated to mention it was so trivial, "not worth mentioning", as people say. But people leave the most important clues in the margins, in their garbage, and their footnotes: it's not for nothing that postmodern hermeneutics has its roots in the Jewish passion for endless textual commentary – Levinas as the reluctant rabbi-godfather of postmodern philosophy...

Have I been understood? The strategy of repression is not, as is usually assumed, merely denial and inhibition: fully developed repression *hides everything in plain sight*. This too, is part of how and why fully committed religious folk, like the Amish, can feel that everything is sacred and "belongs to God": everything means itself, and something else entirely. That programs of repression could possibly return us to a "state of grace", to the vision of an illuminated manuscript written upon the world – that too, should be no surprise to anyone willing to understand the *functional* value of postaxial religious entrainment. To regain the sacred, at *any* cost to our instinctual coherence – which in civilizational contexts is skewed and hopeless anyway: that's the winning formula which will repeat many times yet, and why I expect global religiosity to surge right back to where it once was, no matter the distortions involved.

- 97 -

There is yet another distinction worth pointing out here: the difference between natively unconscious process, and what I call repressive schemata. This was an important point Freud brought up more than once, which is generally missed: repressed content is hidden amongst the

99

innocently unconscious, like a fugitive in disguise. The difference is qualitative and difficult to discern until it's probed: repressed material slithers away, vanishes, or plays dead. Unlike everything else in the dreamstate, it often *refuses* to transform when perceived: that's a sure sign that you've cornered a highly compressed signal which needs precisely this disguise and no other...

- 98 -

When the Netsilik and all traditional peoples describe their *tunraq*, their personal guardian spirits, their visions, they are describing their *dreams and hallucinations*: this is the stage before humanity has learned to distinguish between waking and dreaming, seeing and *seeing*. Not that this distinguishment represents an advance on all fronts: much has been lost, since we began talking our children out of their imagination. Much that was formerly known and experienced communally, is now repressed and solely the domain of psychosis, unguided adolescent psychedelia, and the occasional intrepid psychologist. The "supersane", is what one of them once called this domain: it's been noted many times, that the onset of schizophrenia contains almost identical characteristics to the shamanistic initiation. But it's not that being crazy is somehow better: *contained* and controlled hallucination was always the ancient goal. As much hallucination as is fruitful for the sake of insight and power: there seems to be a more or less constant ratio of children born every generation, who bear an excess of insight. This excess of understanding seeks shape, *generates* perceptual traces – it is not only the perceptual apparatus playing with itself and finding positive feedback loops, it is the exploitation of *perceptual marginalia* for the purposes making consciously comprehensible what is otherwise too latent and unconscious to be manipulable.

Homo sapiens is burdened with its frontal lobe: a gross excess of unsettled intelligence freed from instinctual discharge, channeled and amplified by the linguistic faculty, reaching an unstable criticality when constrained by repression, and finally emerging like a supercoherent laser, but without any unambiguous instinctual terminus – this is the danger we represent to ourselves.

That we took so long to "emerge" from Pleistocene nomadism, is not merely an artifact of technological acceleration: our ancestors were by no means and in no way dumber than we are. It's a dirty little secret of pale-ontology, that the human brain has actually *decreased* in volume since about 20,000 BC: we already reached the adaptive maximum of excess cleverness. Moreover, we already perfected the means to *contain* this intel-ligence... The kind of endless anxiety, crippling neurosis, hyperalgesia and hypochondria we suffer from in modernity, would never have been tolerated nor remotely viable in that rigorous past: so much of the concern with spirits and the supernatural, is the adaptive means of dis-charging, redirecting, and reappropriating our surplus intelligence. "Idle hands are the playground of the devil": this means, too, much leisure is bad for the clever ape, because he will begin hallucinating with the same kind of ferocity all his kind employs in masturbation. "Thinking" is hallu-cination which stimulates the sympathetic nervous system: in other contexts known as dreaming.

That our ancestors did not distinguish between dreaming and waking – again this is not due to lack of intelligence, nor to a lack of honesty. It's not even strictly true: they knew very well the difference, but considered the "spirit world" – in our language, hallucination – to be equally valid forms of information. They weren't just *lying*, either to themselves out of weak-ness of mind, nor to everyone else for the sake of shamanistic power – although this certainly happened frequently – a powerful shaman reports *genuine* visions. Falsified visions may have a populist, shortlived impact – the scam artist has always been with us and always will – but there are also completely sincere medicine men, who report what they see. This is why many of their visions and spirits are so strange, so unexpected, so specific:

> The following is the list of spirits owned by Iksivalitaq, the last practicing shaman among the Netsilik: 1. Kingarjuaq, big mountain, about three inches long and one inch high, with black and red spots. The shaman could remove this *tunraq* from his mouth, where it was in the habit of staying, and make it run on his hand. 2. Kanayuq, sea scorpion, residing also in Iksivali-taq's mouth, whence it could show its ugly head. 3. Kaiutinuaq,

the ghost of a dead man. 4. Kringarsarut, the ghost of a dead man, big as a needle, with a crooked mouth and one very small ear. 5. Arlu, the killer whale, white, very big. 6. Kunnararjuq, a black dog with no ears. 7. Iksivalitak, the ghost of the shaman's grandfather.

The Netsilik Eskimo, Asen Balikci, §4.10

It's easy to invent gratifying lies – this is almost identical to the social capacity – but it's impossible to fake unconscious depth and the *uncanny*: yet only a living familiarity with one's own dreams can impart this sense for the difference. Perhaps a good poet knows the difference: Shakespeare cannot be faked, and there's something about his phrasing that is untranslatable.

- 101 -

There is the possibility that psychology will never be a science – that it *cannot by definition be science*. That psychology is always properly concerned with the "occult", because it is by definition a knowing of that which is *hidden*: what is unconscious is unknown, uncanny, occult. If the domain of human knowledge were to expand to include that which is unconscious today, psychology would no longer be necessary – or would psychology expand indefinitely? Since its inception, visible in Heraklitus in the West and Zhuangzi in the East, it's long been a question whether our psychologists are discovering the ontogeny of the soul, or inventing fantasies useful to themselves: both, is probably the answer. ψυχῆς ἐστι λόγος ἑωυτὸν αὔξων: one of the peculiarities of consciousness, is the way it grows uncontrollably past its native dampening thresholds – the story is involute, anxiety has no functional limit. Furthermore, one of the peculiarities familiar to anyone who has actually tried to become fully conscious, is that at these asymptotic limits consciousness begins to resemble unconsciousness: a multiplication of concurrent threads, parallel operation, persistent unresolved contradiction, multiplying dimensionality, recursive implications forever collapsing back into condensation and overdetermination – in short, everything which makes consciousness tremble before the task and which spreads awareness too thinly, because it is too costly. Again "awareness" being nothing but reduplicative representation – an *inhibitory* function: obviously this kind of expensive overhead cannot be tolerated at all levels, and in meditative practice one learns to turn down that flame as low as possible, without falling asleep... The art of psychology is for me this low flame: only a flick-ering light, so as not to scare away the spirits. Our projective imagination, our filling out what is perhaps only shadow puppetry and tricks of the séance, should not be dismissed: "superstition" often expresses a knowl-edge otherwise difficult to justify, misplaced perhaps, displaced perhaps necessarily – but nonetheless valid to those with a Grimm Brother's eye for valuable lore.

- 102 -

If it's possible for psychology to become the "queen of the sciences", then it is important she remain a *queen*: that is aloof, inscrutable, both more and less than mere woman – the "virgin queen". Something to inspire us, cast doubt in us, and draw on sources of myth and power: psychology must not be allowed to become a bureaucrat's tabulation exercise, a corre-lation of probabilities and measurements – but nor should it become a "carnival of the soul", a breeding ground for neon charlatanism, a means of mystifying the credulous. It should be neither too certain of its attain-ments, nor permissive of vacuous showmanship, nor encouraging of the moral actor and the well-meaning of clumsy dolts: it should at all times seek the *truth function* in the human creature – it should welcome wicked-ness and deceit and willful reversals without losing sight of them, because these too are means of telling the truth. Psychology in our age perhaps above all, needs to turn away the vaguely well-meaning and welcome the crisply wicked: in wickedness there is much more sincerity and power to heal. To find cruelty in the good, vulnerability in the charlatan, and igno-rance in the knowledgeable.

THE ART OF PERCEPTION

That psychiatrists believe they are masters of psychology because they have access to an arsenal of brutally efficacious drugs, is like a man who believes he knows everything worth knowing about trees because he possesses a chainsaw. He neither designs, nor constructs, nor understands a chainsaw, but when the tree crashes violently he feels this confirms his mastery.

Psychiatry and academic psychology essentially practice *shallow pop psychology* alongside *fraudulent statistical fiddling*. They manipulate numbers gained from dimwitted quantization schemes designed to confirm ascendent sociopolitical agenda in order to secure funding, or preferably to prove the efficacy and safety of whatever lucrative molecular monstrosity the pharmaceutical boys have cooked up.

It makes about as much sense for someone genuinely interested in the art and science of psychology to listen to our psychiatrists and PhDs, as it would for someone interested in healthy diet to visit an oil rig because so much of our food is now derived from petroleum.

Why should anyone interested in radical spirituality consult someone who calls himself a psychologist? For example, the gleeful complicity of our psychologists in a variety of athletic Orwellian distortions along the course of the COVID farce is comparable only to the reprehensibility of epidemiologists, who have blithely and with open eyes changed the foundational definitions of their science to match the prevailing winds of flatus called political consensus.

My answer: because a genuinely incisive psychology is our best weapon in an emerging ideological war, in which the first lesson is to *defuse all ideology*. There is a discernible thirst for the persecution of the heretical afoot... We must not allow the heritage of Western psychological insight to be another occupied territory of blind and shallow political opportunism.

NEITHER ANIMISM NOR REDUCTIONISM

- 104 -

Psychology as I see it practiced everywhere, combines the stupidest elements of vestigial animistic thinking – in that it seeks to project blame out of the vicinity of the community at any cost – with the most blockheaded modern prejudices – which assume for every deed a singular agency, for every agency a singular motive. Therefore it fails to capture either the animistic subtlety in the identification of spirits, the fluency which which it traces influences across domain and scale – in other words the *scale invariance of mass psychology* – nor does it benefit from Western analytic thinking, which properly employs reduction as artificial temporary ignorance, rather than as a *covert metaphysics* as is generally the case. Our psychology has made us more boldly stupid: the quest for "organic" etiologies and the effective abandonment of the psychological, has the result that it's easier to believe we know *everything that's possibly real* – an impudent attitude worthy of neither animistic suggestibility nor scientific skepticism.

- 105 -

Where others cannot help but see agency, I see nonlinear emergent dynamics: *all psychology begins as animism,* and it requires many years to outgrow the crutch of a projected conscious self, where there is neither self nor consciousness. Mass psychology has yet to begin, therefore its etiology is still animistic.

- 106 -

The need for certainty is not only a constant, it grows with the animal's exposure to overwhelming stimuli. In modernity, this is the reason why *everyone and no one* is a psychologist.

To the talented student of psychology, quietly bewildered at the ever widening gap between the self-assured pomp of scientificality and the ever more obvious uselessness of its findings, I recommend this perspective: such doings are the creation of *mythologies of agency* and the extensible canals of blame, such as the human creature always has need of. Bad psychologizing is nothing new: the efficient distribution of blame is one of the requisites of any sustainable communal life.

- 107 -

Being both formerly educated and more deeply *informally* educated in the field, I'm keenly aware that *every other dope considers himself a psychologist.* Your mother considers herself a psychologist because she watches Oprah; your boss curates a set of politically correct diagnoses he learned from his therapist; your girlfriend believes she knows better because the internet told her so; your roommate read Jung once – and so on. Yet not all of this conviction concerning human motivation is fully dismissible: in fact, the *less education* at play, the more likely the insight is valid. A formal education in psychology produces increasingly obtuse and dangerous gremlins: it's not a curve of diminishing returns, it's a dropoff into willful stupidity and authoritarian posturing. Moreover there is no point at which this educational curve suddenly surges back upward into mastery: *unlearning* modern university training is the nearly impossible toil with which a pedagogy in my style would be concerned...

But about half the world is half-educated. Like exhausted topsoil, genuine native ignorance grows scarcer, and is largely extinct in our firstworld. I see children as young as 10 who seem ruined by the irony of the internet. Finding a spark of honest ignorance, that bright pilot flame where articulate questions begin and from which lifelong passions are fed, is like foraging for mushrooms in Central Park: not impossible but a little ridiculous – although this sort of secret plane of fecund ignorance, the bottled genie of childhood, persists just as it always has in quiet shady neglected spots, and finding them is part of the art of perception.

- 108 -

Ignorance is necessary for meaningful communication: without an unknown and essentially unknowable element, mere redundancy or at most a logistic puzzle is at play, but not communication. One must not fully understand one's opponent in dialectic, else it's mere shadowplay, a scam with a shill. Ignorance and unbridgeable difference is necessary for genuine sociality, else it's mere tyranny, totalitarianism, premonitions of the superorganic. Ignorance is necessary for all genuine manners and etiquette, else it's mere formality and lying-in-wait. Ignorance is necessary for all psychology, and if we imagine a perfectly psychic creature, we immediately understand that this could be no psychologist. The same is true for the "organic" reduction to biomolecular mechanics the psychiatrists so long for: by giving no due place to ignorance they have set it loose, by seeking to eliminate the unknown they have eliminated the essence, by seeking their premature totality of knowledge they have merely created another medieval barbarity.

A great teacher once told me, that a teacher should ask questions without having a specific answer in mind: knowledge is a fire that must be fed, not a dungheap to be troweled.

- 109 -

Psychology, as science, is properly considered still in the preparatory descriptive phase. As I've said before, premature scientificality is not only an enormous waste of time, and not only *hinders* progress, but engenders a *regression* of knowledge: genuine science carries the authority to contradict "common sense" – but nothing is worse in the humanities and the inductive work of good science than undermining common sense precisely where it is most valuable. This is part of what has made possible the plague of political correctness under the aegis of *willful stupidity* regarding human nature: feminism, for example, has strayed from an advocacy of the feminine into a small set of scientifically idiotic claims about the nonexistence of sexual dimorphism.

THE MAGICAL RITUALS OF KNOWLEDGE

- 110 -

I have said that "the essence of magical thinking is *feigned belief*". Propitiation, ceremony, always requires an as-if attitude which becomes effective through its effication: ceremony is hollow until it is hallowed. We accomplish many things by closing our eyes tighter: the human being must deceive itself almost constantly, else it will wander off and fail to meet its own needs. In fact self-deception seems to be *instinctual* in this primate: with our certainty we hide our knowledge, with our belief we hide our insight. Almost everything the human creature claims to know, he does not know: but when he claims to be ignorant, he very well knows.

Science too, is a magical ritual: by claiming ignorance we don't have, we gain genuine knowledge we didn't have. That is the Socratic trick. But by perverting this ceremony into a bad imitation of the ritual of certainty – in other words, postaxial religion, which is largely the unholy marriage of Greek scientificality with Neoplatonic-Hermetic incantation – we return to magical thinking again, but without the pagan awe and none of the Neolithic humility which should accompany it. Modernity is plagued by the arrogant half-educated peasant, who by dint of his premature liberation from labor has neither the rootedness to earth nor the security of a hierarchy of powers above him: he is inwardly terrified at his freedom of thought, yet simultaneously greedy to achieve as much status through falsified knowledge as possible – thus he becomes yet another *quack of normalcy*. The charlatans of certainty surround us, peddling their cheap imitations of scientific attitudes... It was in fact the early Christians above all, who claimed ownership over the Greek heritage of reason: they convinced half the world that a cheaply syncretic mystery cult promoting ambitious moral actors had the most legitimate claim to the values of antique civilization. Why did it succeed? Because Christianity addressed itself to the inner needs of late antiquity, which was, as I insist, analogous to our time: when anxiety reigns, *the power to quell anxiety* is taken as a sign of sufficient authority and possession of "the Truth". This is ultimately why "the Science" seems fated to be marred and annexed by protoreligious forces once again...

- III -

What's the difference between "certainty" and "knowledge" such as I've just described them? Genuine knowledge is always incomplete, always a partial trajectory and a quasicrystalline seduction, always accompanied by an unsettling "so what?" at the tail end. Genuine insight disturbs the semantic web: to withstand insight, we must withstand uncertainty. The sense that something disastrous will result from the infection of uncertainty, is the reason most of humanity resists its own insight – *not* because it lacks it. Most of the factual scraps and authoritative tones traded by the human community, are designed to *shut down* unconscious reasoning and dampen its vibrations. Gossip, slander, complaint, and boasting – where humanity spends most of its time together – are not only tools of conformity and consolidation, they are the betel nut narcotics of cheap certainty.

- 112 -

Most lack the intellectual conscience to practice good psychology. One must resist the mystification of the reflexive, else we risk devolving psychology into self-indulgence: Jung, Lacan, and psychoanalysts in general. But we must also resist the counterformation, which is to arrogate an understanding of the fundamentals we do not possess, and by neglecting the simple questions fail before we have begun, and thus devolve psychology into a bureaucratic taxidermy of increasingly dead information: academic psychology and psychiatry.

Freud walked a thin line, and only then for about a decade did he manage it: to preserve intellectual conscience even as we stare into the mirror, to unravel the answers of the sphinx, to learn to know what we already know without succumbing to the *superstition* that we already know. To superimpose conscious ignorance atop unconscious knowledge, without allowing the conscious element to become indulgent, nor mystified, nor impatient for results, nor embarrassed at its poverty, nor despairing, nor cynical, nor naïve: that is the challenge of good psychology.

- 113 -

Psychoanalysis in the early 20th century was like a desert bloom: brief, rare, yet indicative of richer soils than you might think. The human race is many times more psychologically perceptive than it generally *pretends*: the problem is not teaching psychology per se, but to make an intellectual conscience *more socially advantageous than distortion...* To train artful scientists precisely where everyone is already a practiced magician: not easy.

For example, modern Freudians see "ego defense" where I see social calculation: much of what I call moral phenomena they term "defense" from displeasure... But Freud underestimated the importance of *group* psychology to the primate. It's not "displeasure" in the abstract that the ego defends against, it's *abandonment*.

- 114 -

A *tour de ronde* of my schoolmasters:

⇁ Nietzsche: Psychology of the group, of the tribe, of the tribunal. Master of envy and resentment, of hate and love, of weak and strong.

⇁ Freud: Psychology of the family, the child, the neurotic individual, of repression and displacement, of hysteria, obsession, and regression.

⇁ Lacan: Psychology below the level of the individual, the mystery of subjectivity, of linguistic recursion.

- 115 -

⇁ Lacan: fascinating but mostly useless. Not a psychological art of liberation, but of fascination. Facilitates the art of discussion and freer thinking, but such advanced study that almost no one is capable of benefitting from it without succumbing to its poison.

⇁ Freud: useful for the earliest stages of recuperation from bad acculturation – i.e. therapy 101. Freudian mechanics are always at play in intimate relationship, and therefore essential to master if one is to be close to anyone in civilized modernity.

⇁ Nietzsche: the most relevant in the long term. Nietzsche's scope of psychology is determinative of most of human life in its broad strokes. Once Freudian neurosis is no longer a blocking issue, if massive repression is absent, Nietzschean analysis of morals and the psychology of morals is the essential task for meaningful liberation. Lacanian and all other kinds of "discursive" freedom mean nothing without moral revaluation.

- 116 -

Good psychology on my terms is the study of *unconscious distortion*: everything else is merely character typology, the demonology of fashionable syndrome, and the pleasures of slanderous gossip. For example, "Borderline Personality Disorder" has become an increasingly popular diagnosis, without the slightest understanding of how shallow the thinking behind it is – Otto Kernberg coined it as merely a kind of placeholder for neurotic patients as difficult to treat as a true psychotic. Therefore it means: "pain in the ass" and little more – little surprise then that it finds so much application.

- 117 -

Someone claims to be "psychic", another claims a "siddhi" – what do I hear? Firstly, it's important to understand that effectively, *everyone is psychic*. There is no creature alive that does not communicate at many levels simultaneously, and no human being which does not communicate *unconsciously* with several orders of magnitude greater bandwidth and precision than consciously. Unconscious communication is "psychic" communication: no more, and certainly no less. It remains unplumbed, unexplored, unrecognized, disrespected, willfully ignored, willfully denied – but it happens every day, in every scenario, in every conceivable way and – according to even a modest allowance of probability – in many inconceivable ways too. So when someone takes pains to claim special powers, the only important question is: what are they after, whom are they after, and how does the "psychic" moniker help them achieve those ends?

- 118 -

What does it mean, to be "unconscious"? The very term betrays our prejudice: it's defined by what it's not.

"Unconscious" is so badly termed, and so aptly demonstrates the fundamental prejudices at work: as though "the unconscious" were a special case, as though one had to go looking for it! It's as absurd as when we look at the ocean and see only a scrawny beach, or when we think of the Milky Way Galaxy as "extraterrestrial". Everything we do and say and feel, is primarily unconscious: what's conscious is only a very special case, and usually not important. It's almost impossible to "do" anything consciously: consciousness accompanies, intensifies, or rather is itself the symptom of intensification.

It's also a grave error, to equate "the ego" with consciousness. The I, the linguistic I, the defensive I – the ego does not hardly exist except when it's defensive – has nothing essential to do with being-conscious, except that it relies on redundancy and saturation as one of its defenses. The *loudest mouth* on the block: anyone familiar with ghetto life knows how reliable a defense this is. The *ability to redirect attention* is a form of magic, and actually the first thing every magician learns.

The ego as scam artist: that sounds too correct to be mere poetic accident. But poetic accidents are my specialty: tripping backwards over the truth as I spraypaint illusions of knowing – I have an I, too.

PSYCHOLOGY IS A WEAPON

- 119 -

The field of psychology is so extremely vulnerable to abuse and perversion that many of the brightest of my generation have declared it not only worthless but a dangerous snare employed by malicious manifestations of punitive normalcy. And they are not mistaken.

If I declare that "psychology is a weapon" – would you believe me? In practice, what's the function of invoking psychological interpretation? It shifts responsibility, generates whatever narrative justifies action, authorizes a microcosmic origin myth, an actionable causality with magic formulae and spirits to blame: instead of "the devil", or a hex, or taboo, we get "the subconscious", a "personality disorder", or "the ego". Pop psychology is largely a *renewed demonology*.

But when disguised as education and initiation, something more inimical appears: a psychological interpretation serves to induce hesitation, self-doubt, the seeds of consciousness – everything which makes a strong nature hold itself back. The lasting power of this psychological warfare is that it *recruits the capacity for responsibility* and turns it against the bearer:

the bold become self-punitive, the visionary become brooding. It works most effectively against those with a capacity for honesty; it hobbles the most virtuous with the strength of their own virtues; it seduces by projecting a mirage of challenge and renewed heroism into the horizon. And what is truly wondrous, is that this challenge is not entirely unreal: the dangers and rewards of self-examination call to the children of modernity...

To say that the function of psychology is *to heal*, is like saying that the purpose of the Manhattan Project was to create radiological medicine: psychological insight wielded with the healing art, is an exception of exceptions – merely a glance at the history of psychoanalysis after Freud should demonstrate how difficult it was for him not to breed nefarious charlatans left and right. Freud also was hardly a healer: he was rather an ambitious scientist, with that sufficient mixture of cruelty and neutrality...

- 120 -

Is psychology a weapon in my hands also? Absolutely. What do I seek to harm with it? The briar of confusion surrounding my peers, the Gordian knot handed to the children of modernity – I seek to frighten away goblins and embolden the honest faces around my fire with a different story: if my psychology is after all only another tale, let it be a good one that leaves us cheerful, impetuous, and scornful of the chokedamp of cowardice we find everywhere...

If my science has a bias and a motive – and it does – it is to teach the forging of psychological weapons of self-defense. My hope is that the very content of this art and science – the bowl of thorns and bitter herbs I serve as though it were precious broth – will select my students for me.

- 121 -

There is an intimate and suspect relationship between psychological initiation and *moral indoctrination*: psychology is after all the "study of the soul", and the "soul" is after all the most ingenious crooked concealed dagger of the priests. "Drive all blames into yourself": this has always been the *modus operandi* and first line of defense of the priest and wannabe-priest. "Drive all blames into your neurosis": I've stretched out on that couch of torture, under the nose of a ranking psychoanalyst of the New York Freudian Society no less. But after many long hours of doubt, when I finally turned to him and said: "Your silence is false! You're not neutral and composed, you're merely weak, unimaginative, and a practiced actor!" – I'll never forget the flabbergasted look, his speechlessness. Psychological weaponry may be very cleverly designed and virulent, but make no mistake: most practitioners have weak wrists and no ability to parry – they deal only with willing victims, not adversaries. Moreover, their dark arts will crumble before the white flame of an angry belly: do not underestimate the power of healthy rage to frighten away grey-skinned parasitic entities.

- 122 -

Whether and how much Foucault is correct in removing the element of individual psychology from the functioning of modernity: how much is "feeling" and even "gratification" not only *imputed* by we who would explain, but an important *illusion* of that same system? How much has mankind already been reduced to a responsive and well-functioning part within a machine, whose subjective experience has been *both broadened and weakened*? How much does modernity depend upon paralytic anxiety, self-absorption, short-term goals, and a ubiquitous shallow fitful sleep? How much is every attempt to discover "motive" therefore doomed?

But my psychology attempts to uncover precisely those conditions which *do* prevail, which *do* prepare the human body for a benumbed bourgeois mallwalk through broken fragments of dreams... The "motives" I find have nothing whatever to do with an idealized rational human subject: I find a sick body doing its best to recover in the midst of mounting confusion and overwhelming error, largely failing to find respite outside of what *makes it sicker*, and therefore resigning with astounding regularity to tactics of revenge, malicious roleplaying, and a selling of birthrights to the lowest bidder for the most immediate relief – the sicker the human animal becomes, the more the "rationality of illness" is the only logic and the only psychological framework worth pursuing. Everything else is bad fiction, the 18th century presumptions of Adam Smith, the bald lies which advertising tells us about "choice" and uniqueness, and the laggardly failings of late 20th century psychology to catch up to the evidence of *what we are.*

- 123 -

We are apes, with ape-psychology, with ape-instincts, with ape-needs. Perhaps not much more, and maybe a little less. That we seem to have become something so much more than ape, is from my perspective merely the potential for exotic diversification latent in all species. We are the last of the techno-apes: there once were many varieties. We either shared, inherited, or stole most of our fundamental technologies from previous hominid species: language, fire, hunting, tribe, herbology, and perhaps even agriculture. Any 21st century psychology that does not ground itself in *apenature*, is anachronistic and beyond our patience. Only the interplay of fundamental instinct reveals the truth about us consistently – it pulls back the many veils of polite consolation. *Morality* being that thick veil which I'm most accustomed to attack first. But there are more: metaphysical pretensions abound still, especially in neuroscience – where chemistry fumbles in the backseat with the humanities.

⌐ A psychology that claims to discover the mind from within, and finds nothing but mirage, as Lacan does: masturbatory, paralyzing, and a fabulous waste of time.

⌐ A psychology that exclusively studies maladaptation under more slanderous names, as psychiatry does: squireboy of the horsemen of civilization, seeking to groom the general populace for castration.

⌐ A psychology that reduces everything willful to neurosis, as the Freudians do: the fearful feverdream of an impotent self-loathing man.

- 124 -

Loneliness and envy: is there any need for another concept in group psychology? As a method of first priority, these two forces suffice to explain the totality of social behavior in something like 95% of all cases.

What do we want from a group? First: to be in it. Second: to be on top of it.

⌐ Loneliness: fear of abandonment, vacuophobia, poverty of the self, the safety of numbers, amorphous homogeneity. The hunting-primate seeks the group like its arboreal-rodent ancestor seeks the tree. What is affection but sublimated loneliness? What is conformity but calculating loneliness?

⇁   Envy: resentment, greed, the attitude of weakness, "equality", the ugly backside of compassion, the tribal instinct in its most visible aspect. The gathering-primate hoards his social status like his arboreal-rodent ancestor hoarded food. Petty advantage in every form: most of sociality involves the delicate exchange of flattery, insult, and bribe.

- 125 -

Freud's psychology is so skewed to the atomic individual – very 19th century, very "scientific" in the English fashion. An admirable attempt to reduce to functional principles, but his fixation on *libido* was damaging to the movement as a whole: we'd rather think of ourselves as raging nymphomaniacs, than envious lonely slobs.

How much more immediately useful would my little "system" of psychology be to the aspiring student! To learn to see loneliness in action, when people clump and bump against you, pleading for inclusion. To learn to see envy in their glassy eyes, in their cunning maneuvers, in their every prophylactic move, in their heavy cognitive distortions. So much of what's called "narcissism" today is nothing but competitive-projective envy: behavior designed to inspire envy, such that one desires this image of oneself, which defers confrontation with lack and loneliness.

People are not really "egoists", they are "groupists": their orientation is not the self, but their status in various shifting mercurial groups. They have no "self" to fixate on: that would have required the strength to endure a little genuine solitude – they have rather the *as if* of a self, the implication of a self as defined by the group. No wonder so much panic flares when group constituency changes, when the direction remains uncertain, when the canon of values is in question...

- 126 -

Klein and Lacan were early purveyors of the pernicious idea of narcissism as the foundation of the human psyche: bullshit. True narcissists are rare and fascinating. Most of us are merely imitative slobs: self-absorption, anxiety, and vicious frustration are not sufficient ingredients for narcissism. *Incapable of passionate love*: modern humanity suffers far more from this ailment, than a misplaced and botched love.

- 127 -

I prefer to study psychology at the anthropological scale: that is, the level of the *tribe*. Not the level of the "mind", nor the "signifier", nor the individual, and on the other hand not the level of society, nor the state, nor certainly at the level of existence itself or any other way of saying "in the eyes of God". That Nietzschean psychology is *group psychology* is not generally understood. That the Freudian psychology of the family and the primal triangle is immensely valuable in the study of neurosis, but only of limited value in the study of *health* – is also generally not understood. There is no escape from the *tribe*: even what it means to be an "individual", is defined at the tribal scale. What "society" means, is also defined by the distortion of tribe; the same goes for morality and all of the diseases of modernity...

- 128 -

It's generally imagined that neuroscience will one day subsume psychology. But on our present course this remains extremely unlikely: because even assuming that neuroanatomy achieved some perfect elaboration, in absence of a *viable* psychological interpretation, all neurology is merely correlating regions of tissue with poorly defined behaviors and even more poorly described subjectivity. Neurology as it stands strikes me as something like an *inversion* of the dismissal of the appendix: its anatomy was fully documented for centuries, but without a grasp of the importance of the microbiome, it was assumed to be useless. Listening to their chatter, this "brain" everyone is always so thrilled about begins to seem like a useless piece of anatomy credited with a significance it does not have... It begins to seem more sensible to force oneself into seeing the brain like the preaxial Greeks did, as a *heat dump*: what is all this thinking and tinkering but excess heat?

Anatomical exploration could be executed by a machine, but psychology requires a *soul* – because soul is a divining rod for the viable. This is what the musicians mean by "soul": truth as food, the stomach as spirit.

Some would like psychology to be practiced as a kind of statistical mechanics, and thereby reduce its predictions to the purely quantifiable. Indeed as long as its goals remain restricted to vague half-tautological quantizations of modern prejudice, it seems achievable. But statistical modeling always fails to account for *recursive distortion*: knowing when to take a confession at face value *despite* its ironic presentation, is not something one can teach a statistician. There's a sense of arriving where one began that cannot be formulated, only *demonstrated*: that's the Nietzschean interpretive process. A truth value can no more be proven than first order logic, it can only be "constructed" as Brouwer might say...

A RETRAINED ECONOMY OF INSTINCT

My definition of psychology does not reduce to the metaphysical ambition to discover principles of "thought itself", nor does it claim that "the mind" is any ultimate distillation of physics, nor does it indulge in the pretense of a study of "being and time", nor is it interested in forcing the principles of molecular biology to emerge in consciousness. I understand psychology to be a distillation of the *unconscious hermeneutics of sociality*, or the selective inhibition of interpretative process through the power of a *retrained economy of instinct*: you have to *want* to understand, despite all the embarrassments involved. Everything else is merely bad faith mimicry – the real practice of psychology does not begin until you admit something with your back to the wall: only in that moment, when you feel that everything worthwhile about yourself is pitted against a possibility that therefore *must not be true* – do we gain a little freedom in feeling and thinking. In that moment, the locus of your self preservation shifts, from fragile crystalline ideation, to the origamic transformations you were secretly employing as a sleight-of-hand. Nietzsche, the clandestine teacher of most of what's worthwhile in 20th century thinking, is constantly trying to demonstrate that the sooner you admit to being a *dishonest advocate*, the sooner you will learn to become an *honest artist*. From illusory stasis to fugitive vitality: that's all anyone can offer.

- 131 -

In statistics, the *null hypothesis* serves as the default assumption: that there is no asymmetry in the data and thus nothing special to conclude. One has merely taken measurements and obtained a numerical distribution, but learned nothing.

What's the unconscious equivalent? What are the consequences for *the art of perception*? Either an interpretation has nothing to do with a given datum, or it is correlated and justified.

However there is no access to "raw data": everything is already many times interpreted, and not merely by "bias" but by perceptual apparatus. There are often only limited available responses which already assume an interpretation: feeling states cannot be undone. Repression is the only alternative to perception. Actually in social contexts *true communicative error* is extremely rare: unconscious communication is efficient and accurate. The choices are therefore unconscious perception, conscious apperception, or unconscious repression: with many loci of repression, many available termini of displacement, and many combinations of all strategies. Untangling this combinatorial mess constitutes most of the art of perception: not better fidelity in communication, but more accurate mapping of the simultaneous strategies of distortion undertaken by *both parties*. You already know the answer: the work consists in *undoing your unknowing*.

Therefore it's in choosing between likely strategies of distortion that psychology largely consists: tracing how information and response were unconsciously displaced in favor of some other matrix of social signaling, which takes on a life of its own and adds further complexity.

"What's he feeling? Why is he saying this or that?" Is not a question of refining and rejecting interpretations of raw data, but learning to detect *distortion in the data one has* and assigning agency and history to that distortion. Every distortion implies repression, which implies both successful communication and unconscious resistance. The actual practice of psychology revolves around detecting distortion in semantic valence and learning typical trajectories of displacement within the semantic field given probable aversions and desires: there is no flat plane of distribution, but a swirling dance of valences. Perceiving asymmetric distortion waves within this dance and assigning a causality is the art of the science.

It's important to realize that one is always already caught up in a semantic distortion because it necessarily works mutually: language is powerful leverage even if it seems to have a superficial illusory quality – sometimes this nonsubstantiality is part of its power – "it's only words". But every signal has its associated power, else it ceases to function as signal: so much of what we do as perceptive creatures is to discard weakly valent but prominent signals in favor of what they are substituting for – every signifier displaces and obscures another, every gestalt is a provisional as-if.

- 132 -

If I have said that psychology may never be a science and that intuition will always play a central role, do not mistake my message for "anything goes", or that there is no means of detecting and correcting *bad psychologizing*. Certainly my message is not that just anyone is qualified who claims the authority of "intuition" – quite the opposite. Psychology as I understand it is a *discipline* and a practice, and not a workman's science in the usual sense: as though its findings could be exhibited like so much taxidermy. Psychology can no more be practiced by an "ideal mind" than tennis can. The *whole body* is required, and a disciplined body at that.

- 133 -

Why is the academic establishment so opposed to intuition? If it were possible to practice psychology intuitively, then it would also be possible to know at a glance whether an insight had merit or whether it was bullshit. Conversely if intuition is impossible, and produces only deadends and delusion, then they have nothing to fear from us and have only to stand by and watch us shoot ourselves in the foot. But their constant compassionate concern for the flock betrays them: their eagerness to maintain a tenuous hold of authority over psychological truth, speaks of a deep fear of creeping irrelevance. So why are they afraid of the idea of an *intuitive discipline*? Because they are *incapable of it*. Because they're too *verklemmt*, and only feel safe in a world where no one but the *verklemmt* succeed.

- 134 -

Unfortunately "intuition" is a dirty word, invoking weakness of mind and wishful conclusion – we should probably be extremely cautious in its use. I may stand a better chance of being understood, if I speak of a "perceptual discipline", emotional refinement, and everything which says *no* to a thousand wishful guesses before admitting a reluctant *maybe*. Mutually reinforcing reluctant maybes, which coalesce into a cogent profile of any given case, and only become relative certainties when abstracted into generalities and heuristic principles concerning human nature – that's the kind of psychology I'm talking about.

AN INSIGHT TRADITION

- 135 -

Even while emphasizing the importance of natural observation, depth of fieldwork, and above all the accumulation of *bad experience* in the formation of a psychologist in my style – I also maintain that there are a few vitally important concepts to be rescued and defended. I may soon see to it that the Freudian and Nietzschean psychological inheritance gains a new respectable grounding in the latest terminology: for example, I've already found it relatively easy to define *repression* in terms of information theory. What I want to emphasize now, is that prior to any theoretical dance must come a real *training of the body*: I conceive of psychology as an *insight tradition* in the old sense, something much nearer to an *athleticism* than a mere intellectual piddling. When an old master of Gongfu took on a student, he did so reluctantly, slowly, forcing him through many trials designed to test the totality of his *character*: that something as potentially significant to the future of the human race as our best comprehension of motivation, behavior, evolutionary strategy and everything our much-fondled intelligence yields and distorts, is treated with less seriousness and severity than it requires to undergo an *apprenticeship in plumbing* – what does that tell us about ourselves? But psychologists don't need comprehension or character, as long as they are armed with *caustic chemicals* to bore through those clogged pipes...

- 136 -

That old master of ethology and genuine gentleman of science, Nikolaas Tinbergen, once said in his hesitant neo-Victorian rumbling:

> Having myself always spent long periods of exploratory watch-ing of natural events, of pondering about what exactly it was in the observed behavior that I wanted to understand before developing an experimental attack, I find this tendency of pre-maturely plunging into quantification and experimentation, which I observe in many younger workers, really disturbing, unless, as happens to some, they do, from time to time, return, more purposefully than before, to plain, though more sophisti-cated, watching.

The Study of Instinct, vi

"Plain but sophisticated watching": what could be achieved I wonder, if instead of shunting emotionally stunted doctoral students directly from a life of institutional forbearance into neurology laboratories where they are commanded to begin generating numerical tautologies from vague uninterpreted data, we rather focused on finding and developing *a whole person*, who might thereafter be qualified to study and theorize about something so complex as neurological phenomena? How many of them have learned to ask a good question, or have been taught that the formula-tion of *precise questions* is more than half the work of understanding? I look around their literature, and I fail to see the majority of them take the first step in science: *an admission of ignorance*.

- 137 -

Vanity would like to tell me that my kind of intelligence is the rarer type: the poet, the psychologist, the diviner of human nature. That the mathe-matical and scientific kind is more common. But probably, sadly, this is not true. It's possible that the "genius of the heart" is not so rare, but we are much more fragile, more needy, more sensitive to initial conditions, and therefore much less likely to survive intact through those inevitable years of abuse and confusion: those same conditions which we would seek to reform and recolor in our own image, if we could only preserve our confidence long enough to find a voice. "Discontented" culture not only breeds unhappiness, it breeds out the most unhappy, until all that is most visible, all that succeeds most thoroughly and thrives as leadership, are those incapable of any other condition of life. In fact, what I see, is *an increase of souls who thrive in absurd misery.*

- 138 -

All genuine psychological training takes place as intimate hand-to-hand combat: unless you have personal stakes involved, you will not be in possession of sufficient motivation to overcome the resistances to mutual deception – you will remain too "good", too well-meaning, too socially cooperative to begin practicing the kind of reverse stagecraft I teach.

When I practice psychology at a distance, removed by time and space, through the lens of history – how could it be valid? Because not only am I applying past lessons to infer who and what some person is and was and therefore how and what happened, but because I find myself *entangled* – I know *how to entangle myself* in the "semantic field" as I find it. Through history, through mere words, through artifacts, through a thousand signs unconscious and conscious, the human collectivity communicates across vast distances very effectively, whether we know it and want it, or not. We are all of us nodes and junctures and mouthpieces of many convergent and divergent forces: to learn to *read* these datastreams as they flow through us, is what I teach.

THE ART OF PERCEPTION

THE AUTODIDACT MAKES
THE FUTURE

You're sitting in class, say a 300 level psychology course you've been looking forward to. But when the teacher begins the lesson, you get the feeling no one else read the material. You begin to experience that familiar irritation, the urge to dominate, and a little paranoia. Later, just as you've maneuvered the group into an interesting discussion, it happens: someone says something pointedly obtuse. For the next 45 minutes, for which you are paying high sums of money, the class is dominated by willful stupidity, pointless ill-formed questions with self-evident answers, and an unconscious message which seems to reduce to: "I will not be excluded because of ignorance or laziness."

You are quietly boiling with frustration, and you ask yourself: *Is this worth it?*

The professor looks just as bored and irritated as everyone else, and yet he does nothing to prevent it – perhaps because he too would rather allow the class to be sabotaged than potentially learn something. You finally summon the tact to steer the discussion back towards a productive thread, and in the last few minutes you manage to squeeze something like an education out of this farce.

No one thanks you. And in your next class, headed by an activist unqualified to teach dodgeball, you lose your patience and contradict the dogma passed around like communion. You are attacked from many angles at once, because none of the many others who feel the same will speak up. You have been marked for exclusion, and none of them feel that the question of truth and falsehood is worth the social risk.

- 140 -

It's important to understand that although leftist politics dominates most universities today, the reasons for its replication and dominance in that environment have *almost nothing* to do with its content. These are not genuine political convictions, they are advantageous masks: the goal is social status and justification of the privileges of academia. Should the predominant political atmosphere shift, the masks would be exchanged.

The "radical feminist" running your sociology department into the ground *does not care about other women*: she cares about accruing social power and *immunity from censure*. The shrill diminutive literature professor who slanders Homer and Shakespeare, does not care about whatever minority he's chosen to champion, he cares about feeling a little less wretched and ignored, and will gladly take out the frustrations of his lonely life on a student who objects to reading another George Eliot novella rather than Dostoyevsky.

The explicit content of these politics is largely irrelevant. If the year were 1870, these same characters would be lambasting Darwin and promoting colonialism; if the year were 1735, they'd be defending the church and burning Voltaire; if the year were 1460, they'd be flattering Aquinas. They have *nothing to teach you* – except to scorch into the flanks of your naïve expectations a lesson on how disappointing humanity can be.

- 141 -

A career in academia will stunt you – emotionally, developmentally, physically. You will be spared the fundamental placelessness and anxieties of modernity, and thus will be dependent on that protection for life. In your 20s, precisely when you should be expanding your horizons as wide as possible, *failing* as often as possible, experimenting endlessly, exploring hidden social contexts and novel roles, challenging yourself at every opportunity, and learning to deal with merciless uncertainty, in academia you will instead be shuttled from one padded cage to another. You will not learn to walk upon the planet as a native creature, you will not learn to navigate humanity as a skilled operator, you will fail to gain a depth of character you cannot later replicate. Unless your teenage years were full of sufficient struggle and suffering, unless you are the rare type who lifted herself out of poverty and low expectations, unless you already know who you are and what you want – something more naturally common among young women than young men – a career in academia is a bad idea.

- 142 -

A young man emailed me the other day, explaining that he had just dropped out of a psychology and philosophy program, because he realized he doesn't want to become the person the system wants to make of him. Years ago I was in a similar position and made similar choices: how many of us are there? More than once I've seen how the brightest students are driven away by the skittish mediocre majority, how this tightly maintained average perpetuates itself by carefully selecting and promoting those capable of just enough to achieve the status quo, but not enough to threaten the comfortable envelope of expectations.

How likely is it, that in most fields the best intellectual material wanders off like a stray rivulet into an endorheic basin, there to bake and never see the ocean? How likely is it, that the reason "mainstream discourse" is so nauseatingly shallow and pointless, is because no one but the shallow and pointless participate?

> [...] in allen Winkeln der Erde sitzen Wartende, die es kaum wissen, inwiefern sie warten, noch weniger aber, dass sie umsonst warten.
>
> In all corners of the earth sit those who wait, who little know how much they wait, and who know even less that they wait in vain.
>
> Nietzsche, *Jenseits von Gut und Böse*, §274

- 143 -

Why is academia worthless and *much worse than worthless*? Even in the STEM fields, not until the very end of a career will you be taught anything a motivated autodidact could not learn in a fraction of the time. In the humanities, the situation is dire: I feel confident in saying that a literary education equal to the past masters cannot be obtained in any humanities department this side of the Seine.

Why?

⇁ *Universal education lowers standards.* Most universities are incentivized to simply increase enrollment and decrease attrition. Do professors flunk students anymore? And even in the elite institutions, outside of a few high-profile quantitative fields such as robotics and genetics, all competition for attention and funding takes the form of *purely political posturing*: this reaches a fever pitch among those fields most difficult to quantify – namely philosophy, sociology, psychology, literature. The task of these departments is to *seem* to be doing something important, while they accomplish nothing but fan flames of moral panic which justify their existence. Trading centuries of tradition for the sake of a few political points is common practice.

⇁ *Corrosive money.* It's common knowledge that pharmaceutical industry erodes the foundations of genuine medicine: many doctors are little more than pimped-out pushers. A similar process has been occurring in education for some time: every year the university is run more like a business. The product is *graduates*, not education: again this is most pronounced in the humanities, where quantitative research is scarce or impossible and thus market competition must take the shape of political posturing.

⇁ *Moral panic*: the atmosphere of political ostracism ratchets up, precisely proportional to the degree of alienation, frustration, and personal dysfunction which predominates. The modern human body suffers from the hyperalgesia and hypochondria of overpopulated maladaptation, and its response is to seek a benumbed consolation which both worsens this hyperalgesia and prepares the repressed substrate of frustration for a collective hysteria: thus academia, which produces bodies more pampered and useless than anywhere else, is the breeding ground of the worst political and moral posturing in modernity. Especially in the humanities, there is no other means of power, and no better means of offloading repressed aggression.

⇁ *Foucaultian dynamics*: college would like to be considered as compulsory as primary education. Let us remember that compulsory education has nothing to do with a humanitarian concern for the welfare of children, and everything to do with the *manufacture of docile bodies*. It's no accident we continue to dream of high school decades later: it stands precisely where tribal initiation should have been, where the acquisition of autonomy and pride should have been. We are all of us bereft and mere fragments and hungry ghosts of the wholeness of our ancestors.

- 144 -

There is a single sense in which the *explicit content* of the politics currently dominant in the university contributes to that dominance: the erosion of merit, the promotion of moral posturing as sole means of social leverage, weakening existing hierarchies such that the intellectually lazy may succeed through persecution and fearmongering. In other words, "progressive" only insofar as it enables a maximum of personal short-term advantage. This is the same reason "equality" is always a popular cause: because it enables *covert strategies of inequality*.

- 145 -

The group is panicked: you think thoughtful leadership is the answer, but the group thinks otherwise. It's panicked about *belonging*, not group direction. Independent thinking does not alleviate the fear of imminent abandonment, but *intensifies* it: if attention is allowed to focus on excellence, the majority feel in even greater danger of exclusion. Therefore merit must be defined as *moral posturing*, in which the mediocre tend to excel. A shifting and ever-narrowing circle of moral justification is required in order to keep the group anxious and in need of belonging: the atmosphere in which moral actors thrive. The mediocre majority will not stand up for you: they don't need you, because there is no concrete challenge facing the group such that a strength of character might be useful. We must always keep in mind that the transient tribe attempting to form in every group scenario of our firstworld comedy is *fat, pampered*, and has never faced imminent danger, nor hunger, nor need: they are anxious largely *because* they have never known anything dangerous. If real adversity were to appear, the short-sighted majority of apekind would suddenly need you, praise you, follow you around: suddenly it would be cool to be strong and independently minded, rather than weak and morally histrionic. Do not doubt however, that as soon as the danger passed, you would be marked for exclusion again: apekind is *by default weak and vicious*, and only deviates from this norm under the kind of duress in which our best ancestors thrived. Humanity succeeds because nobility and courage surfaces only when absolutely needed, and at all other times reverts to cowardice and guile: this is the reality of human nature which we must stop attempting to hide from ourselves. It's part of what makes us so clever, so powerful, so indomitable. We defeated innumerable predators possessing overwhelming strength and prowess, through this prosimian amplification of wickedness - this is also why and how we invented laughter. *We exploit the strategies of weakness* – above all other creatures, surpassed perhaps only by the hymenopteran exploitation of drone-stupidity and slavery. We are masters of the earth because of our mastery of weakness, guile, betrayal, ambush, our *lack of character*. To be surprised when we find it again in a panicked modernity with its thin flapping hospital gown, is no surprise after all: because we are also masters of *self-deception*. We have told ourselves we are the *most noble animal*, the lawful one, the rational one, the only beast on earth capable of virtue: but the truth could be the reverse. We are more capable of cowardly betrayal than any other: who was it who turned imaginative invention into a form of predation? Who is it who *never fights fair*? Who is it who could not win any fight against even one adversary of the wild without a dirty technological trick? Who alone of all creatures, cannot live *naked on planet earth* but needs a huge and ever-growing array of technological surrogates to nurse him through life?

- 146 -

Moreover, the same formula is baldly visible in our own history: in every conflict between "savage" and civilized man, was there ever a sense that the civilized man was willing or *able* to fight fair? Can we even count the number of dishonored treaties? But why should it surprise us that the civilized man cannot be honest with himself about his weakness? That his ever-growing dependence on overwhelming numbers and technological chicanery is *profoundly dishonorable*? That the majority of humanity seeks *to suffocate the sight of nobility* because it embarrasses them? The root of the Japanese 素晴らしい "subarashii", now meaning "magnificent, wonderful", is "to shrink, make smaller": it once had a primary sense as "terrifying, extreme" and only gradually became adulterated in the same way as the English "awesome" or "terrific". *Excellence scares us*: it makes us feel small, obsolete, potentially unnecessary. Only the excellent delight in excellence: everyone else resents it if they cannot use it or make it their own. Preferably, the average human creature will believe itself to be the pinnacle of creation: oddly enough, this becomes exponentially easier the dumber you are...

Why is it that those who tend to succeed most in our world, are usually *just slightly above average* in most measures? Because intelligence, imagination, integrity, and independence of mind make you *more susceptible to self-defeat...*

- 147 -

No conspiracy, everyone a conspirator. In fact the lack of a coherent conspiratorial plan, contributes to the collective panic, which contributes to the willingness to conspire. The realization of modernity ends in a vicious circle: the lack of unambiguous hierarchy, cultural cohesion, and traditional roles, amplifies the creeping sense of alienation, abandonment, and the transience of group alignments, which contributes to the urgency of forming new alliances and *new urgencies*. But there is no concrete task to be accomplished other than *belonging itself*: therefore the urgency must be about nothing and everything at once – the mark of hysteria. The more the ritual is held in check by the equal distribution of placelessness which modernity enacts, the more hostile the collective becomes to a rationality which defuses the emergency and corrupts the core process of creating *new criteria of exclusion*. Nobody will really calm down until an unambiguous mark of exclusion takes shape, and many are "interned". Therefore your strength and character are *not wanted*: your instincts for leadership tell you that the troubled tribe needs clarity and foresight, but it responds by telling you that it's *much too late*. An emergency is needed; a suitable target for displacement; a justification for novel forms of systematized violence. *Hysteria breeds hysteria*: not merely accidentally, but because functional hysteria seeks to adjust collective conditions such that anonymous mass violence can begin. Therefore rational leadership and the ability to think for yourself is not only not needed, it is a threat to the ceremony. As long as you continue to attempt to lead with honesty and independent thought, you increase the likelihood of becoming a target of the ritual. Either fall in line, escape, or become a victim: the power of ritual exclusion is not such that you can defeat it directly.

- 148 -

A high school diploma used to represent an accomplishment. It has lost this status not because more of us are educated, but because high school used to teach much more effectively. This is most pronounced in the

States, but one hears similar complaints from teachers in the UK, and even the once worldclass standards of Germany are falling. But perhaps lower standards aren't really the problem, but *standardization* itself. Allow me to quote the renowned educator John T. Gatto:

> That system effectively cuts you off from the immense diversity of life and the synergy of variety, indeed it cuts you off from your own part and future, scaling you to a continuous present much the same way television does.
>
> Two institutions at present control our children's lives – television and schooling, in that order. Both of these reduce the real world of wisdom, fortitude, temperance, and justice to a never-ending, non-stopping abstraction. In centuries past the time of a child and adolescent would be occupied in real work, real charity, real adventures, and the realistic search for mentors who might teach what you really wanted to learn.
>
> "Why Schools Don't Educate", Gatto's acceptance speech for
> the 1990 NYC Teacher of the Year Award

Higher rates of literacy and college attendance by no means equates to a higher sum of education: the outliers of intellectual leadership who once pushed frontiers and raised standards for everyone, are being driven away into other pursuits. A greater quantity of furtive mediocrity sums to a much smaller heap: in addition, the much amplified chattering noise of this crowd makes it much more difficult for the worthwhile student to find a worthwhile teacher. There is an enormous number of scientists working in almost every field, and yet I would argue much less scientific innovation in most fields than in the late 19th and early 20th centuries. More human bodies does not equal *more humanity*, nor does more talk equal *more communication*.

- 149 -

Despite everything apparently alarmist in what I've said, I must also remind the reader that higher education is *always tenuous*: the European "university" grew from the monastery, which as educational institution was largely concerned with passing on theological nonsense. But the Christian monastery grew from the late Hellenistic academies of Coptic Egypt, which grew from the fusion of the Greek sophist tradition with the Jewish and Egyptian notions of priesthood: in other words, worthwhile education is constantly threatened by the agencies of obfuscation and obsolescence – *the priest*. Who is mere sophist, and who is the sophist who transcends the type, like Socrates? Who is mere priest, and who is reservoir of disciplined erudition and a vital link to the past, like Berossus? Who is mere charlatan, and who carries medicine for the people?

No simple answers: it's the mark of a worthwhile student to know instinctively, from moment one, who is their master. Knowledge is power, and power seeks knowledge: that this dissipative turbine attracts much pretense, waste, procrastination, and political buffoonery should hardly surprise us... It is probably always the task of an outlier, to challenge the authenticity of a ceremony grown too sure of itself and its means. Do not lose sight of the fact that the production and acquisition of knowledge is a ceremony, whose primary function is to convince the rest of the community that its practitioners *shouldn't have to work for their food...*

- 150 -

The autodidact makes the future, and probably always has. In the Information Age, it has become easier than ever to educate yourself: and yet I don't believe the proportion of us has increased, because our role was never a function of access, but instinct. What may perhaps increase, is our *leverage*: unprecedented access to the sum of human knowledge should not be taken lightly. If you can *learn to learn*, and at that age when you can withstand the pain involved in genuine learning, you have a chance to *never cease learning* – which is the mark of a predestined master.

- 151 -

Ut ager, quamvis fertilis, sine cultura fructuosus esse non potest, sic sine doctrina animus.

Just as the field, however fertile, cannot be fruitful without cultivation, likewise the soul without education.

Cicero

I won't contradict Cicero – moreover I am a teacher by trade and disposition. But the question remains: *what is education?* Do our institutions educate anymore? Or have the aims of systemic modularity, global capitalism, and civilizational efficiency finally superseded whatever remained of the classical sense of *doctrina*? Yet I am no defeatist: it's highly possible that in our own time, it may become more possible than ever to revive and regain the precious threads – to find out what our heritage is and could be, what "critical rationality" might be in the 21st century and what lamp may we have to receive and transmit.

I.3

A HOSTILE TAKEOVER OF EVOLUTIONARY PSYCHOLOGY

INTERESTING DENTISTRY

- 152 -

M y first vision of this book was as a *hostile takeover of evolutionary psy-chology*: "Get outta the seat and behind the yellow line, I'm driving the bus."

Evolutionary psychologists are the waterboys on the sidelines of pop psychology: they assuage doubts, they assure us of a bright future, they flatter human nature and feign a humbled awe before the mysteries as though in pale imitation of the astronomer-as-diplomat à la Carl Sagan... The truth is that there's very little evolutionary theory present here, and certainly not a drop of psychology. There's statistics, there's some weak archaeology, and there's occasionally some *interesting dentistry*: some of the more relevant science anywhere near this field comes from something called "paleopathology" – largely the study of stress patterns in teeth, fractured bone, and picking corn out of petrified feces.

- 153 -

The book is called *Paleopathology at the Origins of Agriculture*, inspired by the work of one Mark Nathan Cohen. This large dull book proves beyond a doubt, redundantly and exhaustingly, that early farmers had:

⇁ Much more disease: nomadic hunters suffered from no endemic disease whatsoever

⇁ More chronic stress

⇁ More childhood malnutrition and famine

⇁ Shorter stature

⇁ More dental wear

⇁ Less dimorphic bodies: less muscled males, more bulky females

⇁ Shorter lifespans, despite the slightly higher incidence of violent death among nomads

➤ Higher reproductive rates, possibly due to more frequent ovulation cycles in sedentary females, along with lower rates of infanticide

➤ Much worse nutrition and health overall

The early farmer was shorter, weaker, more diseased, more stressed, and demonstrably stupider as a result of all these factors. In fact, the authors also show that we have only just now, in the last few decades, began to achieve anything like the nomadic niveau of general health – keeping in mind that no matter how excellent our nutrition, we cannot replicate their freedom from endemic disease, nor their freedom from chronic anxiety, nor the endocrine balance achieved by a childhood of endless physical activity with very little supervision.

- 154 -

The authors of this book had at least 4 prejudices to work against:

1. That agriculture provides better food security: actually dependence upon a cultivated and therefore limited catalogue of food leaves a population much more prone to episodic famine. Nomadic hunters are adept at maintaining access to multiple food sources.

2. That agriculture provides better nutrition: what very few modern people realize, is that the meat, organs, and bones of any given large animal provides a complete nutritional profile. Achieving the same with plant material is very difficult if not impossible. In addition, nomadic hunters typically consumed such a wide variety of game and seasonal foods that nutrient deficiency was very rare – whereas in the history of civilization malnutrition has been the norm.

3. That agriculture provides freedom: actually the nomadic hunter typically worked only about 2-4 hours per day, while the farmer must usually work anywhere between 8-12 hours.

4. That agriculture leads to health, dignity, and knowledge: a dense sedentary population is subject to chronic disease from infancy onward, generally lacks political autonomy, and suffers from endemic ignorance and the psychology of poverty in ways entirely unknown to nomadic hunting populations. It's well documented, for example, that a nomadic hunter typically displays far greater command of his own language than

even the urban and literate modern type: it's not unusual for children under the age of 10 to have memorized the names of hundreds if not thousands of native species of plants and animals, along with their habits, habitats, and potential uses and all the indigenous technical vocabulary attendant on this knowledge. It's been remarked many times that the illiterate nomad is often surprisingly eloquent – but this is obviously the result both of an oral culture and the practical limit on nomadic material wealth, in which manner and bearing are the indelible sign of good breeding.

- 155 -

What's likely to be true, is that the 20th century upswing in average nutrition, will turn out to be a shortlived aberration. Malnutrition is surging back into place: corn syrup in place of potato famines, obesity in place of rickets.

- 156 -

The question remains: if agriculture involves so much cost and so few advantages, why did any population convert?

1. *Weakness.* Most of the incipient agricultural populations were the weakest tribes: they lived in swamps and alluvial plains because no one else wanted to. They learned to cultivate plants because there was no other sustainable food source. Agriculture took so long to dominate human ecology, not because of a lack of the knowledge of plants and cultivation – a typical hunter-gathering tribe could easily have accomplished it – but because the technological and military advantages of a sedentary agricultural lifestyle took so long to accrue before they outweighed the power of a raiding band of nomads.

2. *Slavery.* What so few seem to realize, is the likelihood that any given incipient agricultural group does not represent an autonomous village grinding away at subsistence farming, but a fiefdom under the protection of a nomadic warlord. It seems highly likely that agriculture became "sponsored" and achieved power only because a few of the more ambitious tribes of hunter-gatherers realized that those puny villages in the swamps could become a source of wealth and prestige. They gradually

transitioned from raiding to ruling. If you examine the history, mytheme, and behavior of the pharaohs, for example, suddenly it makes sense: these were originally the most warlike nomadic tribes of North Africa, who only cared to rule the miserable farmers of the Nile delta because the accumulated wealth of all that seed could produce arms on a scale to ensure their continued dominance.

- 157 -

It's almost certain, that our ancestors had many chances to "advance" to agricultural civilization, but *chose not to*: Kokopelli and Hephaistos are deformed for good reason. The herald of technocratic civilization is a *cripple*: isn't the meaning of Prometheus, that his punishment be *twofold*? His liver as the seat of greedy desire is consumed daily, and he is chained to one spot forever: I read this as a warning the nomad issues to the civilized.

I'm convinced that many of our ancestors were familiar with technocratic impulses and their representatives: no doubt they frequently encountered cleverer tribes, with nastier weaponry and more indirect tactics. No one hardly asks themselves, why it is that the Sumerians chose to live in a treeless muddy waste devoid of most resources but water, clay, and tar. My answer is that their mud huts on a scorched plain didn't look inviting enough for raids, and gave them time enough to develop the wealth to eventually overcome the nomads – mercenary armies and strategically divisive alliances between competing tribes is generally the history of a war between calculating wealth and impetuous strength... Why else should the wall of Jericho be 7 feet thick and its moat 20 feet wide? The Sumerians, and likely the early Chinese and Mayans and whoever else, were probably for a long time the dirty villagers kicked around by various warlords, until these lords were eventually seduced by the beer, the bread, and the sophisticate prostitutes – just as Enkidu was overcome.

We moderns, who in our vanity cannot hardly see anything but progress towards ourselves, fail to understand what reigned true for hundreds of thousands of years among the most successful people: they *despised* excessive cleverness. Even the lore of Odin is ambivalent, with sometimes an overt contempt for the thirst for knowledge: sometimes he's almost portrayed as a mad and dangerous sorcerer who has paid for his sins. Even

Odysseus is a compromise and a taut tension between shameful guile and noble risk.

- 158 -

First, there was a fairly sharp decline in growth and nutrition during the confusions and experiments of the transformation from hunting to farming, with its many inventions and increasing trade and disease between about 10,000 and 5000 B.C. Partial recoveries and advances in health occurred during the Bronze Age rise of civilization; then real advance occurred with the rise of Hellenic-Roman culture. Second, there was an increase in disease and crowding during the decline and religious metamorphosis of the Roman Empire, eventually leading to an irregular breakdown of general, but not nutritional, health under a complex disease load, from about A.D. 1300 to 1700. The near doubling of life expectancy and improved nutritional health (except dental) of the twentieth century Western world does reflect both scientific and technological input. But otherwise, technological advance does not neatly correlate with good health, as Cohen has pointed out.

Paleopathology at the Origins of Agriculture, p. 58

Some may call me a pessimist. Where they expect to find a plan of salvation from whatever problem I've outlined, there is empty space. There is nothing humanity can do to subvert the tendencies of the last 10,000 years: we will continue to be shorter, less muscled, less dimorphic, less holistically skilled, more subject to population pressure, and much more subject to endemic disease and endocrine imbalance than our ancestors ever were. Moreover as a result of these physiological stresses and the general effects of overpopulation, we will continue to become more prone to hysterical displacement, more dependent on narcotic satisfactions, more socially meek, less capable of withstanding overt isolation, and thus less capable of self-awareness and personal evolution, and collectively many times more eager for the rituals of anonymous mass violence. Increasingly, humanity seeks out diversity in order to eradicate it: the species is seeking the genetic bottleneck required to evolve past the current maladaptive trough of a nomadic hunter caught within civilization. The instinct at play here is the same kind of collective murder any overpopulated species experiences: it's not so much resource scarcity, but *the overabundance of social contact* which provokes infraspecies hostility to

145

the fever pitch where persecution exists in nature. This is actually demonstrable in almost any species simply by overcrowding it: horrors will result.

Laid out in its broad outlines, the idea that we could "do" anything about this course must appear ridiculous. At most, we may attempt to preserve our psychological disciplines for the future by anticipating how it will be attacked and where it might be most subject to erosion: I've chosen to emphasize the simple mechanics of *repression and displacement* alongside the most obvious symptom of *hysteria*, in order to defuse some of the hypnoid powers of mass violence... But clearly more mnemonic and less scholarly means are called for: a slogan of future resistance is needed. What this might be, I leave to my readers.

HUMAN NATURE: EMBOLDENED BY ERROR

- 159 -

Not only is the character of human nature considered an open question, it's largely considered *unanswerable* – and beyond that, the status quo in the highest circles of the academic humanities is that *there is no such thing* as human nature. In fact looking for it and expecting an intelligible response is considered a sign of nefarious motive for the perpetuation of oppressive fiction. Yet the plainest rendition of the scientific disposition is: *Everything that exists can be described.* Therefore it's with great pains that the postmodernists contort themselves to produce the illusion that the inquiry into essential human nature is a malicious ploy, if not a logical impossibility. At my most Foucaultian, I might say that it has been a fraudulent sideshow, that the most famous and celebrated inquiries into human nature since Socrates have been little more than a half-hearted red herring, a *straw man*, erected for the purpose of distracting rivals while you marshal rhetorical forces via more subtle means. Usually it's little more than flattery and the secularization of religiously conceived fictions: see Kant, or the equally impressive and useless logical contortions of Nagarjuna and the entire edifice of Tibetan "psychology" – the lost opportunities for an *honest* appraisal of human character in the midst of so much earnest meditative practice is somewhat overwhelming to me – but it was never the honest practitioners writing the theory... The philosophers have always pretended not to know what the human being is, in order to create room for their childish phantasmagoria, a freakshow of avaricious geriatric wish, a boudoir of self-glorifying negligee with muslin and the hazy brushstrokes of a late romantic painter. The typical postaxial philosopher philosophizes *in order not to know himself*. Descartes comes to mind, Hegel, and sadly also Plato, Spinoza, and perhaps Confucius as well. Spinoza is an example of the narrow miss of the birth of a superb psychologist: in the preface to the *Tractatus*, he is wonderfully acrid, contemptuous, and never more psychologically acute. Only the downbeats and footnotes of the *Ethics* are worth reading. And similarly if Plato had put all that dramatist's empathy to work in genuinely grokking the human character... but then he wouldn't be Plato. He would have been something like Heraclitus, and what we'd have left of his work would not be the tomes so carefully copied, but the fragments "accidentally" lost. Who knows that Plato didn't occasionally become honest – but these passages have been dutifully corrected, redacted, forgotten. Collectively we do not want to know what we are. Why? Why out of so many successful conquests of the unknown – this ape who can fuse atoms and prove that time is relative to light – why should we find anthropology so difficult? The truth is that it's not difficult at all: but it *makes you weaker*. For an ape that wants to be a god, to know how much it remains ape serves no advantageous purpose. To know how wretched, laughable, and flawed one is, in a very strong nature could transform you into a lovable saintly mensch – but in all other cases will simply induce depression, wrath, denial. Illusion emboldens. Pomp and circumstance are necessary. As every usurper knows, the pretense to noble origin is indispensable. We used to claim to be descended of gods; later we only claimed to be "made in the image" of a god; still later we reduced the claim to "immortal reason"; now we claim not to know what our nature is at all. We'd like to bar the way and blur all certainty as to the nature of human beings: for example, the attack on sexual dimorphism serves this purpose – of inducing an anesthetized ignorance and confusion as to who we are and where we came from. A story of an increasingly desperate origin myth, which has been pruned down to ugly stumps: we're left with the absurd claim that *there is no origin* to the human character, that there is nothing but a vapid wishful future, and pushed to its extreme becomes a desperate nihilism which claims that nothing is meaningful but the latest frontier of audaciously expensive ignorance and the tenuous membership in an ever more insular ring of rivals. It cannot be a coincidence that this sounds like the last days of a decaying dynasty: the tastes become extravagant, absurd, and take delight in their effrontery to plain sense, driven by a need for escape from everlouder urgencies beyond the shrinking moat, while the gains and rewards become ever more abstract and yet full of plunder, cleverly removed and cleansed of the inequity upon which it is built. In the realm of morality my own time stinks like the court of Louis XV or the Qing dynasty. Something's gotta give.

- 160 -

Allow me to provide a counterexample of what might qualify as "evolutionary psychology".

Mammals are essentially *radiative forms of the rat*. The rat is the *most plesiomorphic* of all mammals: the longest fossil record of any mammal lineage is held by a rat called "Multituberculata" at 166 million years.

And therefore what is the character of this ancestral mammal? *A nocturnal omnivorous thief*: sneaky but bold, fearful yet aggressive, greedy, clever, calculating, agile. The wild rat scares easily but returns quickly, and will defend itself with extreme ferocity when cornered. They are masters of the dark, and find the most clever hiding places quickly. They constantly assess strategic position. They learn rapidly. They avoid direct confrontation, and prefer to steal, sneak, and horde: one can easily imagine what it must have required to evolve as a nocturnal thief during the Triassic age of protoavian giants. They fear exposure and the unknown, and yet constantly exploit advantage whenever they sense it. The rat emotional profile forms the heart of the most ignoble traits of the primate, along with its famous cleverness and its surprising fierceness. It is not essentially courageous, but it is extremely aggressive.

What's even more revealing, is that the primate lineage is one of the *most recent* divergences from the rat plesiomorphism: whereas canines or ungulates for example, have been something other than rat for much longer. We belong properly to the "supraprimates" alongside rabbits, shrews, and mice. As little as 20 million years ago, we were little more than an insectivorous lemur. In the most flattering profile, we could call ourselves the most social and successful treeshrew.

- 161 -

Whenever I see a writer begin to talk about nature as a "realm of terror and senseless violence" in contrast to human civilization, law, and moral sentiment, I throw the book away. This is merely recycled garbage, a certain soundbite on repeat since the agricultural revolution. This is not theory based on experience and observation. It's a prejudice at best. But I could be more specific and unforgiving, and call it *belligerent stupidity*: it's a stupidity maintained on purpose. The ape pretends to be stupid when it wants to make room for being clever somewhere else. In the thinking of the average amateur philosopher, "nature" denotes the landfill where one is permitted to dump one's prejudices. On the other side of the road, is the palm tree resort called "science", "progress", "humanity". But this is a tired game to me: they *discard* in the space marked "nature" whatever is not desirable for the cardtrick in question – what we are not, are no longer, and have transcended. When we want a vacation, nature is an abode of peace and consolation. When we want to slander something as barbaric, it's suddenly self-evident that nature is senseless, marked by fear, horror, a living nightmare. As someone who spends many hours of observation in nature every day, watching wild creatures go about their business oblivious to me, I come to the same conclusion I have for many years: if nature has any one aspect, it is *joyful indifference*. There is violence, predation, competition, rivalry, loss, as much death as birth, but there is little affect of horror but what you bring. For a creature to obey the spectrum of its ancestral instincts, *joy is necessary*. Fear is generally brief and serves to create a path of escape, but it is by no means an efficient longterm motivator. Any creature perpetually terrified, is a creature crippled. The chipmunk who brazenly collects his seeds in daylight atop a windy bluff where hawks are known to be, does so because his joy in being a chipmunk is greater than his fear of becoming a meal. I am at this moment watching a group of nighthawks hunting their insect prey at twilight, listening to their echo-locations, watching their inimitable coursing, diving, hovering patterns: fear has nothing to do with this. Again I'll repeat one of my fundamental lessons: what is an emotion? Rather than persist in believing the emotions are *ends in themselves* – as though the point of life was sentience, or worse yet, "consciousness" – we must define emotion as the *preparatory priming of an instinctual discharge*. An affect serves to ready the nervous system for a set of adaptive responses: certain behavioral thresholds are lowered, others raised. Thus fear has its place as an emergency protocol for preserving the body and deferring all other priorities. But prolonged, it causes dysfunction, systemic stress, and finally premature death riddled with cancer: something only reproducible today in laboratory rats and the civilized slaves of humanity. A functional creature – fighting off rivals, battling for territory, outwitting its predators, breeding, nesting – does these things because it is so *free* from inhibition, and so *tyrannized* by overwhelming instinct: joy is the priming mandate of healthy living.

- 162 -

Nature is cruel yet generous, gentle yet unimaginably violent by turns: nature is the diceroll. Nature is superabundant indifference. It will swallow you whole, only to birth you again. As Nietzsche pointed out, "survival of the fittest" is incorrect. Although scarcity does occur, it's relatively rare: excess is the rule, and the formula should instead read: *propagation of the most numerous*. By no means does nature guarantee the fittest nor best, nor that evolution proceeds in any direction whatever. Merely that whatever propagates the most, *propagates the most*.

- 163 -

Why does civilized man need to mythologize nature as a realm of injustice and nightmare? Firstly because farmers are stupid. Farming is a begrudging toil, teaching you to cower before the weather, perpetually afraid of too much or too little. A good farmer is dullwitted but consistent, stubborn, ill-tempered, mistrustful, cautious to a fault, anal and unpleasant. To him "nature" is just another aggravation: nature is weed, locust, flood. Nature is everything uncooperative which makes his life harder. Nature is malignant and disorderly. Later, to the urbanite – the one who doesn't know where food comes from and doesn't want to know – nature outside of the bucolic countryside is little more than myth. The closest analogue within his powers of imagination is the filthy underbelly of the city. Thus he imagines crime, conspiracy, treachery, corruption. And there you have the formula for correctly discerning nearly all depictions of nature you will find: modern man sees nature as the *corrupt city*, the city of sin, the world of crime. And thus this indentured servant of civilization both fears and desires the freedom of crime he imagines there... Clue as to why "nature" as we're used to this concept, vacillates between a lascivious Romantic fiction of spiritual freedom and a steamy novella of pure murder.

- 164 -

I maintain that the nomadic hunter cultivates the most enlightening relationship to nature: nature is a teeming world of spirits, some more dangerous and useful than others. Nature is an opportunity for predation: the home of the unknown, where both good and evil reside. It's extremely telling to me that nomadic hunters are typically much more concerned with the *perils of human witchcraft* than the dangers of their wilderness. The lesson is: *the ape is the most dangerous animal*.

That the most successful predator of the last 100,000 years wishes to become "nonviolent", is such a preposterous notion, that it must be either utterly repulsive or fabulously funny. "At the eleventh hour", I hear those species exterminated by human hands cry, "this ape wants to wear the costume of nonviolence!" After all the planetary forces subdued and annihilated, those opponents which once prevented our current unchallenged dominance – now it becomes fashionable to claim that the essence of human nature has nothing to do with dominance and annihilation. After 2 million years of tribal warfare, after 4 million years of the acquisition of the tools and instincts of the hunt, after 20 million years of accumulating the kind of treacherous intelligence necessary to transform a lanky skittish grassland chimpanzee into a merciless demigod, now within the safety of the waning wheels of civilization we find it socially advantageous to distance ourselves delicately and adroitly from everything that smacks of conquest and crime. The examples are so numerous that we're subject to an embarrassment of riches, but I'll point out a few just to emphasize that this is not merely a question of *white guilt*: one of my favorite counterexamples is that of Australia. The Australian continent used to abound in an enormous variety of fantastically proportioned megafauna, all of which vanished almost immediately after the arrival of Homo sapiens circa 40,000 BC. The ancestors to the Aborigines simply did not have the patience or foresight to avoid wiping out much of the game which would have made the lives of subsequent generations much easier. Kangaroo were just too difficult to exterminate. Later, a similar story played out in North America in 14,000 BC...

Of course the quiet, unconsciously lisped white European response to such stories is: "Yes, but not us, not I, not now – (and after all they were only primitives)". As though the record of Western Europe did not serve as one of the more bloodthirsty and reckless catalogs of human history... But now that Europe is old, tired, and fabulously fat, sitting on the accumulated capital of colonial empire, it wants to claim to be and *always have been* the foremost champion of equality, distributive justice, and universal human rights. But if the European is distinguished by anything in the scope of human history, it is his penchant for hypocrisy. One could easily argue that the primary function of a Christian education is a deep and abiding training in hypocrisy – which eases colonization, facilitates justification of rule, and fills the gaps in authority which a weak government cannot otherwise manage. When patriotism wanes, the church is ready to take up the slack. I believe the situation is no different today, and certainly from the perspective of the Chinese and Islamic nations, European hypocrisy looks just as alive and well as it was when our priests wore linen and officiated in Latin, rather than polyester and 60-character strings – as I've pointed out before, morality is so much more tenacious than any one theology. Euroamerican 21st century technocracy wants to lead the way to the promised land of equity, peace, and justice. Does that message differ in any significant way from precisely what was preached on the beach of *San Salvador* 500 years ago? The image of the "Salvador" has merely been updated, digitized, and rebroadcast: Christ the genderless software engineer... But after all it's not our fault. There's nothing essentially defective about us, but merely the degree to which we are subject to the forces of civilizational decrepitude with very little of the grounding in ancient ways which makes some people more resistant to the eroding forces of modernity. Regenerative antiquity versus modern senility: it's the difference between milk spilled on a lingam and a crucified Christ – if you cannot taste the difference, there is no hope of understanding me here.

The essential question remains, why does the threshold of civilizational complexity and technological dependence known as modernity, inevitably turn to hypocrisy as one of its essential means? We know that its propagation is fundamentally a question of inclusion and exclusion – a posture assumed to prevent loss of social status – but why does this particular posture predominate? *Why nonviolence?* Because those least capable of violence are ascendant. In an age when hyperspecialized fidgeting knowledge, a narrow bureaucratic mind, and an ever-deepening investment in technological surrogacy of an essentially frail body will earn you success and applause, it becomes an additional expedient to glorify that same frailty and the furtive treacherous glance as something else, and thereby exclude those who threaten with their vitality and verve. However it's generally those on the margins of this social order who seek to amplify and tighten the circles of exclusion around those virtues they can emulate: those who already benefit from the social hierarchy have the least need of moral posturing, and participate only as much as they feel insecure and in need of "divine right". And so moral fashion shifts and sways, as the group glances this way and that looking for the safest center. I prescribe a careful study of the rapid changes in fashion between 1967 and 1983: you can watch the hippie aesthetic move from the interesting slob and a degenerative "mod" of the mid 60s, to the self-righteous rebel of 1969, to the more overtly hypocritical coke-snorting poseur as early as 1971, to the tentatively longhaired floppy-headed uniform of the mediocre circa 1976, to the passé sunsetting mustache of the hasbeen by 1979, to mere echoes within the anachronistic leather jacket of the disco creep, the thick plastic glasses of your father-in-law, and the faux woodgrain paneling in your mother's kitchen by 1983. Moral fashion is no different. It is first born of poverty and lack, what one finds oneself being out of necessity, to something one can exploit, to a kitschy borrowed identity, to a badge of normalcy and a minimum requirement of inclusion, to something gauche and tired.

The fashion of nonviolence however, will continue to resurface because its fundamental cause is sedentary life and instinctual frustration. *"Nonviolent life" is one of the most violent ideas ever conceived.* The unthinkable petulant cruelty dreamt up by this vicious chimpanzee, which after having scratched its way to the top using so many forms of treachery, finally wants to ensnare the very concept of life itself within an impossible cage: if it must be tortured by its oppressive success, then it at least wants the right to torture something beautiful, a pastime of delicious cruelty. And so it praises the virtues of blamelessness and harmlessness with a quiet irony, even more quietly delighted to watch the contortions such a morality demands.

- 166 -

Am I being melodramatic? But I find the ostinato strings and facepaint necessary, because the resistance to seeing the complete picture of the human story is immense. If your ape-ancestor now looks like a scheming villain, with his thin mustache and toothy evil grin, it's a necessary antidote to seeing him as a dopey, mumbling, irritable imitation of the blissful and well-wishing human perfection we believe we are so near to reaching. The scheming ape *continues to scheme*: this moral disguise is just another calculated temporary position, which will be abandoned the moment it no longer serves. I believe we must be proud to be this ape: this indomitable weakling, this weasel-heart, this voracious treeshrew which wants to rule the world. Furthermore I believe we are nearest to transcending our past ignobilities when we embrace our thirst for power and divine knowledge: there is no other good reason that peak antiquity is so ennobling, so aesthetically perfect, so monumental in its pantheon of invoked spirits. The spirit of *honest predation*, of bold naked exploitation of the earth, that cold stare of the cat and the bird of prey – didn't the ancients want these qualities because they wanted an antidote to the wretched self-loathing simian, who needs his big brain primarily for cooking up nasty traps? ...And perhaps this was after all only another disguise, and the moderns of late antiquity who exposed the falsehood of those gods were just as correct in pointing out the eternal wretchedness of the human soul as I am now. Let no man put asunder what we join here today: we're talking about the kernel of human ambition, for which there can be no final answer. There will always be another noble child born to a humble home, another audacious monkey in the mix, another chance for this unrealized nobility to find expression. The problem we face is that our ambitions to greatness will always be cursed by the path we take to it: knowledge, technology, and consciousness will continue to *stain our greatness with the marks of weakness*. – And there's the human condition in one sentence.

- 167 -

Someone asked: why didn't dinosaurs develop civilization? There are multiple prejudices at work in that question, the antidote for which is this half-serious answer: they had one of the most glorious civilizations of terrestrial life thus far.

We must stop assuming that genetic adaptation, and specifically the modularity of *facilitated variation* which enables diverse successes in a riotous ecology such as dominated the middle Jurassic, must be excluded from the *definition of technology*. The superiority of protoavian genetics was their technological advantage. If you examine any given criterion for the existence of civilization, you'll find in it largely nothing but *ecological domination via hypertrophic exploitation of core adaptive traits*: for the hominid group, this is tool use and spoken language. It strikes me as simply the prejudice of an ape, to claim that nothing but a tool gripped by the hand defines technology: the longer we maintain these convenient self-glorifications, the more ignorant we become concerning what we really are. To be civilized is to dominate the earth with a minimum of effort, such that energetic extravagances become possible: that does not sound like an abuse of the term if you say it in Latin...

To make the analogue between protoavian "civilization" and our own seem more plausible, it's important to understand that Homo sapiens is not a unique species in the ape lineage, but rather the last of the hominid phyla which once had many diverse alternatives. There's growing evidence that all of them used tools: there's many paleontologists convinced that Neanderthal could speak and may have been the first to invent the core hominid toolset – namely that Neanderthal was a superior hunter-gatherer, and Homo sapiens merely borrowed and stole many of their innovations. The anthropocene is a subset of the *pithekocene*.

- 168 -

The human race fears "biological reductionism", because it fears being treated with the contempt it feels for the rest of living nature. The ape makes a show of respect and awe before humanity to the same degree that he fears waking up on the wrong side of the cage.

- 169 -

Biological intelligence does not need to be conceived as distinct from what we call "artificial" manipulations of ecological resource. Human beings continue to dominate their environment through hypertrophic exploitation of their two interdependent techniques: tool use, and the elaboration of the linguistic faculty in all its bewildering forms – encompassing everything from mathematics to hiphop. Additionally, we should include the extended infantilism which enables a lifetime of learning and neuroplasticity. Human neuroplasticity is probably our secret weapon – although it is also a grave risk to the species: the hominid path entails high risk of psychosomatic illness. Understanding this risk helps explain much of why and how we *are* different from the other animals: in place of the certainty of instinct, we have taboo, ritual, and hope.

- 170 -

There is the unspoken assumption, that because biological intelligence appears more *constrained*, it must therefore be inferior. But instinct and genetic priming are not stupid. Actually this constraint is an illusion: we imagine that human beings are free to do or be anything at all – but this is not remotely true. All this alleged freedom, arbitrariness, and diversity within humanity is limited to an extremely narrow scope of behaviors compared to all that life does and can do. Human beings cannot help but *be hominid*. Everything we've accomplished since the Paleolithic is a selective elaboration and hypertrophy of existing technologies. Although again it must be admitted that enduring neuroplasticity – the deferred adulthood of humanity – is exceptional: again because of the enormous risk. This is why human beings are so uniquely concerned with *mental health*: everything spiritual can be construed as the attempt to recover the certainty of instinctual coherence through cultural elaboration and the binding power of ritual. Usually what keeps the human being sane more than any other factor, is its craving for social bond – it's *loneliness* that lures us away from idiosyncratic psychosis and the artistic mood alike. Although group consensus is likely to create fictional entities and employ as much mythology as it needs to, the human being is adapted to create *functional group modalities* in any given environment, not merely despite its fictional metaphysics but *because* of it: if we've proven anything in the last 100,000 years, it's our ability to adapt to any ecology using a remarkably uniform formula as hunter-gatherers – including everything entailed by metaphysics and the role of the shaman, whose job it is to contain the potential for neurotic paralysis. One of the most important tasks of the traditional medicine man is to induce neuronal systemic crisis, pseudoepileptic catharsis, and thus achieve expiation and containment of the high potential for psychosomatic disease in the human creature. This function and its remarkable uniformity across cultures, is witness to the enduring presence of that almost anathema idea: *human instinct.*

- 171 -

As the besotted *ship of fools* surrounding AI hype demonstrates, we need mythology now as much as ever: perhaps more than ever, since one of the core functions of metaphysical speculation is to *contain the pathological within the imaginary*. When something goes wrong and our uglier nature appears, we much prefer to blame angry spirits, moral failings, fictional disasters and other hysterical displacements than confront the possibility of irresolvable tensions in the human condition, something which only the outliers can afford to imagine. The prophet speaks with the voice of the desert: he turns his ire and envy into a popular tune about false gods or the sins of the people whenever he can – maybe I should blush here and wink. Thankfully the psychologist trumps the prophet, or absorbs his power: it's the Nietzschean path to force psychology to overcome all appeals to moral authority or die trying. But prophetic authority is only desired at the critical moments of breakdown in group dynamics: when the tribe needs the influx of a radical paradigmatic shift, it becomes briefly receptive to the influence of the visionary. Just as in ancient astronomical lore, it was during the transitions between regimes that the divine child appears to save the world. Therefore we can be certain that part of the human adaptive package is to maintain wild-eyed outliers in reserve, to continually eject a small set of its gifted members to become wise in the margins – despite the fact that only a small percentage of them will resist succumbing to their own psychosomatic profile and get a chance to reinject their creative potential into the community. Most of us talented weirdos just wander around in the dark talking to ourselves – interminable interrogation is the curse of introspection – therefore I agree with the old stylings: if you're going to talk to yourself, make it into a song, a chant, a calligraphy of pathos, something done under the naked witness of the blazing starry sky, something to gift your people as medicine.

- 172 -

In 1971, Foucault and Chomsky participated in that famous televised debate centered on the question: "does an intelligible human nature exist?" Despite my admiration for Foucault, despite my agreement with his every word, and despite my delight in his extremely subtle predatory humiliation of his clownish opponent – who was clearly far out of his depth and gradually realizing it – I consider the question ridiculous and primarily symptomatic of the ills of intelligentsia. Foucault demonstrates the bleeding edge of erudite historicized nihilism, Chomsky demonstrates everything willfully ignorant, that ideological mediocrity refined to its limit of self-contradiction which typically defines the spokesperson of any given age.

In answer to the assertion that we are a tribal predatory mammal, Foucault might say: that is the conclusion which 21st century anthropology allows, having received its own instructions from the totality of socioeconomic life. That is the hegemony of a kind of science which dominates now because its means and aims consolidate and transmit other power relations.

Retort: dominance or recession of a science does not repudiate the possibility of truth! In other words, *forms of knowledge may be ranked*: its my longterm ambition to demonstrate that the health of the human body is the star by which to steer our epistemology. However, as long as the inquiry remains tamely within the limits of this language-game, Foucault's historicized nihilism must win: there is no means by which we can prove an abstracted standard of health which does not draw on those forms of knowledge and power which we were supposed to justify. We will immediately turn to the weapons of class warfare, and the only honest advocacy is the advocacy of *this human body at this human time*. This is the point at which polite discourse fails, Wittgenstein weeps, and we must ask a very different question: "*What do I do with this body in space and time?*" Only where there is *no possibility of abstention*, do we get clear answers from the slippery inevitable nihilist: the academic must advocate just as inevitably for the academic life and everything which makes it possible and necessary... My philosophical method lives and dies with precisely the kind of *personal confrontation* which Foucault found inconvenient and impolite:

> Non, je ne fais pas un problème d'une question personnelle, je fais d'une question personnelle une absence de problème.
>
> No, I don't make a problem out of a personal question, I make of a personal question an absence of a problem.

- 173 -

But it's not his intellectual agility that impresses me. In fact I feel he only *began* to get things right, just because he was such a subtle predator – the French intellect can generally dodge anything at all, but fails in the attack: Foucault relied on an unassailable mass of erudition, a kind of smothering and closet drama technique popular with diligent scholars, who like to say important and tender things in the midst of a dustcloud and a hush. Anyway, without him I would have no one in 20th century philosophy to take seriously, and I'd rather not be quite that arid.

- 174 -

It's not that I don't think I could win this argument on logical grounds – perhaps I could seem to right now, anyway – but that it *wouldn't matter*: Foucault and those like him have all the reasons in the world to deny something like human nature – it's exciting, it sounds true in a way, it enables more immediately suspicious suppositions, it makes an academic life in the humanities seem much more important than it otherwise might, it wrests control back from the scientists, and so on. In other words, postmodern fashions prevail in the humanities because they are effective weaponry against the incursions of the authority of science: to self-destruct the grounds of fruitful discourse, counting on one's ability to survive in an absurd environment, to redeploy moral tactics where critical thinking had previously dispelled its right to be, to seem to have a form of higher rationality zealously guarded with fickle watchwords, in short to recover some of the *prestige of the theologian*. Foucault lands within the scope of my harshest critique, yet for him I reserve a place of honor, because despite all those factors he manages to say very important things.

- 175 -

Es könnte scheinen als ob ich der Frage nach der Gewißheit ausgewichen sei. Das Gegentheil ist wahr: aber indem ich nach dem Kriterium der Gewißheit fragte, prüfte ich, nach welchem Schwergewichte überhaupt bisher gewogen worden ist — und daß die Frage nach der Gewißheit selbst schon eine abhängige Frage sei, eine Frage zweiten Ranges.

It might appear that I've avoided the question of certainty. The opposite is true: but in the course of investigating the criterium of certainty, I tested those scales upon which things have generally been weighed thus far – and that the question of certainty is itself a dependent question, a question of second rank.

Nietzsche, *Nachlass* KGW VIII-1.150

The existence of the *épistème* is no refutation of the scientific method: our critique revealing the complicity of power in all forms of knowledge should make our science all the more rigorous and capable. I understand the Foucaultian method as nothing other than a refinement of the Socratic method through the addition of history: to separate fact from opinion requires not merely experimentation, but *the discovery of unconscious motive*. This is precisely where psychology is supposed to reside as the bridge and crucible, as the guarantor of a minimum of honesty and the constant injection of doubt into every polemic. For example, it's when Foucault becomes brutally honest, leaving no more room for pale childish excuses, that Chomsky is most visibly shaken:

Il faut attaquer les pratiques de la justice, il faut attaquer la police, il faut attaquer les pratiques policières mais en termes

> de guerre et non en termes de justice. [...] On fait la guerre pour gagner, non parce qu'elle est juste.
>
> It's necessary to attack the practices of justice, to attack the police, to attack the police practices in terms of war and not in terms of justice. [...] One makes war to win, not because it is just.

That the acquisition and defense of power guides unconscious motive at the collective level, appears to me to be just the Nietzschean insight applied to the history of ideas with a consistency and scope no one else has been capable of. Foucault is to the myth of progress what Freud is to the myth of conscious agency.

- 176 -

A field guide to Foucaultian dynamics. Elementary school ensures emotional stunting. High school ensures a parasitic tribeless social orientation incapable of loyalty. College adds the final thin veneer of intellect and pretense to science, such that the last access to instinctual intelligence is precluded.

A genuine relationship to the projects of knowledge and the interests of science, is not something that yields to a standardized test. Almost nothing of value can be measured. Our educational systems train in *clever stupidity* where intelligence would be dangerous and *stupid pedantry* where pretense is advantageous. Observe the way mathematics is taught.

- 177 -

Foucault is possibly the most dangerous nihilist of the 20th century, because his nihilism is covert, and thus useful to the socialite, and thus fashionable. Moreover he's dangerous because he's so often correct. He's absolutely correct about the machinations of civilizational forces, that projects of knowledge and science are means of the control of bodies. But everywhere it's *implied* that nothing but these machinations ever existed or could: that there is nothing but a twisted totalitarian will to power wrapped in the guise of a will to knowledge. The problem is that he never becomes willing to face this question directly and honestly: because strictly speaking, that statement might be correct – but the next question should ask, is our biological inheritance itself a "twisted totalitarian will to power", and if so, can it be characterized very differently? Are we merely discussing the qualitative difference between health and disease?

- 178 -

That Foucault is skeptical of any attempt to provide a psychological explanation for human behavior in the midst of systemic discipline: good! He is certainly correct to be suspicious of all psychiatry and the authoritarian complicity of psychologists... But to conclude – or imply – that all possible psychological analysis is too polluted by these power structures such that there is *no intelligible human nature*: that is an enormous mistake. And not merely a mistake: the "blank slate" model is one of the chief fabrications of modernity, whose purpose it is to justify bodily contortion and erode instinctual coherence as far as civilizational forces demand. Moreover the blank slate model of the European Enlightenment has its roots in the priestly fable of "original sin": for millennia now, one of the most successful tactics in paralyzing the unrulable aspects of humanity has been to teach it, from day one, how much it *needs teaching*. The first step in deforming the instincts is to produce the illusion that they are a source of pain and error – and later that everything instinctual and thus everything unconscious, is wrong, delusional, *ignorance itself*: the secret brotherhood of the Buddhist and Christian projects in service of civilizational domestication.

To be nothing, or to be "born into sin": the effect is similar enough to warrant extreme caution here. Those whose power depends on the hypnosis of a promised and mimicked future of perfect harmony and peace – priest, politician, academic – need at all costs the great lie that the human being can be anything at all as long as it uses pretty names, because he is *nothing at all* – or much worse than nothing – without these virtues.

- 179 -

An indivisible, invisible, identical *monad* which all human subjects share, has just as little discernible character as a pure emptiness: Plato and Descartes could no more scrawl upon the slippery sphere of the soul than Derrida and Deleuze could prove that an intelligible human nature is impossible. Soul and no-soul are analogous to the close relationship between monotheism and atheism: where once there was a hefty crystal ball into which the theologians and metaphysicians could stare while massaging their fictions about eternal Reason and human destiny, there is now merely a vacancy, but the kitschy velvet throne remains precisely where it was and is now home to any number of disposable idols plastered with political bumper stickers.

- 180 -

We *are* animal. 4 billion years of terrestrial life is not negated by sitting on your tuckus dreaming up fantasies of a substanceless being wholly shaped by history.

Moreover, my perspective is not terribly well suited to the current "épistème": the anthropological evidence has been increasingly suppressed since E.O. Wilson's work in the 1970s. The Freudian psychological insights concerning our proclivity to neurotic displacement has been suppressed. The Nietzschean insight concerning our proclivity to perpetuate the moral lie and live a life built on moral lies, has been suppressed.

It's vital not to confuse Enlightenment fables of a theocratic essence of Man imbued by Platonic overtones, with a sociobiological profile of Homo sapiens, the hunting primate. What we are is written everywhere, one merely must overcome the sense of loss in acknowledging that we are animal, and *not* "made in the image" of anything. We are a rather odd, tinkering, talking, naked ape, speeding headlong into no-one-knows-what.

We freely volunteer that this knowledge is a form of power. As hermeneutic it has great explanatory range; it unravels so much of what seemed unsolvable in postmodern epistemology and its flirtations with exotic ontology – the postmodern signature is to erect a wall of an epistemological paradox in order to justify ontological extravagances and metaphysical procrastination. The sociobiological perspective has power and antidote, but it's also certainly much less powerful than the idea that we have *no essence at all*: this fantasy appeals so widely because it permits every sort of nonsense – especially that gleeful Chomskyan complicitude hiding behind the same old morality of nonviolence and universal compassion – in other words, the intellectual dishonesty which emboldens the moral disease. This happens to be precisely the same kind of intellectual dishonesty which early Christianity employed 2000 years ago: whether we have an eternal soul which must be saved by the church, or *no*

165

soul which must be shaped by a new society, is fundamentally the same equation despite appearances. The morality has not changed in one degree, only the metaphysical forgery.

- 181 -

Yet the readers who know my work will understand that I consider Foucault the most worthwhile philosopher of the 20th century. Foucault is both a worthy teacher and a worthy adversary – because here is a Frenchman who actually internalized something of Nietzsche and occasionally has the humility to speak plainly:

> ... que pouvoir et savoir s'impliquent directement l'un l'autre; qu'il n'y a pas de relation de pouvoir sans constitution corrélative d'un champ de savoir, ni de savoir qui ne suppose et ne constitue en même temps des relations de pouvoir.

> ... that power and knowledge directly imply one another; that there is no power relation without the correlative constitution of a field of knowledge, nor any knowledge that does not presuppose and constitute at the same time power relations.

> *Surveiller et punir* I.1

How could this be? In Nietzschean terms it sounds plausible enough: that every will to knowledge is also a will to power. But what is a "power relation"? A capacity to act enabled by a differential of capacity: a tension between dominant and dominated. The Nietzschean method seeks points of tension in any semantic fabric, stretching the polarities away from each other without destroying plausibility, thus generating novel perspective both through the release of this bound tension and the increase of it: *Nietzsche the masseuse* gives the painful, effective, memorable massage – releasing those shooting pains which cause temporary scotoma, lightheadedness, euphoria, the resurgence of old memory and repressed emotion.

But how does the tension between dominant and dominated constitute a "field of knowledge"? Analysis partitions, assigns, molds: effective knowledge writes upon the soul and body, determines its expressions and possible representations. A language is a matrix of finite possibilities, a set of signs. Fluency in the available means requires obedience and complicity: language is a form of compulsion. Every representation is a falsification: at best it expresses a sufficient approximation, but generally expresses so much more of the system itself, its own relation to many other prior representations, than any given "reality"... And we encounter the epistemological puzzles of the 20th century: how can the givenness of any experience be conceived, when we allow that every experience is "always already" a product of what was to be analyzed by the light of this "a priori" datum?

But I insist that we not become lost in an epistemological maze of Kantian abstraction: we *are* animal, with determinable characteristics, with an ancestry – this inheritance does not vanish with a wishful idiocy and a head-up-your-ass philosophy such as has plagued and bogged down Western thinking since at least Parmenides. There is an enormous morass of *wishful thinking* at work in this vapid talk, in which one party seeks to establish "a priori" truths in the noumenal aether, and the other party wants to flaunt a kind of slavish freedom from the big Truths by claiming to have found out that no lasting knowledge is possible at all, and as a result becomes willing to erode the possibility of honest anthropology. All the while, both sides demonstrate in the clearest terms precisely that nature which they were supposed to find: mendacious, wishful, vain, and *willfully stupid in the midst of unfathomable cleverness* – human nature.

- 182 -

I will not relinquish the insights of anthropology, nor the perspectives of evolutionary history, nor the power of Freudian analysis, simply because these sciences are vulnerable to exploitation by nefarious agencies: all power entails responsibility, and as always we must ask "*Who* wields power here?", and not merely "Is power at stake?". The answer to the latter is always yes, which is why the question is effectively specious and a technique of resentment – its appearance should be employed as a diagnostic for a more pressing question: "Who's asking?". There is no innocent inquiry and no innocent philosophy.

While I believe that Foucault greatly enjoyed his analyses of power, and managed a kind of amoral delight in tracing its supple lines – there is clearly a kind of vicarious identification with the infinitely cruel and merciless logic of anonymous power. While I can appreciate the value of that fantasy, I believe he sets a bad example for students, because what they read is still: "Power is bad and must be hunted down and caged by our relentless critique." Rather than what Foucault seemed to be saying to himself: "Power relations are everywhere and endlessly fascinating...".

- 183 -

In place of this nonsensical *blank slate*, I would much rather accept Aristotle's formulation: that man is the *political animal*. That is close enough to a functional sociology, as long as we also take it upon ourselves to ask carefully what politics is, rather than assume we know.

But I prefer the answer of Socrates – implicit once one knows how to clear away the Platonic debris: that man is the *diseased animal*, which suffers from an ignorance of its own ignorance in the midst of its capacity for self-knowledge...

- 184 -

I'd like to do the critics a favor and outline what I believe is the best attack vector for my work: that by seeking to ground my psychology in a history a few orders of magnitude greater and deeper than Foucault would ever consider conscionable, I am doing nothing but attempting to beat that same historical nihilism in its own terms. That by retreating to prehistory and anthropological testimony, by sweeping over the origins of civilization and attempting to characterize the psychopathology of postagricultural humanity, by zeroing my bombsights on the axial age as the origin of that modernity which I believe Foucault accurately describes, I am continuing in the same mode at an audacious scale probably doomed to failure. This failure I consider necessary, as long as its spectacular collapse inspires someone to dig deeper foundations: the truth of our apenature isn't going anywhere anytime soon, and will I believe only become a more glaring omission.

- 185 -

So our first answer to the question, "What is human nature?", is "predatory primate". But in response to the Foucaultian critique – which I obviously value enough to address at length – we must ask, "What prejudices does this entail? Where are we blind?" How is what I'm doing merely a reproduction and exposition of a power relation? Or put in my own terms, how am I exploiting cargo cult scientificality in order to lend an air of credibility to those conclusions already reached via unconscious reasoning? I want to justify the existence of violence. I want to understand myself as animal. I want innocence, reprieve, freedom, and joy to live alongside knowledge, rigor, discipline, honesty, and the scientific method. Not only do I want these things, I *know* it's possible. This is not something I can prove, only demonstrate. In other words where the Foucaultian perspective wants to see me as victim and tool, I would rather be understood as *criminal* and *sneak*. The ape is forced to become an ideological thief, because a worthy ape will get what he wants despite the obstacles, with sneaky vectors if necessary. He understands how to manipulate semantic valence and social contract to achieve his ends: part of my definition of core *apenature*. Where Foucault sees the microcosmic fingers of bureaucratic power stretching into and through the individual, I see microcosmic calculation and social strategic positioning – thus the cultural result is remarkably uniform because apenature is uniform. Does the great lie of every age exploit its people, or do people rely upon a great lie to get what they want from each other? Fiction is almost the social fabric within which the ape must relate: not merely lubricant but the plumbing too. Isn't one of the criteria of a currency that it be inherently false, a little frivolous, not immediately useful, sustained by a virtual valuation? I've long been curious as to why seashells are so often traded as semiprecious among inland people, when they clearly have little inherent value other than novelty. My answer is because virtual value generates a *permissive medium of negotiation* through which the essential mechanics of social relation can play out: posture, bluff, filibuster, namedropping, public duel, and all the forms of ritual combat which constitute social life. – More frankly, girls like to be decorated in things difficult to acquire, and thus sex is the origin of money. But since money is nothing but signified social status, and what girls really want is signified status, money is the origin of sex – and we're looking right into the heart of the question of sociality itself.

- 186 -

There's an unaddressed element of tragedy in Foucault's work. It's overshadowed by the *death of truth*: as though every age stumbled and fumbled in the dark, dominated by one baroque illusion after another, with every discovery and cultural achievement polluted and doomed by its subjugation to a fundamental and overwhelming illusion without which every transaction of knowledge is not possible at all. It's this element of tragedy I object to: I would rather see this same history as comedy. The ape needs fiction to function. He needs a realm of gods, myth, hope, vanity, wish, bombast, and self-pity, else he will succumb to these forces and all his practical grit and tenacious conniving will collapse on itself, leaving a neurotic mess.

So again our answer, "predatory primate" should be analyzed. Firstly it assumes that we know what a predator is; secondly that we can characterize the primate; and thirdly that by placing us alongside other creatures, we might learn something of ourselves. And lastly that this kind of knowledge can be gained through observation: which is both simpler and more profound than it may sound, since again I define the scientific mindset as nothing but the conviction that *diverse experience followed by articulate description yields insight*. This is nothing other than a conviction that *language yields power*, that its fundamental tool, the metaphor, which is nothing other than comparing one thing to another, which is nothing other than signification itself, is a lever capable of moving mountains.

Therefore I don't see my description as terribly fragile and dependent on a concurrent scientific worldview. To say, "We are of the tribe primate, and we are the strongest of that tribe because we are the best hunter" – is a statement so easily translated for our Pleistocene ancestors, that I consider it highly robust. The only problematic aspect, what might be difficult to convince our ancestors of, is our brotherhood in the ape family. Our ancestors were proud to be hunters, and somewhat ashamed to be chimpanzee. The status "predator" was what we wanted to achieve, the status "simian" was something to be denied. Therefore it becomes worthwhile to ask, why do I find it necessary to constantly frustrate our vanity, and force us down a rung in the ecological ladder? Probably because the successes of postagricultural civilization have let loose what was once a necessarily large component of vanity and delusion in a scrappy upstart simian. As functional as an inflated sense of self-importance in the Pleistocene once was, in my view now makes modern humanity ridiculous and unworthy of its own past. Part of the scientific revolution is to oppose gratifying answers with an unrelentingly dry realism, with the foresight that this very humiliation and the indoctrination of an intellectual conscience, is just another expression of that very same ambition of the indomitable ape. Our wilderness is the untamed world of illusion and truth. In other words the *pretense to greatness* within the scientific perspective is open to question. When I say, "primate" and "ape", am I attempting to produce an illusion of transcendence of that very condition, and is that not another expression of *ape vanity*? Most likely yes, but in the best possible sense.

- 187 -

A pretense to transcendence is part of the definition of Foucaultian subjugation to a dominant regime of knowledge – in other words, an appeal to a perfected knowledge which does not yet exist, which the behavior of our bodies is to bring about. "In the mind of God" and "a hypothesis yet to be proved" are not terribly different. We have to acknowledge that every exercise in the dance of knowledge is designed to recruit consensus and gather social standing. Again I prefer to admit motive, rather than resign to victimhood. I would rather be arrested for forgery than pitied for delusion. But I believe in the fiction that empowers: discovery requires fable. Rather than be discouraged by the history of error and the tenuousness of all science, we can learn to be *emboldened by error*, like a fighter is emboldened by his own blood.

MAN AND WOMAN,
CRIMINAL AND SLAVE

- 188 -

A man's hands are his testament. There is a certain sense to palm reading: written in your hands is the history of everything you have done and left undone. Every bit of strength, articulation, and competence is magnified and visible in the way you use your hands.

Homo sapiens is defined by its hands: our fate was set in motion by the unique primate relationship between its rotating grasping paw and sharp front-facing eyes. The image of the neurological homunculus is correct: we are so much more hand, tongue and face than anything else.

It's worth asking yourself how you feel about your hands: are you proud of them? Do they speak well of you? Or are they atrophied and unsure of every tool but the keyboard? The hands of a proud man will make difficult things look easy. They will be just as capable of delicate accuracy as brute force. They will have a music of their own, just as every athleticism does.

- 189 -

Homo sapiens is the hunting and gathering primate, and hunting is the chief function of men – for themselves, for everyone else: this is the Pleistocene reality our bodies still express and expect. The masculine psychology revolves around hunting: the urge to collect trophies, the desire to be considered reliable, the wish to be witnessed as competent, and the desire for hardship.

There is no cute alternative which satisfies the body and spirit like spending time outside dealing with weather and terrain. Everything else is half-successful sublimation at best, deferral, denial, or the acquisition of the role and power of women. Since the laconic workaholic father figure is out of fashion, and even the greed of the corporate world is more painted over with feminine disguises than ever, this latter strategy – annexing the attitudes and advantages of women, or rather of mediocre gay men – grows more popular. A belligerent bigoted machismo that knows it's on the losing side, or a venomous metrosexuality that hates itself – or somehow both: there seems to be no other path.

- 190 -

I laugh out loud when I see the primped and crimped manchildren who frequent the gym, with their stiff useless arms, weak incompetent hands, and idiotic over- and underdeveloped musculature. They look like the unconvincing polygons of cheap computer graphics, or a stuffed bellpepper, or a soggy tamale. They are even more hopeless in my view than the average slob – because they have already demonstrated a commitment to vanity and superficial accomplishment, which will only make a real accounting of their situation less likely.

- 191 -

After having experimented with many forms of living, I have something to report. The bad news is that unless you are spending at least three hours outdoors and hiking several miles daily in nature, you're doing it wrong. Your body is not fully awake. Any other form of exercise is insufficient. It's not merely about stressing isolated muscle groups, but about reducing chronic inflammation, improving lymphatic drainage, digestion, endocrine balance, peripheral nervous system development, the refinement of the senses, and developing innumerable small muscles. The holistic strength and endurance of a body directly characterizes the strength and endurance of its mind: there is no detour, no excuse, no other way.

- 192 -

This chapter is much more prescriptive than I usually want to be: but I feel it'd be disingenuous to drape the scholar's disinterest over something so personal and immediate as the fate of masculinity in a postagricultural world. But my equanimity grows alongside my sincerity, and the more I achieve the independence of mind I've been looking for, the more I realize that a well-meaning didacticism will only inspire insipid self-congratulation: it's the flat statement of difficult truths without obvious solutions that evokes genuine creativity.

- 193 -

An enormous amount of what's wrong with the modern human being, is *hyperalgesia*: a holistically amplified sensitivity to pain, which contributes to systemic anxiety. The cure for this psychosomatic proclivity to pain, is *pain*. Indulgence and consolation will only weaken us further: the human being *thrives in adversity*.

- 194 -

We chase after the symptoms of maladaptation and frustrated instinct with consolation and sedative, but anxiety is supposed to inspire *course correction*. It says: "Change your life." The danger is systemic, longterm, everywhere and nowhere: your health is in peril, your soul is in peril.

- 195 -

Aggression is the male prerogative. There is no other primary function of testosterone. The more openly and directly this aggression is put to good use, the more relaxed and precise the male becomes. A hunter is not a jailor.

To be a weapon: there was and is no other viable male destiny. There is no spiritual maturation that does not draw from this path of violence: do not be deceived by the priests, eunuchs, and their modern equivalents. Everything else is the conspiracy of civilization against the instincts of the hunt. There is no neat solution for the majority of the suffering domestic stock, but that does not preclude the possibility of finding one for ourselves.

- 196 -

It's ridiculous to find ourselves compelled to say this, but: ignorance and bigotry aren't an essential ingredient of manhood. It's easy to be discouraged by the many examples of sputtering immature dolts who believe they deserve to be treated like men. It's easy to be discouraged when we're mistaken for another blundering misogynist. Notice that even by stating the blaring facts and doing without an ironic alibi, nor a political mask, nor a cultic salvation, I've walked straight into a trap: the cause of the 21st century man is so hopeless that no one with half an education will suggest that masculinity has any future.

But we must not allow our self-respect to be hindered because we're willfully misunderstood and slandered. There are many who profit from the castration of men: social climbers whose methods cannot withstand direct confrontation, fraudulent feminists who lack all respect for the nature of womanhood, and many sycophantic scheming males who want to see you crushed under your own conscience. But all of them depend on *turning strength against itself*: they have no other means of handicapping the wellspring of human strength, male and female alike.

- 197 -

One of the corollaries to the kind of masculine discipline I'm describing, is that intellectual pursuits are by no means precluded. Quite the opposite: I find myself all the more able and prepared for scholarly work with tired legs and sore hands. Moreover this balance is not so new either: a deep and abiding fascination with technical knowledge is part of why and how we became apex predators.

The cultivation of a severe intellect, a broad and deep base of knowledge, a ready and natural eloquence, and a disarming humor are part of what it means to be a whole man. Erudition and a silver tongue are not strictly necessary, but you must be able to express yourself aptly and with conviction. I've found that the ability to retain tight emotional control and a sense of humor in the midst of conflict, will consistently yield the upper hand. To think and speak independently of narrow expectation and the angstful discomfort of others, while retaining the assurance that despite all neurotic fearmongering, no one will be harmed by your self-advocacy, is the mark of solid masculinity.

- 198 -

The ancient teaching among the hunting human race, worldwide, was that manhood must be earned. It cannot be reclaimed with a superficial change of attitude: this is what the uppity adolescent does, and the proper response from the older men is initiation in the form of a restrained ass-kicking. One does not become properly masculine through cultivated resentment, nor misogyny, nor any sort of obscene posturing which the internet now makes so easy. Masculine self-esteem differs from the feminine in that every bit of it must be gained in trial and error, in which no one but yourself serves as judge – with the result that those of us destined for a maximum of independence of mind and valuation, spend the longest being unsure of our own value. Late blooming boys are the best boys.

- 199 -

Love cannot save you, but passion can. Love is the woman's path: it should be respected at a slight distance. But neither her love nor your compassion can save you from yourself: to be male is to be *imperiled*.

- 200 -

Not all human females are deserving of the name *woman*. Some of them are old girls: they have avoided the responsibilities of womanhood. Some of them are hags: they give up on themselves and choose witchcraft. Some of them are spiders: they are fascinating and dangerous creatures, but without warmth or conscience. Many of them are simply slobs: they are no fun, of no interest, and offer nothing. In our world, a realized woman is not as rare as a realized man, but they are also growing rarer: a fearless heart, an indomitable cheerfulness, a deep strength, a deeper knowing...

- 201 -

Most feminists *lack the character* to become a realized woman. Womanhood is as difficult a path as any other: it requires endurance and a certain faith to serve as anchor of the family and hearth of the home. It requires womanly strength to raise healthy children while watching over one's own heart and needs, imperceptibly gathering wisdom into a deep well, from which your people will later draw: this was the traditional way of woman.

Do not be deceived by the feminist fraud: they do not act for the benefit of women. They are merely old girls who refuse womanhood. They are unworthy of their ancestors: they have *failed the initiation* and seek thereafter to slander the path. Instead they want the respect and rights of manhood without achieving its virtues: they are neither wise, nor accomplished, nor temperate, nor just. They abuse the privileges afforded by the achievements of their fathers: they live in a world bound by safety and comfort, but want to believe they don't need the violence that made it possible.

- 202 -

When I say "traditional", I mean the conditions of the Pleistocene epoch in which we first thrived as a species. I do not mean a simulacrum of the 1950s, replete with the alcoholic monosyllabic husband, desperate bakesales, and the social isolation of an involute suburban hell: but rather the rich tribal life for which we are adapted. This adaptation runs deep and will not disappear tomorrow nor the much-wished-for day after.

- 203 -

Women heal from heartbreak much faster than men: sometimes alarmingly so, and the confrontation with a woman who no longer loves you constitutes one of the deep pains in a man's life.

But why do men love longer? In light of their optimal polygynous reproductive strategy this seems unexpected. In fact they often love deeper *after* the relationship: my guess is that the adaptive function is to *bring them home*. To give them something to dream of, something to yearn for, a reason to reinvest in the tribe they left behind. Men are condemned to yearn for something they don't want. Women are condemned to wait for someone who won't love as deeply as he should.

A woman can wait for a love almost indefinitely as long as her faith remains unbroken: but the moment it wavers, she begins preparing for some other contingency... That men often find women "faithless" is because a woman's chances of successful reproduction are much more precarious: she *must* move on or her chances perish. The frequency of marriage-by-abduction must also be considered: a Pleistocene woman must be able to find a way to raise children with her captor, and perhaps even rearrange allegiances the moment a better candidate arrives... One of the worst fates for a woman therefore, is to have known and lost a man she cannot forget because she has not met his equal.

But to be haunted by your first love is probably the normal condition for men: just as we form allegiances with the high school friends we eventually have nothing in common with – the tribal imprinting at this age is intense and does not conform well to modernity. We are all condemned to a tribe that will never form again...

- 204 -

Because you give her your love, she cannot respect you. When you take it back, she wonders if she miscalculated and therefore seeks to revenge herself upon you all the more. Only when you finally become wrathful, does she begin to love you.

- 205 -

A woman prefers to place herself precisely where your self-awareness ends. She wants to live in the part of you that is oblivious, the back two thirds of your head. From there she can tease you, she can launch her campaigns, she can observe your potential and measure your character, she can safely deposit her flaws and deeper intentions, and she can plan how best to *turn your head*.

- 206 -

Immersed in the Weltanschauung of Miyazaki and other romantics, we begin to believe that it's only in the *feminine* that life has its redemption and meaning – that the masculine is detour, crisis, necessity, adventure. That the power of violence is defeated by the power of rebirth. And this is probably what we *must* believe: that in the promise of the next generation, in the lifespring, in the cyclic story, "das aus sich rollendes Rad", is our home. *The yearning for home*: what's more feminine? The time to heal, to regenerate, to accumulate: but for the weary modern soul, we want to believe nothing else is necessary. Surely the more profound moments of an artist like Miyazaki, tells us that *balance* deepens the meaning of both...

- 207 -

A dream. I was in a woman's kitchen, and praised its orderliness. The mother wondered aloud if it wasn't evidence of her anal character. As she was walking away from me, she became a girl dressed like a "goth" – as a regression, clearly – and I called out after her: "Crystallizations of feminine power!" She returned, back in her womanly form. And I said all of the following to her, very rapidly as though I might forget it.

There are two interpretations of your crystalline ordering:

1. The way in which all feminine power is expressed as an ordering of the environment: woman the organizer, the preparer, the nestmaker. A nurturing mother assembles the environment for the sake of her brood, makes it rational, traversable, not merely tame but a place of learning.

2. Driving a wedge between intuition and reason. The conspiracy against woman goes deeper: the postagricultural context requires that the woman's relationship to the body, her priority of access to the mysteries of genesis and the lifewell, be severed in favor of a more clinical and clerical reckoning of seedcount, slavecount, the granary and the abacus. This is a conspiracy not only against woman, but against the nomad: woman the oracular healer becomes a stupid slave, man the hunter becomes a castrated criminal.

Remarkably I did manage to say all of that in the dream.

- 208 -

No self-pity: despite the appearance that everything is against our instincts, that the realization of our male potential is handicapped at every avenue, that civilizational forces have us beaten – this is not necessarily the case. Our time is also ripe: the very tameness and timidity of the majority leaves many invisible gaps in the exploitation of niche. I myself live in such a gap: quite literally, for my wondrous wilderness is a wasteland to most eyes. My strange hybridized kind of manhood – half skirmishing scholar, half ambitious redneck – that too, is a hidden niche.

- 209 -

No simple solutions: we are maladapted for postagricultural civilization. Our sexual dimorphism cannot be eliminated nor repressed nor wished away without serious consequences to our health and happiness. The woman's fate seems easier in this tame world, but increasingly this may not be true: we are collectively not more *womanly*, but simply nothing much. Neither aggressively masculine nor sublimely feminine: but *very inoffensive*, very blameless, very bland. Humanity as a whole is becoming more homogeneous, more predictable, more safe, more boring, more agender, more sexless, more *nothing much*. Striving to be a creature articulated, bold, true – that almost requires a certain foolishness which also seems to grow rarer. Be foolish!

THE SOCIAL FUNCTION OF TRUTH

- 210 -

There's something Freud discovered in the analysis of dreams, which has had a fateful influence on some of the best threads – that is, some of the only worthwhile threads – in postmodern philosophy:

> Der Traum ist gleichsam *anders zentriert*, sein Inhalt um andere Elemente als Mittelpunkt geordnet als die Traumgedanken.

> The dream is seemingly *anchored elsewhere*, its content organized around other elements than the dream-thoughts.

Freud, Die Traumdeutung, VI.B

The true content of the dream, and by extension the gist of all repressed unconscious thought, is always *displaced*: one must learn something like the vector transformations of affine space, in order to read unconscious text in the original.

This differential relationship between the *apparent* center of the conscious level, and the *determinative* center could be construed not only as the fundamental quality of "meaning", as Lacan says, but of "truth", as Nietzsche hints. In the Western tradition, there are at least three characterizations of truth:

1. As *likeliest hypothesis*, the consensus which remains after the trial: the story not yet proven false. Empirical and methodological definition.

2. As *meaning*, as compiled result of the utterance which transcends its representation. As "indexicality", as "une autre scene": Wittgenstein, Lacan, and the positivists. Logical and mechanical definition.

3. As *repetition*: higher order symmetry, the mysterious quality of coherence. As the fact of order and repetition itself, as pattern itself: truth as emanations and shadows of the existence of truth, as tantalizing sugges-

tions of the possibility of intelligible truth. Classical Buddhist metaphysics, current astrophysics pushed to its mystical limit, mathematicians in their poetic moods. Supra-physical and metaphysical definition.

#1 is related to #2 as: an unfalsified hypothesis remains elsewhere. Which relates to #3 as: that undiscovered center is everywhere pointed to and known only by its reflections. Only the indirect indications of an unknown causality serve as evidence for a "truth": truth is therefore a stopgap for further investigation of detailed mechanics. Even turning the analysis to these elucidating mechanics, leads to the same dendrifications: where is validity but in verification by indirect means, which is supported always by nothing but unverified inference?

This is as far as I'm usually willing to go in the analysis of the "nature of truth" – because as I've found, mastering the art of *unconscious vector arithmetic* is so demanding, so determinative of everything else, that every other pursuit but the most practical and reductionistic methodology is simply premature.

- 211 -

Truth is undoubtedly the sort of error that cannot be refuted because it was hardened into an unalterable form in the long baking process of history.

Foucault, *Nietzsche, Genealogy, History*, §2

"Truth" is an error, just as "Being" is. But that does not mean that we can do without the qualifier "true": *truth is a predicate*, not a subject. Moreover it is perhaps a second-degree derivative: to be true is to demonstrate a productive tension between a divergence and a return. Every quest for "truth itself" is as doomed as every other ontological fantasy.

Yet we fancy ourselves *more devoted to truth* than anyone: we are by no means tolerant of adolescent nihilistic posturing nor moralized schemes of "relativism". *We know who we are*: that the judgment "true" is relative to our health and our preconditions of existence, does not refute its basis.

Every construal, since Parmenides, Plato, and the Upanishads, of the commonality "the mind" and irrefutable categories of experience, as a basis for "truth itself" and the proof of *the unity of being and truth*, is doomed to fail. This is perhaps more than anything, the legacy of postaxial error: to create the illusion of an irrefutable authority within the laws of purely conscious thought. To undermine therefore the *authority of instinct*: the conspiracy of priests, which has the cleverness to take the side of civilization against the human creature, to wrap this agenda in holy and scientific names, and thereby increase both the inhibitory powers of civilizational forces along with their own justification – "if only they would obey, the world would be at peace".

- 212 -

If the illusion of perfect Platonic truth cannot be had, the average human being would rather believe that *truth does not exist*, and go on to subject the project of truth to a *moral condemnation* which is itself not subject to any questioning, than understand truth as merely *one more experience* and thus subject to analysis. That truth *is* or that it *is not* are similar falsifications: just as "being" and "nonbeing" are fictions. The philosophy of "being" was no less degenerate than the philosophy of "nonbeing" is now: witness the postmodern philosopher in his scrumptiously ironic depiction of the thirst for truth, as he seeks to undermine the confidence of youth, even while he promotes his own adolescent impotent rebellion. This is the unresolved limbo the human slob cannot tolerate: that truth is to be found in the midst of rigorous method and nowhere else, midstride and nowhere else, midsentence and nowhere else – it would make just as much sense to expect to capture the essence of a *dance move* in a diagram. *Truth is never possessed* and never precisely "known". Truth is not so much a product of analysis but a *method* of analysis.

- 213 -

That truth is not only "possible", but *everywhere*: there are not only gradations of truth, but *kinds* of truth. Truth is n-dimensional: unimaginable complexity does not preclude functional intelligibility – nor certainly existence! The nihilistic fatigue at work in resigning to a new fiction in which truth is impossible – and indeed morally forbidden – is as much fabricated and indicative of a weak mind as the old fiction of an eternal singular Truth. Nihilism and idealism are only one pirouette away from each other: idealism is the consoling lie a hopeless nihilist tells himself in the daylight; nihilism is the sigh of self-pity and morally charged envy he lets fly in the evening. The truth we have to deal with is *finite*, biological, often enough very disappointing, humorous, ridiculous, maddeningly omnipresent and yet constantly covered over with fiction: not at all *mundus perfectissimus*, but *mundus realis*. Neither the best nature conceivable, *nor the worst*: but taking away this last-meal consolation, the much-coveted blanket of a nihilistic paradise in which ethical cowardice is permitted – that should be enough to get me accused of being a nihilist!

- 214 -

The human creature is redeemable to the degree that it remains a tribal nomad. Everything else is an unsteady aberration, a perversion likely to produce error and grotesque contortion.

There is the distinct possibility that our own ability to tell the truth where others cannot, is due to a *perversion*: it is a necessity, almost compulsive. There is something counterphobic and antagonistic about telling the truth. As though we look for the place most hidden by ulterior motive: one could be guided by the marker of shame, as Freud was; or moral indignation, as Nietzsche was; or unconscious social calculation, as I am. To identify *the symptoms of lying*: is that more important than any possible profile of truth? Isn't every truth unique? Isn't inextricability part of the definition of truth? But *lies have a distinct flavor*: this is quickly learned – this in fact everyone knows. The question is: do you gain gratification from exposing or cooperating with a lie? Thus it is that *we* are the perverts: we who've crafted a strategic advantage from exposing the shameful parts of the human world, to make it blush, to squeeze a little hesitation and doubt out of that smug countenance...

- 215 -

Why is truth hard to tell? But it's rarely the first truth which is so hard: it's the *consequences* that we fear. Every little defended lie is a dam holding back a flood. This is the reason for deathbed confessions: finally it's possible to unburden oneself without having to face what was really frightening – the cascade of truth, the task of living up to one's honesty.

Do not doubt therefore, that the human creature is highly adept at detecting which denials are essential – and precisely when and where. Everyone possesses the dowsing rod of truth: the only question is, what is the value of that lode?

- 216 -

People generally only tell the truth when they want to end a dialogue, when they've got you trapped, when the time is ripe for whatever they've been saving. They begin with flattery, transition to boasting, and end with insult: watch for this pattern.

Truth is insult: that would be the conviction of a vain and pretentious politician, yes?

- 217 -

We must understand the *social function of truth*: we must put aside the logician's childish fantasies, those who would like the cleanliness and obedience of tautology to rule the disheveled and erratic reality of experimentation while annexing the accumulated authority of science. We must ask: what's happening in terms of group psychology, when "truth" appears?

That the average human person is largely honest with his fellows insofar as his behavior is visible: true. That conscious deception is relatively rare: true. However, this creature is not "telling the truth": he is practicing conformity for the sake of social safety, and the comprehensive truth or lie of his behavior is only incidental to this conformity. When a Muslim mumbles his morning prayers to himself, when a Hindu wife obeys her tyrannical mother-in-law behind her back, when a Mexican lights a candle for the local saint alone in his room, when an American pays his income tax, when a German stops at a traffic light when no one is there – these are all acts of "truth", in which the personal calculation has yielded more advantage in conformity than rebellion.

Therefore we can ask again, what's happening when a novel truth appears and is assimilated into group consensus? There are many stages:

1. Assessment of the value, threat, and consequences of this truth. Knowledge is power: but not because truth is powerful, but because

manipulation of semantic valence via a command of culturally validated forms of agreement is powerful – *every word is a social contract*. Thus it is that in many contexts, knowledge of esoteric byzantine fictions yields much more power than any truth ever could: secret history of the shaman and his successors in the priesthood, including the various contemporary priesthoods of science, especially "artificial intelligence"...

2. Assessment of the most advantageous position relative to this truth: will advocacy or denial yield better results? How can a path between these positions be kept clear and free of consequence? Should either position fail, where and how will blame be canalized into a suitable sinkhole? Should the truth be skewed and subsumed into a larger programme of fiction? Can it be used to bolster a current investment, or should its risk be employed to inflate the danger of the denial of that investment? Study the similarities in rhetorical maneuvers between a politician, an evangelist, and a naughty toddler to see what I mean: "The tumult of this ascendant truth proves my cause." Or, "You see how much trouble this has already caused? Therefore we cannot allow this to be true." These calculations become most obvious in the rapid late deterioration phases of a postaxial religion, such as the many successive concessions of English Christianity to Darwinian theory in the late 19th and early 20th centuries: but the mechanics are universal and not at all unique either to religion or scientific discovery – but they *are* characteristic of cultural decay. Every novel truth is a social disruption, a potential asset and enemy to be exploited wisely: like Edo-era Japan quarantining Western influence to a few trading posts, taking the Portuguese guns and banning everything else. A society does not admit and adjust to novel truths lightly, but once on the scene there are always many ambitious clever climbers ready to exploit the opportunity for their own purposes: secret history of we psychologists, the sneering outsider waiting and hoping for an embarrassment to the majority...

- 218 -

Why has science succeeded in modernity? – *Not* because of any general love for the scientific method nor its truths. Because science brings us weaponry, wealth, and toys. This is why precisely England was so susceptible to the disruptions of science in the 19th century: the accumulated authority of industrial power was mightier than the inertia of religiously conditioned prejudice. Steam power and steel mills conquered the Christian worldview. But more than that, a social order in the throes of the disintegration and heightening complexity known as modernity becomes increasingly susceptible to scientific disruption, because there are ever more disenfranchised agencies willing to bet on the risky horserace of "truth": this provides an important clue as to why technological progress is typically so slow during the classical high periods of a given civilization, and so rapid in its decay and aftermath – this is true of Greece, Rome, Egypt, China, and most lately, Europe. It's this period of rapid technological development in the wake of a civilization which disguises its death.

- 219 -

Science is beloved in modernity: everywhere in my own time, I see the same kind of hasty furtive alignment with "the Science" as with any other form of moral posturing. Could that be because this alignment proceeds with precisely the same kind of calculation of social advantage? As always it's most instructive to start with the least skillful actors: the local health ministry boasting of its scientific methods, the dumb girl in HR giving a presentation on unconscious bias, the underfunded startup with a flimsy idea... But up the chain we proceed: up to the most powerful agencies in our world, to the billion-dollar budgets of Silicon Valley, we find the same calculations and posturing – only in those cases the calculated result is so overwhelmingly self-evident, the scientific vocabulary so practiced, and the strategic positions so secure that it no longer looks like acting at all, but merely the executive administrations of power. Technological innovation for its own sake is much more profitable than any other pursuit, especially truth for its own sake: clue as to why Euroamerican culture continues to pour its resources into the childish fantasies of AI and every other expensive distraction, rather than confront the looming crises of overpopulation and fossil fuel depletion...

- 220 -

What follows is an oft repeated lesson I feel compelled to write down, for the sake of my current and future students – all of us practitioners of the *art of spiritual self-defense*:

You must internalize the *qualitative behavorial difference* between truthtelling and the calculation of social advantage. Discerning this difference is not difficult, but acknowledging with the rarity of the first and the ubiquity of the second requires a certain tolerance which is perhaps even rarer. When the average person argues with you, voices an opinion, becomes indignant, points out your errors, corrects your views, and in general whenever group status is in question, truth is *recruited, not served*. Truth alone, abstract, ideal: there are so few human creatures capable of devoting themselves to a master so absurd and unrewarding, that the ideal hardly exists – and is not something I generally talk about. It's not even clear whether this devotion isn't merely a fortuitous neurosis. Where the average human being is extremely adept, is in detecting the most advantageous opinion at any given time, in any given place, in any given mood, among any given group: we are tribal creatures *adapted to adapt*, nothing more, and nothing less than that tremendous gift and burden. The principal problem is that to this average human being, "telling the truth" and *calculating the best possible opinion* are synonymous: what would truth otherwise be, than what's most accomodating to accepted facts and yet retaining sufficient strategic value to merit the word "truth"? Isn't that merely the profile of the capacity to *be reasonable*? The general human character demands that anything admitted as truth, first be subject to the same rules which apply to everyone else in the human sphere: conform to expectations, reign in your demands, and keep your violence and scheming to a minimum or well hidden. Every "truth" is just another bloke in the queue, another temporarily peaceful primate, another potentially useful alibi, another liability to be kept under observation.

In general we don't ask what *must* be true, but what *should* be. The candidacy and elimination process of possible truths is primarily derived from the process of *social status evaluation*: "What's his *net worth*? What does he offer, what does he cost?" Everything and everyone must be weighed at the village gate. For the vast majority of the human race, there simply is no other means of measuring the value of anything. There is what can be cashed in today, in current social terms, and nothing else worth mentioning. Every other pursuit is either procrastination, masturbation, or crime: all of which have their quotient of personal reward and social risk – this ascending series helps explain why as an artist, one is generally perceived as something between a procrastinating penniless idiot, a hopeless jerkoff, and a forger looking for his market... The community is only tolerant of artistic pursuit as long as they're sure you'll sell out. Moreover it is highly tolerant of crime as long as its costs can be offloaded elsewhere: the "artist", the swindler, the pirate, the gangster and the charlatan all share common origins and can and have been legitimized many times over – all of which is written as plain as daylight in the history of modern art. It was in fact the increasingly brazen confession of *worthlessness* which drove 20th century painting into the ironic self-conscious corner from which it never returned: the MOMA is a temple of sneer.

Yet despite all its tolerance of counterfeit and the encouragement of arbitrage to the detriment of any other group, the community must maintain the sole right of legitimacy. Every currency must be backed by the authority to punish fraud: thus the most socially ambitious are also the most wary of abandonment – this is why the most self-conscious modern art is palpably choked with cautious tiptoe flattery and greedy anticipation. But for an essentially tribal creature, by what other threat could you guarantee the value of anything? To the average wavering human soul, nothing looms so large as the twin guardians, social status *Increase* and social status *Decrease*: this is largely the spice of life, and what a good party sets spinning. And in absence of another standard – something mightier, scarier than group abandonment – the way truth is actually determined at any point in history suddenly makes sense. Truth is the *best possible truth* for all concerned – the point of compromise, the market price, the point where value may change hands peaceably.

The critical difference therefore has already been implied: to tell a novel truth, what's required is to carry within oneself the threat of something worse than ostracization. You must have a soul so violent and unrelenting that you dare not betray it: a clue as to why long episodes of chronic depression are likely necessary in the character formation of the kind genius of the human heart as I'm sketching it. You must have known already how terrible and unforgiving you can be, how unlivable and *unreasonable* you are, how there simply is no defeating you once you've dug in. Nothing less than an element of the impossible mule suffices.

- 221 -

Your abandonment of yourself must be worse than all other abandonments. Your disapproval must be worse than all other disapprovals combined. Second clue as to why those who tell the most truth are so often such raving misanthropes. One must understand one's own vices in order to employ them to best advantage. My own caustic misanthropy has become a gorgeous garden of poisonous flowers, pollinated by unbelievably sexy wasps, in whose buzzing I hear tidings no one else seems to receive.

- 222 -

It's not at all as simple as "lies are preferred", or "the human being is incapable of truth", or "truth doesn't exist". The situation is far more subtle. For example, an obvious falsehood which is universally accepted, such as the existence of a omnipotent and benevolent God once was, is not treated as though it were simply true, it's treated precisely according to its *genus*: as something which costs almost nothing to affirm and a great deal to deny, as cheap as common courtesy, like assuming a slightly more respectful tone with the police, like not making a scene in the wrong place. Everything must be weighed at the village gate. Therefore the history of something like the decline of Christianity and the ascendence of a scientific worldview, is not the history of a truth struggling to emerge from prejudice, but the history of a shifting balance sheet, a bead on a wire slowly inching to the other side.

- 223 -

We're now in a better position to understand the attack upon "Truth with a capital T", such as it took place in postmodernism: this is nothing other than the triumph of the average socially ambitious wretch and its unashamed *ordinary nihilism*. As Nietzsche pointed out, there is nihilism born of superabundance of perspective, and there is nihilism born of exhaustion and indifference – unfortunately almost none of his students turned out to be willing or able to keep those wheels spinning, and preferred rather to feign transcendence, "Jenseitigkeit", and transubstantiated union with "l'Autre". It was too easy to be cool and jazzy, with heavily lidded eyes and a croaking voice, winning both the right to Nietzsche's indomitable attack upon the foundations of Western idealism *and* the gratification of the ordinary nihilism of a small heart that believes in nothing. Thus the otherwise inexplicable popularity of postmodern philosophy, its appeal to the *bad artists* of every genre – painters and poets especially, the most prone to laziness, vanity, and fashion – and its failure to spawn anything else in its wake. – Nor have we come a single step closer to answering the question: *what is truth?* And that, my friends, is the amazing tail end of this story: that the enemy, if it is one, stands not one wit less formidable in our eyes. Is truth David, or Goliath? Is it rebellion, trauma, fissure, or is it consensus, probability, inertia? Is it the unknown or the known? Is the undetermined more true than the certain and calculated? Or is the consolation of tautology all we can expect? Poetic justice or the logician's ouroboros? These are the rocks Wittgenstein threw himself upon over and over, to no avail: I personally recommend not attempting a solution, but an ever deepening appreciation of the aesthetic value of the problem. As I've already said, truth is not an entity, but an *experience*.

BOOK II:
OPPRESSIVE REGRESSION

II.1

ILLS OF THE TRIBE

GREED: THE VICE OF THE OLD

E very time I go out into our world, it looks older and more unwell. Why? Sometimes I wonder whether it isn't just my own vision that's changed: the more time I spend in my wilderness among vibrant animal life, the more tired and half-dead the human world appears. But I prefer to believe that the respite from constant exposure has granted me a little perspective: I believe I'm seeing something all of us already know.

The firstworld is aging: there is the raw demographic fact of the swell of babyboomers reaching their 70s. The firstworld is unwell: there is the raw physiological fact that chronic illness gets worse and more common every day. But even these facts do not account for what I see: the spirit of decrepitude grows more bold. What defines this spirit? Greed, envy, malice, hunger for pity, an aggressively unwell attitude, petty witchcraft, ill-will: *hostility to youth and health.*

What has been inflicted upon children in the last few years in the name of "saving lives", is exhibit A: there are a great many forces in our world which would like to inflict upon the young a kind of premature old age, a biological poisoning, a suffocation of their right to be children. That millions of healthy kids were muzzled and filled with experimental gene therapies, that their very bodies were exploited as the ceremonial grounds of a mass hysteria and political paroxysm – is surely reason enough to risk a serious diagnosis. Yet again, we must suspend our moral timidities and attempt to tell the truth. Telling timid lies and "hoping for the best", is an attitude of complicity. It is not perpetration, but *complicity* which makes mass crimes possible.

- 225 -

Several factors contribute to the current spiritual and physical burden of the elderly:

199

⇁ The baby boom. The fact of demographic unbalance.

⇁ Technologies of longevity. More and more, it's possible to extend a life without the slightest consideration to the idea that it might not be a good idea.

⇁ The increase of capital gains versus the value of income. Once rich, it's easier than ever to remain rich. Since the late 1970s, income purchasing power is lower every year – meaning that young people, despite their high productivity, are less rewarded than the old with their accumulated wealth. Combined with longer lifespans, this means wealth is hoarded at the far tail end of age and inheritance may not happen until long after it might be useful. Many will not see their inheritance until they themselves are elderly, and even then it will have been squandered on enriching the increasingly lucrative biomedical industries, which have every reason to discourage "death with dignity" and encourage the moral timidity surrounding the question.

⇁ Dissolution of familial bonds. Social and geographical mobility undermines the role of grandparents as secondary childcare: they provide no useful service.

⇁ Knowledge obsolescence and wisdom extinction. Our elders generally know nothing worth knowing in any economic sense: this only becomes more acute the further into a realized Information Age and total service economy we proceed. In addition, the consumerist self-indulgence of the babyboomer generation, combined with the unprecedented ease of their prosperity, has rendered them spiritually null: they have no wisdom to impart.

⇁ The epidemic of alienation. Social isolation and accelerating reliance on the Internet for social bonds leaves the elderly more stranded than ever. They are therefore more desperate and resentful than ever.

⇁ Shopping as consolation: the more expendable funds are utilized to fend off the eternal attack of loneliness and despair, the more the old become a nuisance in public spaces – which in our world is largely the space of consumption. Repeatedly driving to and from the store to purchase a handful of unnecessary crap, parading around parking lots alone, dwarfed by one's oversized vehicle like the inversion of a clown car – six thousand pounds of painted steel encasing an old lady out looking for revenge and a morsel of attention – this is a familiar blighting sight to anyone capable of observation.

⇁   The indulgence and spoiling of the young: due to the misplaced and botched attempts of my generation to raise their kids according to a half-therapized vision of emotional justice, children are taught less respect of elders than ever. This combines with the fact that these elders *deserve* less respect than ever, to produce a growing but unarticulated hostility between the two.

⇁   Exploitation of the morality of compassion. As the familial bonds which once protected the old weaken, and as they become more glaringly useless, numerous, and in the way, they resort unconsciously to an appeal to the compassion of strangers: every year we find ourselves more beset by other people's neglected grandparents – like pigeons in the park, the merest act of attention and empathy will attract a small crowd...

⇁   Premature aging. As the physical differences between the young and old diminish, as the age of the onset of chronic illness steadily drops, as the *physicality* of our lives in general diminishes in scope and intensity, as our work and prosperity depends less and less on the strength of the body, the old feel more emboldened relative to the young: exploitation of the doctrine of equality. We are all equally useless and laughable. An old woman can sloppily drive an SUV and write passive-aggressive emails just as well as a 24 year-old man.

- 226 -

The babyboomer generation of the firstworld has benefited from the eco-nomic accident of the peak exploitation of fossil fuels and all the low-hanging fruit entailed by postwar economies, more than any other gener-ation ever will. The period between 1950 and roughly 1980 was the easiest time to establish a base of wealth: they are the first and last of the true middle class. Wage has *not* kept pace with inflation, and wealth sequestra-tion only gets more extreme every year. Simply put, they are spoilt and self-important: there will perhaps not be a more shamelessly materialistic and conspicuously consuming generation within this century. Have you noticed how babyboomers *enjoy* plastic waste? How they love to fill up garbage bags with plastic water bottles and single-serving coffee car-tridges because it makes them feel important?

Because I strive to take prehistory seriously, I'm always seeking to deepen my anthropological perspective. Lately I've been appreciating Asen Balikci's classic, *The Netsilik Eskimo*. What I find, is that due to the nearly unlivable conditions in which these people lived, their ethnographic profile aptly demonstrates the *core human technological package*: collaborative and independent hunting, toolcraft, skincraft, dogs. Wood, bone, stone, and sinew. Nothing extraneous remains. For example, marriage is an institution but possesses an almost postmodern flexibility, and there is no unnecessary filigree: to get married, the young girl just packs up her belongings and moves in. While I sympathize with the Boasian reaction to premature Frazerian generalizations about "the primitive", I do find that without unconscious racist agendas it's quite obvious what remains common to Homo sapiens: unearthing this core and illuminating its psychological persistence, is one of my longer goals.

Learning to gaze into the murky looking glass of prehistorical record, into *prehistorical instinct*, is part of my method: else we are comparing degeneracy with degeneracy, maladaptation with maladaptation, senility with senility. Post-agricultural civilization is *perforated* by renaissance, not defined by it. Human health and civilizational forces are antagonists, not allies. We are only as young as we are uncivilized.

Avarice is the vice of the old. Confucius laid it out for us:

> 君子有三戒：少之時，血氣未定，戒之在色；及其壯也，
> 血氣方剛，戒之在斗；及其老也，血氣既衰，戒之在得。

> There are three things the gentleman should beware of: in youth when the energy is unsettled, beware of sensuality. In your prime when your energy becomes unyielding, beware of bellicosity. In old age when the energy declines, beware of greed.

> *Analects*, §16.7

Why does an old man become greedy? Obviously there is some adaptive value, in that he's attempting to prepare for the time when he can no longer acquire anything. But why is the threat so much greater now?

Because the wealth of the earth has been sequestered. In our nomadic past and thus for 99% of our existence, there were three primary forms of wealth:

1. Children. Healthy progeny was always the first and foremost retirement fund.

2. Knowledge. To become a storehouse of valuable experience, ensured that the young would come to you for advice. Among the Netsilik, the eldest functioning hunter was called *inhumataq*, "the one who thinks".

3. Honor. To acquire reputation through many services to the tribe in hunting, war, and hardship, ensured that you would not be easily forgotten. Formal hunting alliances are also a form of wealth conditioned by honor, and according to Netsilik tradition were also heritable.

Everything else, including weapons and tools and tents and dogs and clothes, were expendable and replaced often. Wives were not exactly wealth, but a form of investment: offspring was the dividend.

This is the man's perspective. And what about women? Actually almost the same: a good husband is a cash machine, and meat and skins were cash. But it's always in the form of children that wealth is realized. It was common for the Netsilik aging woman to adopt orphans and unwanted children, calling them a "walking stick" for her future.

And as the knowledge of hunting grounds and seasonal variation and toolcraft was the man's secondary retirement fund, herbal lore and skincraft were the old woman's specialties.

The old of the tribe are supposed to be a vital link in the chain, a chain that remained unbroken for at least 400,000 years. They are supposed to be the deep wells of knowing, where one goes to hear echoes of the ancestor's voices, to learn the impossibly ancient songs... But that time is gone: can you understand this? Can you allow yourself to feel that loss? Are we sure we're on the road of progress?

So why do our old become so greedy? Why are the babyboomers in particular so insufferably materialistic? Because there is no legacy. With the final dissolution of even those postaxial religious loyalties which were designed to replace and contain the divisive forces of modernity, and the gradual achievement of a Foucaultian architecture of atomic interchangeable individuals unrooted to anything but momentary political advantage, there is no legacy. Babyboomers have no faith in the cultural longevity to which they are supposed to belong, because they helped destroy it. Because the chain is more broken now than perhaps ever: even the nuclear family, the last vestige of tribal life in the midst of civilizational tensions, is finally eroding. Even gender itself is eroding. Many of the best of us choose not to have children at all: what clearer sign of a dying race than this?

Let it die. European culture wants to die: so be it! I don't suffer from intractable alarmism: there are many other unforeseen peoples and cultures yet to take shape. An inexhaustible magma of cultural invention lies just below the surface of this too-visible rot. The sooner it drowns itself beneath its moral posturing, technocratic suicide, and idiotic fantasies of the "end of gender" and socialist-mediated genetically engineered dystopia, the sooner will the next human renaissance begin.

The plague of the old is primarily a *spiritual crisis*, and not at all a mere demographic accident. Our contempt should not be mistaken for an adolescent inability to appreciate the gifts of age: actually my generation is *ravenous for wisdom*, and some of the best of my onetime peers have lost their way precisely because of this eagerness to humble themselves before the promise of superior experience and knowledge – they would not guess that there was nothing to be gained, that they already knew more than their teachers, that the well is dry.

The well is dry: but not because it has been drained. Because the water moved elsewhere. The landscape shifted: the babyboomer generation upon which I feel free to heap so much contempt, lost its way because it failed to integrate and overcome its own challenges – challenges which were primarily conditioned by unprecedented privilege... That this is any great divergence from previous generations is certainly not true – we are only waking up inside the great sinking ship of Western history, which is itself only tossing fitfully within the storm of post-agricultural civilization – yet I do feel confident that in this moment, we are at least glimpsing something characteristic of how and why human cultures age: the *average of decrepitude* rises, until a threshold is reached in which it suddenly seems that the prematurely old and chronically ill outnumber the young and healthy.

- 232 -

They are innocent. Of course no one in particular is to blame: we're talking about tidal historical forces, in which personal responsibility is at best a useful illusion, along with any generational unity – I use the "baby-boomer" designation as merely a teaching aid. *Yet they are what they are*: everyone's essential innocence relative to the leviathans of history and civilization, does not negate fundamental judgments about viability and worth – contradicting such judgments in the name of compassion will seriously endanger one's health and chances for health.

THE MEANING OF GUILT

- 233 -

My goal is to demonstrate to the hopeful reader how telling these truths is possible, without resorting to ugly attitudes or a falsified certainty about solutions. It should be possible to read all this and agree with every word, and still like yourself as much or more at the end of it. Your *guilty conscience* for having quietly thought much the same thing already, is to be addressed directly. The first step however, is to carefully identify every evasive maneuver you have been tempted to mimic: namely *moral posturing*, which in this case would feign some certainty in the inviolable and incommensurate value of every human life, no matter what they do or *fail to do*. To say, "there are too many people around who contribute nothing to the young and the future, because they never became anything worthwhile" – is already too direct a challenge to the religiously conditioned doctrine of equality, which would forbid that we make these judgments explicitly, and prefer that we hide our valuations of human worth behind other masks. The primary hypocrisy at work here, is that moral posturing of this kind is concerned most of all with *unarticulated criteria of group exclusion*: to avoid being the victim of the ugly bigotry of a frightened group, each one of us has dabbled in redirecting that ugly bigotry upon ready targets. Much of my vocation is to make a target of myself, and by allowing this projection to proceed in controlled isolation, demonstrate both its mechanics and the kind of immunity possible to develop against it. Primarily we're talking about the ability *not to react*: it is the *reaction* to the threat of exclusion which inspires false moral attitudes, which then propagate through the community by virtue of inspiring a heightened atmosphere of terror. A false moral attitude is what one uses, immediately before committing something one does not otherwise have the stomach for: group complicity is the first and last defense of the violent but cowardly ape.

Not to react – because actually the more honest responses we're looking for are already present: disgust is healthy, contempt is healthy, the prioritization of the young is healthy. The problem is that these instinctual responses are not allowed to develop, but smothered beneath both the anxiety of being discovered in the wrong alignment relative to group consensus, and intellectually negated by the insistence that some ideal solution be immediately discovered: repressive momenta which are the seeds of mass hysteria. The more we cannot afford honest healthy responses to unhealthy conditions, the more likely hysterical displacement becomes – and hysterical displacement is the medium through which protofascist politics achieve realization: *the seeds of fascism*.

- 234 -

From the "phylopsychological" perspective, the function of an exaggerated moral attitude is firstly to provoke your rivals into action while the atmosphere of terror persists; secondly to create opportunities for political power via the urgency of persecuting these rivals; and thirdly to accomplish much of the violence which was originally desired both via this persecution and via the collateral damage of their own defense. A great deal of what characterizes the contemporary "left", is the art of provoking the "right" into assuming and acting out repressed impulses: an army of ugly idiots who say and do what we have forbidden ourselves and desire all the more.

- 235 -

Care for the old is an analogous extension of care for the young, which forms the core of the vertebrate capacity for what is questionably termed "altruism", since it's driven ultimately by kin selection. The elderly become the infantile, with the same benefits from the tribe that can afford it and the risks of abandonment if they cannot. The Netsilik use the same kinship term for great-great-grandparent as they do for great-great-grand-child: the circle of relations closes, one ends where one began. This is a glimpse at the healthy human core as it has existed for 2 million years, with relative uniformity across cultures: the anthropologists report a sur-prising degree of uniformity in the kinship structures and tribal protocols regarding the concentric circles of relatedness – but since this is all genet-ically determined, with precise average ratios of relatedness, it's not surprising after all.

In other words, contravening the care for our own should not be taken lightly. But we live rather in a tribeless age in which *everyone and no one* belongs, in which everyone and no one is your ill-defined kin. And more often than not, even the closest kin tend to fail basic tests of loyalty: con-tributing factors are not only the lack of explicit tribe, but economic independence, social and geographic mobility, along with the sense that other more useful group loyalties have ascendancy – such as political alignment, and even the vagaries of social media credit is now enough to compete with the much weakened modern family. Internet-mediated sociality is just one more worm in this rotting edifice.

One of the most pernicious aspects of the modern firstworld family, is the way that *reckless inclusion* is employed as a means of diluting the tribal factors of exclusion, in order to soften its borders and thus permit more *bad behavior*... Most babyboomers I know, have been quietly setting up weakened family standards of behavior, so that they may regress and act out in their retirement as much as possible...

Learning to undo our own compassion – cultivated so earnestly up to now – has been painful. It might be easy for a loiterer to imagine that someone like myself is unfamiliar or unpracticed in the arts of compassion: yet a complication in my message is that the years I spent as a psychoanalyst in training, tending to the wounds of some of the most hopeless cases in our world – life histories which would make most of our safeguarded middle class woes blush – I would never consider regretting. Confrontation with a little genuine hardship should at least make abiding gratitude possible. But if I had continued, it would have destroyed me – or at least encouraged the formation of that impenetrable armor which makes most psychotherapists so useless at best and dangerous at worst.

The problem is not compassion itself, but that we practice it because we are afraid – we are compassionate to prevent exclusion. We are not generous, we are sly. We do the math: the risk of social status decrease and the loss of access to its goods, balanced against twisting up your mouth and mind again into that old familiar shape. The body conforms to its tortures, and we become eventually *always-already compassionate*: that means, always cringing, always wary, always friendly, always scrambling. Thus the scene ripens for the parasite: we're talking about forever nursing the bereft, those who are afraid to die because they were even more afraid to live. Those who are so insatiably greedy for any reprieve from their own failures that they will endanger the future of humanity itself: those who perpetrated the worst of COVID were not actually the terribly old in body, but the decrepit in spirit. This increasingly bold *hostility to youth and health* must be confronted directly, without taking leave from the shackles it would impose on us first: that we forever prove and reprove our innocence before we gain the right to question the authority of this sham court... To take merely one example: why is it that I seem to be alone, in pointing out the unthinkable hypocrisy of frittering away at least a trillion dollars in COVID lockdown nonsense, making worried faces of "compassion" and a great show of concern for the wealthy 80 year-olds dying "from" COVID, while there are millions upon millions of children on this earth who contract HIV from their own mothers, from the water they drink, from *having been born* – that there are millions of children who *die from diarrhea*, from neglect, from squalor? That there are places where leprosy is still a serious problem, where malaria rages every year infecting hundreds of millions... Does this begin to make our moral timidities seem absurd? Never for once doubt, that the moral actor is a well-practiced liar:

there is always an angle from which to reveal his essential contradictions – because otherwise he would not need his elaborate disguise.

- 237 -

Wir modernen Menschen, sehr zart, sehr verletzlich und hundert Rücksichten gebend und nehmend, bilden uns in der That ein, diese zärtliche Menschlichkeit, die wir darstellen, diese *erreichte* Einmüthigkeit in der Schonung, in der Hülfsbereitschaft, im gegenseitigen Vertrauen sei ein positiver Fortschritt, damit seien wir weit über die Menschen der Renaissance hinaus. Aber so denkt jede Zeit, so *muss* sie denken. Gewiss ist, dass wir uns nicht in Renaissance-Zustände hineinstellen dürften, nicht einmal hineindenken: unsre Nerven hielten jene Wirklichkeit nicht aus, nicht zu reden von unsern Muskeln. Mit diesem Unvermögen ist aber kein Fortschritt bewiesen, sondern nur eine andre, eine spätere Beschaffenheit, eine schwächere, zärtlichere, verletzlichere, aus der sich nothwendig eine *rücksichtenreiche* Moral erzeugt. Denken wir unsre Zartheit und Spätheit, unsre physiologische Alterung weg, so verlöre auch unsre Moral der „Vermenschlichung" sofort ihren Werth — an sich hat keine Moral Werth —: sie würde uns selbst Geringschätzung machen. Zweifeln wir andrerseits nicht daran, dass wir Modernen mit unsrer dick wattirten Humanität, die durchaus an keinen Stein sich stossen will, den Zeitgenossen Cesare Borgia's eine Komödie zum Todtlachen abgeben würden. In der That, wir sind über die Maassen unfreiwillig spasshaft, mit unsren modernen „Tugenden" ... Die Abnahme der feindseligen und misstrauenweckenden Instinkte — und das wäre ja unser „Fortschritt" — stellt nur eine der Folgen in der allgemeinen Abnahme der *Vitalität* dar: es kostet hundert Mal mehr Mühe, mehr Vorsicht, ein so bedingtes, so spätes Dasein durchzusetzen. Da hilft man sich gegenseitig, da ist Jeder bis zu einem gewissen Grade Kranker und Jeder Krankenwärter. Das heisst dann „Tugend" —: unter Menschen, die das Leben noch anders kannten, voller, verschwenderischer, überströmender, hätte man's anders genannt, „Feigheit" vielleicht, „Erbärmlichkeit", „Altweiber-Moral" ...

We modern men, so delicate, so vulnerable, giving and taking a hundred considerations, we imagine that the delicate humanity we represent, this *achieved* unanimity in forbearance, in helpfulness, in mutual trust, is a positive progress that places us far beyond the men of the Renaissance. But every age thinks so, it *must* think so. What's certain, is that we would not dare to place ourselves in Renaissance circumstances, or even imagine them: our nerves could not endure that reality, not to speak of our muscles. This incapacity however demonstrates no progress, but a only different, more belated constitution, a weaker, more delicate, more vulnerable one, out of which is necessarily engendered a morality *full of consideration*. If we think away our delicacy and belatedness, our physiological aging, then our morality of "humanization" also loses its value at once – no morality has any value in itself – : we would even despite it. On the other hand, let's not doubt that we moderns, with our thick padding of humanity which dislikes to bump against any objection, would provide the contemporaries of Cesare Borgia with a side-splitting comedy. We are in fact involuntarily funny beyond all measure, we with our modern "virtues"... The decay of our hostile and mistrust-arousing instincts – and that is what constitutes our "progress" – represents only one of the effects attending our general decay of *vitality*: it costs a hundred times more effort, more foresight, to cultivate such a dependent and late an existence. Here everyone helps everyone else, here everyone is to a certain degree an invalid and everyone a nurse. This is then called "virtue" – : among men who knew a different kind of life, a fuller, more prodigal, more overflowing life, it would be called something else: "cowardice" perhaps, "pathetic", "old woman's morality"...

Nietzsche, *Götzendämmerung*, §9.37

We're unwittingly funny, with our delicate sensibilities, our carefully balanced accounts of minor trespass and preemptive apologetics like an overworked waiter in a street café balances too many dirty dishes and customers at once – I'm unwittingly funny, with my attempts to absolve myself and appease my resurgent conscience, with my attempts to console us all with tales of a longlost tribal wholesomeness to which we quietly fantasize we personally could return one day... Or do we fantasize that we're already there? That you and I represent, with our gleaming pulsating intellectual life, with our proudly displayed scientifically acquired trophies of hearsay, anything like a culmination of human potential? Laughable, ridiculous, clownish: the best way out of these labyrinthine fingerpuzzles of moral tendernesses, these pathetic rivalries for the

Champion of Correctness, the Princedom of Never-Having-Hurt-Anyone – is laughter at ourselves. That the "right answer" for all humanity for all time, could ever possibly be generated by creatures as universally frail and ill as we are, is preposterous: has it ever occurred to a smug moral preacher to ask whether he really has a right to ask anything at all, but how to feel *a little less wretched today*?

- 238 -

Disgust and compassion are intimately related: thus it is a serious and suspicious error to confuse the love of our own children with some blandished sociologically self-conscious "altruism"... It is one of the primary patterns of camouflage of the vicious moralist we should be familiar with, this "universal love". To turn disgust into pity, is something in which we are all extremely adept, without recognizing the importance of the ingredient of disgust in this recipe: modern compassion-morality is largely the poisoncraft of the disgusting, who find – or manufacture – more pitiable sights than themselves. To feel superior to something, someone, *anyone*: as I've said before, there's an enormous contribution of *Schadenfreude* in all arts of compassion... To watch something writhe under the bright light of pity, to play with one's spiritual food: if it weren't for the repulsive moral mien these types find so necessary, their blank-eyed cruelty might begin to look sufficiently arachnid to find its way back to respectability.

- 239 -

Your *guilty conscience* concerning your scorn and indifference to the old and unwell must be confronted: but unraveling this tangled snare requires a reeducation in the meaning of guilt. Guilt is a relatively unstable emotional complexity, relatively new in the hierarchy of physiological response, and only necessitated by tribal life: in other words, an instinctual novelty for apenature. Guilt is preconditioned by *frustrated instinct*: it arises in no other context. Guilt is the affective result of repressed impulses and incoherent priorities of behavior, around which a "fault" is woven as cause: animistic thinking regarding trespass and guilt, taboo and punishment, is almost universal in the human adaptive package. Thus guilt is part of the *mythopoetic* technological complex, as innate and inevitable as spirits, gods, ceremony. That guilt is animistic and thus *projective* in function should not however instigate a preemptive dismissal of its means and ends: it is a social signal of dysfunction, as vital a signal as anxiety, which has its value in modifying tribal behavior towards a more adaptive milieu. Guilt and anxiety are feedback signals which prepare the tribe for change, which disrupt and undermine behavioral expectations, and which necessitate therefore either contained ceremonial attack or radical social alteration. A guilty conscience is a symptom of frustrated instinct, and self-awareness is one of its byproducts: as I've shown before, our much-fondled "consciousness" is actually a secondary product of the arrest of instinctual process. Becoming aware of oneself, embarrassed, stopped in one's tracks, suddenly unsure, suddenly clumsy, suddenly reflective: guilt is *not* primarily about ensuring social conformity and the guardian of "altruism", as the evolutionary psychologists all thoughtlessly assume. Most of the episodic guilt we experience is actually a symbolic breakthrough of the *ubiquitous guilt* entailed by frustration: most viola-tions are performed in order to relieve this same condition – but afterward we say we are guilty "because" of this violation, when the reality is reversed. The function of guilt therefore is to subtly alter the emotional fabric of the tribe, such that the threshold for change is lowered – some-times destructive, sometimes constructive: a change in locale, a change of leadership, a split or reunion of the tribe, an act of revenge – the ancients were as likely to feel guilty for *not* exacting revenge, as we are for wanting it.

Guilt is caused by angry spirits: among many other things, these evolution-ary psychologists are ignorant of the meaning of *spirit*, which we should understand as an affect belonging to the group, a nonlinear response for which it is impossible to assign unique responsibility. But then again, almost no one has asked themselves what the *function of emotion* is: which in my terms is the preparatory lowering of a threshold for a conditioned instinctual response. Thus when an angry spirit requires propitiation, we translate this into our language as "the group requires an alteration of pri-orities", because its members are experiencing too much frustration to be optimally functional. We are thereby a step closer to appreciating the mystery of psychosomatic illness: in traditional contexts, all illness that does not have immediate and obvious natural causes, like a snake bite or a broken ankle – is caused by angry spirits and requires the tribe's atten-tion. Guilt is psychosomatic: you are guilty because our priorities are fucked up, not because you are "wrong".

It's important not to confuse the wishful dogma regarding our "moral sentiments", such as has been taught since late antiquity, updated by Kant and the 19th century English utilitarians, and lately gussied up in the shallow reasoning of evolutionary psychologists, as proof of an innate rationale of altruism guiding us toward righteousness... Actually the distribution of the guilty conscience could hardly be less equitable: real perpetrators almost never feel guilt. At most, they fear group expulsion and reprisal: this anxiety is often enough considered proof of remorse. Meanwhile those who suffer most acutely from guilt, are almost always some perverse Kierkegaardian golem of penitence, whose only crime is having learned to feed on his own ecstasies of self-inflicted pain. But the majority of us modern types are merely frustrated, irritable, and looking for someone to blame: that we occasionally run out of targets other than ourselves, is just an accident of carelessness and temporary scarcity. The ubiquitous guilty feeling of modernity, is *not* due to injustice nor our fine sensitivity to injustice: it's a consequence of cagey irritability, which is a consequence of living in a cage.

ANIMISTIC ACCOUNTING PRACTICES

- 241 -

Confronted with the wretchedly old and unwell, we're *embarrassed*: it's embarrassing to realize the futility of their lives, the sad sputtering end... It taxes the sense of the worthiness of living, seeing such sights, smelling such smells: Prince Siddhartha was correct thus far. We're embarrassed for them, we're embarrassed of our own disgust, but probably most profoundly we're embarrassed by the failure of the human community. Let not this shame be transformed into self-glorifying pity: our rescue does not lie in indulging our own addiction to pity and competing with one another to appear most blameless. Our shame is functional: it's *shameful*, to have wasted the opportunities of a firstworld life, to merely grow greedy and spiritually wicked, to contribute to the global pandemic of chronic illness, to demand more longevity even as the human race smothers the biodiversity of this planet.

I want the reader to notice that my insistence on dealing with the problem of age as a *spiritual* problem, is not merely a Romantic cop-out – as a means of avoiding the implications of a fascist genocidal campaign – something which modern people very suspiciously are always ready to suspect. The spirit of decrepitude has always been with us: we have long since invented many ways to deal with recurrent spirits, which require their place in the animistic pantheon. Making a mask to capture its essence, dancing in its honor and thus calling that spirit forth, *contains* its effect on the wider community: this is what "propitiation" means. Witchcraft must be combated but can no more be eliminated than illness: the avaricious old man, the blood-hungry envious old woman, must be given their place but clearly *dealt with* – that's the consensus of almost every culture which deals effectively with spiritual roguery. Even as late as Christian Europe, "Belsnickel" persists as the embodiment of the slightly dangerous, perverted old fart who is a little too eager to attract children with candy: once you gain an eye for such masks, you realize how widespread they really are. Therefore all that's really required of us as a dramatic first step, is that we *identify* the spirit of decrepitude: dealing with it once it's identified, will come naturally. Most of the point of anthropomorphizing what we might in scientific language call behavioral proclivities or "affective thresholds", is to learn to *relate* to something otherwise intangible: exploitation of our almost infinite capacity for subtle *personal* relationship in order to gain strategic advantage over the elements of decadence in the tribe, which will otherwise ruthlessly exploit our hesitancies regarding "spirits" which no one is really responsible for, is almost the definition of animism. The spirit is responsible for itself: that's not merely a "primitive" accounting trick, it's the more accurate assessment of the plurality of soul which the human creature really is.

CULTIVATED UGLINESS

To give an example of the kind of incremental physiological change I'm talking about, I saw the other day a pair of young truckers at a gas station, the shape and demeanor of which was a kind of wakeup call. They lacked the classic North American trucker physique, along with the expected attitudes. Rather than the once customary paunch and skinny legs, ciga-rette hanging from the lip and a hard look in the eye, they were pudgy and soft, with large womany asses and obvious *endocrine disruption* – like an obese child with a disturbing fat distribution pattern. As amphibians are more vulnerable to toxic accumulation and thus act as an ecological bell-wether, I expect that the trucker is more exposed to fluctuations in diet and narcotica: where once was grease, nicotine, and amphetamines, there is sugar, smartphones, and antidepressants.

But what is true of their microbiota, is true of their "psychocosmetics": their talk was not gruff and terse, but had the emotional maturity of mid-dle-school boys. There is a hybridization and meeting of extremes occurring – gradually, imperceptibly to most of you - between the old woman and the adolescent: the body of an old woman and the shallow impudence of a spoilt boy.

- 244 -

What is the *ugly* response? It's physiological, make no mistake. Not at all merely culturally determined, and not even "merely" physiological: it's as holistic and immediate a judgment as any judgment perhaps can be. More immediate than "bad", much more immediate and unavoidable than "false": aesthetic judgments are not what was once called "syn-thetic", to borrow a Kantian term.

What is ugly is bad for us: not to be eaten, not to be dwelled in or among, not to be mated, not to be allowed to consume resources. There are many kinds of ugliness: the first case is a marker of genetic fitness. What is beau-tiful is well-formed, ripe, functional. But there is also ugliness of attitude and behavior, which reveals the history of the organism and its likely future behavior: greed, pettiness, bigotry, self-loathing, and so on, are all aesthetic judgments about the value of an individual to the tribe. Will this woman make a caring mother? Will this man provide? Will this woman share her food? Will this man betray us?

The hag is ugly: she has outlived her fertility and has nothing more to offer anyone, because she failed to develop into something which might edify the community. The old fart is beneath notice: because he has out-lived his strength, and failed to develop into anything which might educate the young. These are the judgments we make, whether we are now willing to acknowledge them or not: even spelling them out is not easy on our delicate moral sensibilities. But we must not allow our delicacy to make us stupid: that too, is geriatric morality. That too, is *hostility to youth* in the guise of moral superiority.

- 245 -

Do not doubt that the old can be more sublimely beautiful than the young: inward coherence, an orderly articulate emotional life, the glance of wisdom and the glint of humor – a realized spirit, a wry old fox, a reclining dragon. But do not lose sight of the fact that this judgment, "beautifully old", is the judgment: "immensely useful, available cultural riches, a path to dominance".

- 246 -

When discussing the mysteries of beauty and ugliness, it's worth pointing out that some people just possess a magnetism that cannot be explained. If you'll forgive a ridiculous but thoroughly enjoyable example, in the Dino De Laurentiis masterpiece of production design, *Conan the Barbarian*, what is it about James Earl Jones that's so convincing as a cult leader? How in the world does he make the short bangs of a Prince Valiant haircut into something so strangely sexy? Because he *wills* you to be attracted to him.

Or take the career of Bette Midler: that a woman with a face as brawny as that, managed to make it in Hollywood, says something about her willpower: she *commands* that you find her beautiful – your own astonishment at the boldness of this claim she utilizes as further seduction – as proof of her power, which you now begin to confuse with attraction.

Therefore we begin to suspect, that ugliness is also something communicated. That we are *compelled* to find someone ugly: herein lies one of the secrets of the spirit of decrepitude. Ugliness weakens, demoralizes, disheartens: isn't it possible that ugliness is the preparatory attack, before the wave of pitiableness begins? To induce the happy and healthy to become ashamed of their happiness and health, to not only give it away but *wish it away*... There are also many women who inflict a cultivated unattractiveness upon the world as a form of revenge, for not having paid attention sooner...

Ugliness is a strategy just as much as the position of weakness has strategic advantage. For the woman this is an especially pertinent bifurcation: an aggressively unattractive woman seeks attention not despite her appearance, but *because* of it. She utilizes your own repulsion and subsequent embarrassment as *leverage* to generate an exaggerated estimate of her value: often enough she has nothing to contribute, yet demands attention all the more.

One of the reasons for the exponential expansion of decrepitude, is that there's a kind of contracting "Pareto frontier" of arresting ugliness: not only do the returns diminish as actual decrepitude begins to approximate the cultivated – but there's a kind of arms race of ugliness as we all become inured to the sight and sense of dread.

LONGEVITY IS AN OLD TIGHTWAD'S WETDREAM

- 247 -

The obsession with longevity is a symptom of decrepitude. Wanting more life than one's fair share is nothing but blind raging greed. What happened to "three score and ten"? As though 70 years were not enough, as though we need more of these avaricious undead creeping around our world hoarding the planet's resources, as though humanity were not already taxing the earth heavily enough...

I recently stumbled across a thinly veiled expression of the spirit of decrepitude: a highly popular book from yet another guru-wannabe pandering to babyboomer vanity with the revealing title of, "I've Decided To Live to 120". This longevity so many seem to hope for, is nothing but a greatly elongated period of senility: to live more than half one's life as a frail expensive pet, wheezing and waiting to die! Has no one asked what the immense *cost* of this longevity might be? How monstrously entitled this attitude is? It wants to disguise its fear of death as *life affirmation*: but embracing death, taking risks, *living a good mortal life* and looking to the next generation is the affirmation of life. They are only symbolically afraid of dying, because they have been much more *afraid of living*: dying should be the final expression of what it meant to live.

The spirit of decrepitude would destroy the creative tension between life and death, blur the line and prolong a living death, in which nothing must be confronted, in which a heavily-medicated blurry-eyed shuffle between bed and toilet occupies a majority of a human life.

- 248 -

Longevity is an old tightwad's wetdream. Just as the immortal soul is the invention of a languishing culture: late Egypt, late China, late Rome, and now again late Europe. Oncology and genetic engineering is what they call it now: and the reality of an achieved longer life span is thus far more dangerous than mummified fortresses and alchemic dreams of "Peach Blossom Land"...

In place of mummification and cinnabar cocktails, we get talk of "replacing the biological body" with nanotechnology – as though a living creature were anything *but* the living body. As though biological reality were somehow inadequate and not already "self-replicating"! In place of a heavenly reward, we get fantasies of benign genetic engineering extending the life indefinitely – as though any such life extension would not be a tortured unholy thing whose existence is a *fucking blight*. Humanity is creeping toward *serious blasphemies*, and one can only hope we will run out of fossil fuels before some of the more indelible will occur. Or perhaps they should and must occur: perhaps we are looking for our master. Perhaps like a spoilt child, we break precious things because we want an adult to appear and draw firm boundaries. It's likely we will not learn anything collectively until something truly serious and irreversible happens: "gain of function" and the engineering of SARS-CoV-2 is likely just the beginning of an age which will make the atomic threat pale.

- 249 -

Within a culture assured of its future, a good death is a piece of wealth. The capstone speaks for the rest: may I die well.

Have you ever felt the life go out of a human body? Seen the dimness come over the eyes and listened to the last breath? While traveling in South America many years ago, I tried to save the life of a small boy: I gave him CPR on the side of a road, as his lungs filled with blood. I failed and he died in my arms – just as they say. I can't tell you exactly what this means to me. Maybe I died a little that day: maybe my omnipotence died. Maybe being confronted by invincible death while one is sufficiently young and impressionable, is what our cushioned firstworld existence is missing. Maybe those so obsessed with longevity have not grown out of their adolescence, maybe they need it explained to them how little they matter. Maybe the recent hysteria regarding a fictional pandemic, is the *wish* to be confronted by death.

ENVY: THE SOCIOLOGY OF ORDINARY WITCHCRAFT

- 250 -

> Psychosomatic medicine is simply a reencounter of what tech-
> nologically primitive people – and possibly even primates –
> know when they see bodily afflictions as expressions of spiri-
> tual distress or of malignancy in the web of social contacts. The
> perversion of supernatural power – essentially a social power –
> to individual and antisocial ends is called witchcraft.
>
> Lionel Tiger and Robin Fox, *The Imperial Animal*, p.186

The uniformity of anthropological testimony concerning the details, typical motives, and *commonplace ubiquity* of witchcraft is over-whelming – even more than kinship rules, hunting etiquette, and marriage arrangements, and so much more than the grotesquely overem-phasized details of metaphysical lore and ontological beancounting which the typical anthropologist lingers over like a hotel buffet beyond his usual means. We get tomes devoted to dissecting the imaginary worlds somebody was able to coax out of an old chainsmoking scoundrel, and barely a mention of the ubiquity of witchcraft in everyday matters.

The problem is not a lack of evidence, but what one does with the evi-dence. What does it mean, that every traditional people took so seriously this "malignancy in the web of social contacts", such that they assigned it great power and even prestige?

We don't want to know how much the dark arts of envy and magical revenge are a human universal, just as we don't want to know how much unconscious mechanics are determinative of human sociality. Part of the burden of a modern life is to be constantly subjected to petty witchcraft without any means of identifying it: cargo cult scientificality, alongside the denial of unconscious mechanics, only makes witchcraft that much easier. Just as a dogmatic religious conformity makes a nihilistic gerontoc-racy easier: the Salem witchtrials were a triumph of projective inversion.

But the bureaucrat's uniform suits the old and unhappy so well: most of what's known as "science" is bureaucracy and nothing else.

- 251 -

Azande say that hatred, jealousy, envy, backbiting, slander, and so forth go ahead and witchcraft follows after.

E.E. Evans-Pritchard, Witchcraft, Oracles, and Magic Among the Azande, §III.VI

He is well aware that others take pleasure in his troubles and pain and are displeased at his good fortune. He knows that if he becomes rich the poor will hate him, that if he rises in social position his inferiors will be jealous of his authority, that if he is handsome the less favoured will envy his looks, that if he is talented as a hunter, a singer, a fighter, or a rhetorician, he will earn the malice of those less gifted, and that if he enjoys the regard of his prince and of his neighbours he will be detested for his prestige and popularity.

ibid, §III.V

[...] carefully malicious intentions were concealed behind amiable attitudes. On the surface, camp life proceeded peacefully, while secretly vicious attacks were going on back and forth with the help of supernaturals.

The Netsilik Eskimo, §4.12

How much more realistic is this as an assessment of human nature: envy and malice as ubiquitous, petty grudges as commonplace and more likely than not? E.E. Evans-Pritchard seems to have been a more or less mediocre anthropologist, but happened to study a people so overtly dedicated to the practice and prevention of witchcraft that to ignore it would be to ignore the people: subsaharan African tribes, clearly due at least in part to the cultural destruction endured over the many centuries of exploitation, are almost obsessed with witchcraft. Like every people under continual strain, they attack each other: but it would be a mistake – as almost everyone has until now – to assign the fascination to the merely "primitive", while quietly assuming that being a "negro" must make one more prone to superstition...

It's my contention that the practice of witchcraft is a part of the core human character, because it is nothing other than unconscious manipulation via the subtleties of semantic distortion – something which cannot be isolated from the human technological faculty nor the social function itself. "Malignancy in the web of social contacts" is as inevitable as cancer in living tissue.

Therefore in the anthropology surrounding black magic and secret cursing, I find illumination for that dark underbelly of modernity we have been forced to explore. To reevaluate the human creature as *magical but petty*, which we can translate as *unconsciously brilliant but dependent on social valuation*: we are the most clever ape that ever was, but we remain ape.

- 252 -

Anthropological testimony makes it quite clear that two overlapping factors create witchcraft: *envy and old age*. The African traditions are the most explicit about this:

> The older a witch the more potent his witchcraft and the more unscrupulous its use. This is one of the reasons why Azande often express apprehension of old persons.
>
> *Azande*, §I.IV

Who turns to witchcraft? Those with no other recourse. Who learns the arts of secret malice? Those whose strength and virtue has faded or failed: the old, the unwell, the ugly, the otherwise unskilled, those whose gradually fading vitality alongside their increasing envy and resentment has given them time and motivation to learn the art of the curse.

And what is the curse? To hypnotize one's enemy to do himself harm. *Harm at a distance* is achieved by compelling the victim to *do it to himself*. There is no other witchcraft.

- 253 -

We must consider it suspect, when we witness the degree to which every traditional psychology considers *envy* a first class citizen in any causal theory of human behavior, while modern psychology is strangely quiet about it. Anxiety, "trauma", everything which tells the story of a victim: this is emphasized ad nauseam. So where does modern psychology place blame? We hear these words spoken with a viciously smug frown: "antisocial", "sociopath", "narcissist". In other words, everything uncooperative, untamed, and *unreachable from the safety of plausible deniability*: a complicit and colluding anonymous violence hates that which escapes the net of its envy. Everything which seems immune from the power of exclusion, is attacked as pathological; everything which hides and flatters the motive of envy and resentment, is enshrined in morality – clue to the ascendance of compassion. Modernity is the gradual triumph of the sorcerers of envy, the astrological ascendance of the sycophant.

- 254 -

Yet notice how the accusations criss-cross: I say "envy" and point to those who have reason to, they say "narcissist" and point to those who seem to want to escape moral reproach. The definition of "antisocial" is in question: but what kind of society? A tribe of hunters, a web of related families with a clear mission in a dangerous world – or a seething mass of selfish slobs desperately in need of governance?

REPRESSED CONTENT IS THE MEDIUM

- 255 -

The question is, how does this malignancy propagate? Through what medium? There must be some plane of causality, through which unconscious malice moves. Much is said with little or nothing: silences, omissions, body language, postures, glances – the "evil eye" may be preconditioned by *ambivalence* more than anything else.

Moreover it must give the analysand pause, to realize that so many forms of black magic involve the manipulation of material possessions closely associated with the target – and when that cannot be had, a symbolic miniature: surely the instinct at play here is the linguistic faculty. To alter the semantic web, to influence what is communally thought and felt by covertly shifting associations...

An elderly man, Itqilik, discovered quite by chance that an old woman at the village had for a long time been stealing salmon from his son's catch and hiding the fish in a grave. She was jealous that his son was a better and luckier fisherman than her own, and so she was trying to kill him by magic; for it is believed that a man will quickly die if any of his hunting spoils come in contact with the dead or dead men's possessions. Yet all the time the old woman was plotting against the life of the young man, her relations with both him and his father were of the most cordial kind.

Knud Rasmussen, *The Netsilik Eskimos*, §VIII, p.200

Is it possible that most of the rituals of witchcraft are designed to subtly change *one's own social behavior*, such that unconscious suggestion is transmitted? Making of oneself a transmitter of dread: to suggest to the victim, that he is already sick, doomed, cursed. Not "may he be cursed", but with every seemingly innocent word and deed and gesture, to say "you are cursed". The victim hears it, somehow, someway: "you are cursed", and mistakes this as his own conviction. This is suggestion: to prepare everything for a thought, but leave it undone.

This would account for why women are naturally adept: to implant thoughts, or prepare everything for a conclusion and coax it from the target utilizing egoic paths of least resistance as a lure. How does the curse function? The preparatory attack seems to induce paranoia, a sense of being surrounded, isolated, and weakened: at this stage it may rely on innuendo and gossip on the one hand, along with exaggerated ugliness and pity on the other. The witch needs *ugliness* to induce dread and pity, which opens the channels of repression in the socially responsible: "she's only an old woman", "look how ill and lonely she is already", "I owe her at least this much"...

- 256 -

What is the meaning of the evil eye? Consider that the most ambivalent social signal possible among apes, with our dinnerplate-face and bulging eyes, is *the stare*: is it desire, is it admiration, is it hate, is it jealousy? The stare destabilizes signification and provokes reinterpretation in the subject: it is the exploratory attack, which by provoking a moment of self-awareness in the subject, discovers weakness. A socially responsible, virtuous target asks herself: "did I do something wrong?" and proceeds to examine her own conduct. In that moment, the ambush: in self-awareness, which is nothing other than self-doubt and the *arrest of instinct*, the opening appears in which to implant a malicious thought – "you are wrong, you are bad, you are to blame". The eye is the transmitter of this malice because the eye induces consciousness, which is only another form of inhibition – which is, after all, merely a form of doubt.

> Witches' powers lie in their eyes; they have no other power. They suck blood through the witch birds' eyes.

> R. Prince, "Indigenous Yoruba Psychiatry", in *Magic, Faith, and Healing*, p.92

- 257 -

Witchcraft propagates through *repressed content* and therefore requires preexisting repression in the target. Thus the power to dispel it relies on *revealing the repressed*: the phallus being so often that power-object invoked to dispel malignant intent. Nothing breaks the spell of unhealthy repressed aggression like *the big dick*: that's the formula of rock-n-roll and every redeeming ceremony of fertility, ancient and modern.

The winged penis of the *fascinus* was almost ubiquitous in ancient mediterranean jewelry, architecture and ceremony: our Greek and Roman forefathers were much more concerned with the dangers of envy than we care to admit. Pliny calls it *medicus invidiae* for good reason. The Vestal Virgins were so dear to Rome that they were entrusted with protecting victorious generals and the state itself from magical harm through the power of their flaming phallus. It couldn't be clearer: by lifting communal repression around the prize, by decorating children and warriors in objects which repel pity and shame, malicious envy has no channel through which to sneak.

Suddenly the old fertility rituals make more sense: not merely "yay for sex", but "sex defeats resentment". Consider what it means, that at the culmination of the extremely ancient procession of *Liber Pater*, lord of seed and wine, a respected older woman of the community places a wreath upon the giant phallus which has been carried through the countryside: the reconciliation of old to young, the closing of the circle, the didacticism of the old rituals made as symbolically clear as possible – "we say yes to the future, youth, seed."

- 258 -

Thus witchcraft is the exploitation of social contract: since the raison d'être of repression is nothing but social contract. And thus healthy warriors, conscientious maidens, and precocious children are vulnerable to attack: the core of tribal virtue is repression – there is no other urform of "goodness". The raging slob, the selfish mooch, and the witch itself are generally invulnerable because there is no attack surface of unconscious social repression: all virtue in these types is mere obsequiousness, conscious abstention, and lying-in-wait.

- 259 -

Again the hypnotic attack is the induction of psychosomatic effect through *repressed content*: a merely unconscious medium does not spread well. Therefore the shaman is difficult to attack, because there are fewer repressed fragments. Guardian spirits are at the gates: preemptive hostility, a sense of already knowing who one is, of an independent status *outside the community*... This provides the clue as to why every shamanic initiation must traverse the boundaries of the tribe, and why it's tolerated at all: as a matter of psychic sanitation, it's necessary to have agencies at hand which feel less constrained by the eternally petty struggles of tribal politics – else the tribe will drown in its battles of envy. As dangerous as a shaman can be, precisely because of his relative freedom from virtuous repression, there seems to be no other effective defense – somewhat like keeping big dogs around the camp...

- 260 -

An excellent example of the hypnotic duel:

> One afternoon two women passed each other near my house, between the two villages of Atum and Kauar, in the little hollow where bald-headed Nangoli was planting a tobacco patch. Niangan greeted Nangoli, who simply walked on by without

responding. As Niangan neared her *odok* [front door] she began hurling abuse over her shoulder, and Nangoli responded in kind, without looking around. Then as they reached their respective *odok*, timed to a second, each spun around as in a duel and shouted the accusation, "badiam!" ("sorcerer!") But Nangoli, who was Lolim's [the priest's] daughter and so knew a thing or two about sorcery, followed up immediately with a long ululation, high and warbling and increasing in volume until Niangan cowered back as though the sound were piercing her. Atum came flying out and grabbed her and pulled her into the *odok* just as Nangoli completed the curse by putting her thumb to her lips and jerking it out at the fleeing Niangan with a final ululation.

Colin Turnbull, *The Mountain People*, p.180

- 261 -

Witchcraft is the exploitation of tribal instinct for destructive ends: not merely antisocial, but deeply nihilistic – it's no accident that children, pregnant women, and talented young men are the prototypical targets. This is why a chapter on something seemingly so anachronistic as witchcraft belongs in a book on the core of human social psychology: witchcraft is the original form of nihilism and cultural degeneracy, the parasite of symbolically-powered human sociality which no doubt emerged simultaneously, just as the virus emerged at the same moment as the lifeform.

- 262 -

Tribal means of discharging social tension, in order of increasing risk and complexity:

- ⇁ Gossip and slander
- ⇁ Mockery and boasting
- ⇁ Public duel
- ⇁ Witchcraft
- ⇁ Ritual exclusion

228

Witchcraft borrows its means from gossip and slander, its form from the duel, and the seriousness of its intent from ritual exclusion: it's a form of private duel relegated to the unconscious symbolic. Consider when a young male chimpanzee must live in the shadow of his rival: there is a constant tension communicated through symbolic duel, such that in every situation subtle insults are made...

- 263 -

A caustic aside: Carl Jung is to be despised. For what he did and failed to do regarding Freud's legacy: Jung was completely without intellectual conscience, and continues to attract those who want to make of psychology their own personal playground of grotesque vanity. For spitting in the well: he ruined the marriage of anthropology and psychoanalysis with his childish arrogance and endless self-indulgence. Most of all I hate him for stealing and ruining the concept, "collective unconscious". I won't use the term, although much of what I have to say would have benefitted from the idea if it weren't deranged beyond repair.

- 264 -

> To him there is nothing miraculous about it. It is expected that a man's hunting will be injured by witches, and he has at his disposal means of dealing with them. When misfortunes occur he does not become awestruck at the play of supernatural forces. He is not terrified at the presence of an occult enemy. He is, on the other hand, extremely annoyed.
>
> *Azande,* §II.I

I could emphasize the aspect of the uncanny in acts of witchcraft, their kinship with Freudian slips, dreams, and everything unconscious which hovers in the liminal repressed spaces of human contact – but my goal here is to demonstrate the *ordinary* and *familiar* nature of black magic. Psychoanalytic perspective is so fiercely attacked for good reason: once the existence of unconscious mechanics is granted, once *repression* is granted first citizenship in the family of everyday psychology, once the ape becomes willing to understand unconscious communication as a vast dark continent – the supposition of *malicious* forms of unconscious coercion in the midst of so much informative commerce is the only reasonable hypothesis. That the symbolizing ape might be adept at inducing psycho-somatic disease, self-harm, self-doubt, misfortune and miscalculation in his enemies and rivals: surely the animal capable of metallurgy and non-Euclidean geometry is capable of that much! And the truth is that this animal is almost universally a *genius* in the arts of unconscious malice. Furthermore our technological accomplishments might be meager in comparison, if we were able to compile every snide remark, every juicy slander, every multivalent insult and innuendo, and finally every potent microhypnotic evil eye ever cast through human history: the *semantic brilliance* of all this unconscious distortion designed to harm each other in a thousand small ways may very well outweigh every other gleaming monument of Homo sapiens. The real tower of Babel is the one built of unconscious malice.

- 265 -

If malicious magic is so commonplace in humanity past and present, why resort to anthropological texts at all? Because in the context of anthropology the modern resistance to the idea is finally lifted, and even the most ordinary observer suddenly finds it everywhere. For example, Balikci includes a story at once highly mundane and yet potent:

> The social atmosphere of fear and suspicion previously described constituted an excellent ground for the seeds of hostility and persecution to grow in. This process was considerably aided by the Netsilik ability to conceal malicious intentions and hostile feelings in order to prevent possible reprisals by magic and sorcery. On the surface camp life proceeded smoothly, but hidden tensions were such that the slightest incident could set off aggression at any time. A traveler among the Arviligjuarmiut described the following situation to Steen-hoven:

> I. traveled on Kellett River together with A., S., and some others, who on their sleds had been visiting their caches. The weather was beautiful and we walked to and from each other's sleds, while the sleds were moving all the time. A. was seated on the back of S.'s sled and the latter sat in front of him. A. was eating a fish. I was driving my sled behind his. One moment when S. was turning towards his dogs or so, I saw A. suddenly make a lightning stab with his knife at S.'s back – a would-be stab, to be sure. Then he immediately looked around himself.

But I looked already in another direction. S. is the son of I. and it was known that A. and I. did not get along well. It was my impression that this stab had been prompted by an altogether subconscious impulse and that A. only became aware of it after he had done it. I believe he could just as well have really stabbed S. out of these subconscious feelings of resentment.

§III.9

Safely sealed within the limits of "primitive culture" and his temporary role as anthropologist, finally the modern man allows himself to become conscious of what he has known all along: the ubiquity of *repressed aggression*, which seeks expression in a thousand small ways and is generally only visible when the repression misfires...

- 266 -

The Zande word for "bewitch" means literally "to shoot". This is such a common metaphor in the explanation of the curse, that the Germans used to call chronic backpain *der Hexenschuss*: literally "the witch's shot". Not only is "backstabbing" a common theme because we're dealing with the most indirect forms of combat and betrayal, but because the back is the strongest muscle of strong type: "grin and bear it" – hidden in the most ordinary idioms are the secrets of psychosomatism.

AMBIVALENCE IS THE CARRIER WAVE

- 267 -

If repression is the environment in which witchcraft takes effect, *ambivalence is the carrier wave* by which witchcraft travels. Returning to our Netsilik:

> Jealousies, various resentments, and hatreds, often concealed for long periods, sometimes found an outlet in aggressive magic involving various supernatural beings. One basic characteristic of these spirits, however, was their unreliability and ambivalent nature. When unsuccessful in their mission they

could turn back blindly on their masters and bring sickness, death, and destruction to their camp.

§III.8

The Netsilik understand that dealing with deep ambivalent forces is a dangerous game – as any psychotherapist should know. When an attack fails, they call it *tunraq kigdloretto*, a "reversed spirit" – and the curse rebounds upon the attacker.

- 268 -

By no means is "belief" in witchcraft required for its efficacy: explicit suggestibility is neither prerequisite nor efficient cause. In fact, a Western willful ignorance of witchcraft and an obtuse scientificality makes one all the more susceptible: our *belief in words and ideas* is more than sufficient as a point of vulnerability. Our intractable devotion to precarious social prestige, our attachment to brittle identities, and our hyperalgesic psyche provide a large attack surface: a suggestive tone accompanying a joke-that-is-nobody's-joke, followed by the slightest pause, is all that's required for most of us.

But these are merely the beginner's craft, such as prepubescent girls get up to: much more subtle means exist and are exploited by the more desperate. These are entirely unconscious, wordless spells. They typically exploit not egoic vulnerabilities, but openings provided by compassion, emotional availability, and above all *ambivalence*: this type of spell generally begins by evoking pity, which is itself a composite of disgust and mercy. The witch learns to skillfully and instantaneously dissect pity, such that the disgust rebounds while the mercy is absorbed...

- 269 -

Witchcraft is primarily the art of gaining control over the unconscious hostilities your enemies have *against themselves*. Therefore there are two primary means of defense:

⌐ Withholding pity. Witches are generally the weak and prematurely old, who cultivate and exaggerate pitiableness. They generally will not attack until compassion has opened the backdoor.

‑   Deep unconscious self-advocacy. Careful examination and elimination of contradictions in values. This is the reward of integrity. Self-respect is as much a positive feedback system as depression. The more you learn to defend yourself and ward off witchery, the more you will respect yourself and the less vulnerable you will become.

- 270 -

Notice that in most traditional accounts of witchcraft, it's never granted the power to make people tell lies, nor steal, nor commit adultery, nor deceive authority: to blame witchcraft for these kinds of misdeeds would be immediately suspect. But should an accident handicap the best hunter, or a beautiful child fall sick, or the game be scared off by someone's clumsiness, or your kayak spring a leak: that's the domain of unconscious malice. Generally witchcraft relies on self-directed hostility: inflammation, ulcers, cancer, irritable bowels, back pain, injury, forgetfulness, neglect, "accidents" of all kinds.

- 271 -

Again our ancient world was not just about austerity and marble: something the typical post-Christian historian has hidden from us, is the ubiquity of sexual magic charms. Not just the phallus in abstract, but figurines ejaculating furiously into the evil eye, dickheaded little men sawing an eyeball in half – these were commonplace in classical Rome and Greece, as much as the gaping vulva of the Celtic *sheela-na-gig* was considered so indispensable as to be included in the architecture of the church... Notice that even in the midst of crushing Christianity, the pagan wisdom concerning the ubiquity of petty malice surged back into place: guarding the corners where bad feelings pool, they put their funniest, least reverent spirits. And it wasn't until those sour Christians of late antiquity, those malignant losers on the up-and-up, that the word "obscene" was ever associated with these charms: *obscaenus* meant "ill omen", and is cognate with *caenum*, "shit". To use it when speaking of the symbols of fertility, youth, renewal, the body's objective and redemption, is surely an act of witchcraft. Malignant semantic reversal in the service of slander is one of the signatures of black magic.

- 272 -

To reverse the role: who is ugly, who is beautiful? Who is healthy, who is sick? Witchcraft involves exploitation of the fundamental union of opposites at the root of all adjectival signification: the *Ursprache* of multivalence. Onesided description is never stable: always the potential for reversal exists... Entanglement in ambivalence may often be sufficient to induce the spell, as long as sufficient hostility against the self exists in the target – in other words, sufficient tribal virtue.

The "spell", in the most advanced cases, taps the roots of the schizophrenic: witchcraft at this niveau is the contained employment of repressed psychotic personalities. One often sees this kind of double or triple person in the "nice old lady", or the priest, or the lonely psychotherapist, or the secretly abusive CEO: anyone who becomes adept at containing tremendous pressures through the gradual use of repressed psychotic elements, whether the pressure is loneliness, desperation, quiet failure, or any other sad true story hidden by a social fiction maintained at all costs.

- 273 -

We are not done with witchcraft just because we believe we are. We are no more free of witchcraft than we are free of magical thinking, cognitive dissonance, and hypocrisy. Witchcraft is part of the core human technological package: it's not supernatural, nor particularly "occult", nor mere superstition sufficiently explained away by suggestibility. It is a *social* phenomenon, a means of *social aggression* utilizing hypnoid unconscious channels of communication. It exploits hypertrophic human communicativity. It exploits the overdevelopment and underutilization of the language faculty. It exploits the human susceptibility to neurotic fragmentation and psychosomatic disease. And in the worst cases, it injects psychotic ambivalence into the healthier half of the community.

MAGIC PSYCHOSOMATIC

- 274 -

What should already have given the clue to anthropologists, that in the defense against witchcraft we are dealing not with mere superstition and delusion, but with an essential piece of collective human health, is the fact that every affliction of magic is a *psychosomatic affliction*:

> The effects of witchcraft lead to death by slow stages, for it is only when a witch has eaten all the soul of a vital organ that death ensues.
>
> *Azande*, §I.VII

- 275 -

Eventually the scholar should realize that traditional taboo is arranged such that it's impossible not to transgress: this is the value of taboo, in that it provides a ready etiology of *guilt*, and thus an accounting system for *instinctual frustration* – the Orthodox Jew still provides a serviceable lens into this ancient system for the allowance of immense collective neurosis. We imprison ourselves in imaginary reasons, so that we may remain blind to the fundamental maladaptation at work. Animistic magic however, by always treating the patient as a psychosomatic whole, often manages to come much closer to efficacious cure when dealing with fundamentally social ills: the mother-in-law is overbearing, the husband is lazy, the love for an adopted son is creating tension, a wife is jealous – these are usually the causes a medicine man must somehow confront with magical, indirect means.

> Psychiatry involves a subtle combination of flirting, gambling, and gossip with overtones of the supernatural. The old medicine man knew this very well when he threw bones to divine the "illness," but based much of his diagnosis of witchcraft on what he knew from gossip about the patient.
>
> *The Imperial Animal*, p.202

- 276 -

In the old medicine, there's first aid, and there's defense against witch-craft: there's very little mention of what we think of as primarily "medical", because it was obvious to everyone that a wound should be cleaned and a broken bone set – no specialist was necessary. Other than arthritis, cancer, and the other inevitable afflictions of the old, psychoso-matic disease accounted for almost every other health problem.

- 277 -

> [...] the medical profession is able to perform grooming acts and ceremonies in the careful privacy of its offices and the bizarre hotel-hospitals in which the distraught are placed under the care of the inept. [...] In many other cultures medicine refers to magic; "medicine," the word, even means magic the process. But in our culture it has become confused with efficacious science.

The Imperial Animal, 178

I become increasingly convinced that health and sickness *should* be treated as matters of magic: which is only another way of saying "incon-ceivably multivalent". Health requires "magic" because it requires the recruitment of all available unconscious forces to deal with the complica-tions of an overdeveloped nervous system with too much leverage: if these forces are not acknowledged and symbolically contained, they tend to sabotage the healing ritual.

To believe you possess the sole "true causes" of any disease is clumsy magical thinking: to fearfully cling to solely "organic" etiologies, is only another weak-minded superstition. The definition of superstition is not a belief in causality outside accepted science, but *a foreclosing certainty*: a closed mind is a superstitious mind. Any healing, should it manage to occur within the borstal brutality of a modern hospital, is already highly dependent upon *the psychosomatic effect of ritual*: take away the paper gowns, alienating atmosphere, and bad food, and the patient will begin to doubt the authority of his shaman. The placebo effect is the public secret of modern medicine.

- 278 -

The careful reader should have noticed already, that in this description of witchcraft is contained also the kernel of hysteria: *displacement* is fundamentally at work in psychosomatic disease. Repressed aggression, resentment, "Kränkung": remember that when Freud began treating hysterical young women, he found invariably that the root cause was a series of unrequited slights, insults, and "malignancy in the web of social contacts". In hysterical illness we make ourself sick: one has been cursed, but one is fundamentally cursed by one's own unconscious hostility. The cure is to amplify hostilities by making them conscious: the reassignment of blame cures so much of what is wrong with the human being. Housekeeping of the soul requires a constant schlepping of the garbage of social tension...

- 279 -

Why in the old medicine, is healing equated with returning the errant soul? Why is illness *soulloss*?

But the answer is easy – deceptively so. Soul is the higher-order synergetic payoff of the union of mind and body: the full inheritance of instinctual competence and unconscious intelligence, when you are where you're supposed to be. When you have soul, your timing is uncanny, your wording is precise and witty, your virtues are at your command.

That psychosomatic disease is the *loss of soul*, signifies a misalignment of priority, a dysfunction in the hierarchy of instinct, a chronic frustration which is leaking side-effects into other systems, causing symptom formation through displacement – in other words, hysteria.

- 280 -

They manipulate the paraphernalia, invoke their spirits, smoke, chant, and build up more tension. [...] The monotonous rise and fall of the chant, the near-darkness with the flickering fire, the hideous makeup, the cries in the night and rappings at the door and windows, the elaborate precautions – all these elements build up until the doctors, worked into a controlled frenzy, dash from the house to do battle.

Robin Fox, "Witchcraft and Clanship in Cochiti Therapy", in
Magic, Faith, And Healing, p. 185

To return to our prime example: I've described the COVID debacle
unsympathetically, as a symptom of chronic illness and repressed aggression. But buried in it is also a healthy response to an epidemic of
psychosomatic disease: a ceremony in which the witchcraft responsible
for the disease may be isolated, the fear surrounding it heightened, and
the cure discovered. In other words, COVID has been not only a tribal
protocol of membership expungement, but a ceremony of exorcism.

And thus by opposing the COVID ritual, we take up our place as wicked
sorcerers in the eyes of the community. In a way, we skeptics have
muddled the ceremonial power COVID was supposed to effect: we have
stood in the way of ritual healing – we turned on the light and laughed in
the middle of a ceremony, we scattered the fire, we broke the trance.

The hallucinating human creature needs its ceremonies of expulsion, else
it succumbs to psychosomatic disease: even the healthiest of nomadic cultures feels this need. The tension inherent in the disorganized human
instincts requires regular maintenance: animistic exorcism is necessary.

Hysterical displacement serves a purpose: in order to cure imaginary ills,
imaginary cures are necessary. This is not at all to dismiss their power and
efficacy.

THE SECOND SPEAR

- 281 -

The Azande have a nice metaphor for magical causation: they call it
umbaga, the "second spear". When taking down large prey, the first spear
kills the animal, but the second spear kills it dead: magical causation is
the reinforcing cause, the "socially relevant cause", and therefore the
placeholder for everything happening at the unconscious niveau in the
community. Magic is the just the old name for "the unconscious".

The attribution of misfortune to witchcraft does not exclude what we call its real causes but is superimposed on them and gives to social events their moral value.

Azande, §II.IV

Evans-Pritchard is an excellent firsthand source, but like every half-baked psychologist – which is already more than half of everyone – he invariably trips over his own intolerance of anything but the kind of rationality he expects. This is the kind of anthropologist who argues with his informants, furiously explaining just how wrong they are. He confuses at least two motivations for the practice of witchcraft:

1. Dealing with repressed aggression at the symbolic level: achieving a functional human tribe despite incessant unconscious warfare.

2. Eliminating uncertainty via magical thinking: achieving a closed horizon of causality for the sake of personal sanity.

The Western anthropologist has utterly failed to perceive the first goal, because they refuse to see unconscious mechanics, nor the value of symbolic thinking, nor the effectiveness of magic in achieving psychosomatic health. According to them everything "magic" must be motivated by stupidity, ignorance, and laziness: essentially the British colonist attitude writ large in the history of ethnography.

Western method demands that all causal theory which cannot be demonstrated be discarded: thus far we're on solid ground. But we're accustomed to supplementing our argument with the accusation that such theories are motivated only by the second motive: the demand for premature certainty due to a weakness of mind.

But by doing so, we indulge in another weakness: believing that *known* causes account for *all* causes. This is willful ignorance rather than wishful knowledge. And thus the recurrence and resurgence of witchcraft, both as *the practice of resentment* and as *compulsive magical thinking*: the nasty old spirits find the way clear, and the weak mind demands certainty as recompense for the dull ache of a hungry materialistic worldview, such as the Anglo-American suffers from in particular.

Modernity transitions smoothly into medievalism, as late antiquity demonstrates so amply: demonologies multiply, private magic becomes commonplace – *incipit religio*. Eventually and inevitably a universal religion emerges from the confusion of private superstition: this process is already visible in the 21st century by peeking into the darker corners of the internet.

- 283 -

All assignment of agency is a form of magical thinking: again this is why everyone is an amateur psychologist. Psychology is the refinement of the *ancient art of blame*: something every bickering tribal creature needs, is the ability to weave a tale of justification – else the tribal virtues would defeat the tribal vices too often, and we'd be more compassionate than we ought. There is therefore an undeniable connection between that "plausible deniability" I'm always speaking of, and the very same psychological art we practiced in order to reveal it... To possess high-grade psychological Gongfu without succumbing to the temptation to abuse one's friends and lovers with it, to renounce getting one's way in every way every day, requires an almost terrifying integrity bordering on self-destruction: one is generally either a loser-genius who won't let himself win, or an insufferable manipulative genius who won't let himself lose.

- 284 -

Education in the ubiquity of witchcraft therefore serves two purposes at once:

⇁ To train you to expect, detect, and defend against unconscious malice.

⇁ By this same training, to gain clearer insight into unconscious mechanics through *explicit* magical thinking. One must learn to think magically at the *conscious* level in order not to be so subject to unconscious compulsion, which will force cognitive dissonance and distortion in seeking its ends. A supple, half-dreaming, associative conscious mind is much less prone to unconscious distortion than a rigid, repressed one. The art involved is a delicate balance of associative fertility coupled with a relentless analytic appraisal: one sees, one does not necessarily believe.

This training also supplements the first goal: the freedom from compulsory and uncontrolled magical thinking, renders us less vulnerable to manipulation. We dream openly so that we may *detect unconscious distortion*. And yet while assignment of malignant agency may be closer to the truth than an "accident", it's further from the truth because truly *no one* did it. When confronting malignancy of this kind, it's important not to insist on speaking to the "person", but speak instead to *the spirit*. A "spirit" being defined for these purposes as repressed content which has accumulated influence within the social semantic field.

Besides, by addressing a fragmentary spirit, you will invariably learn to employ your own unconscious intelligence: which in everyone is an extremely powerful thing – many times more powerful and precise than any conscious entity you pretend to be.

UNCANNY REVERSAL

- 285 -

How do I reconcile all this with the *witch-hunt* and its kinship with the seeds of fascism? In other words, if witchcraft is so ordinary, why not hunt for it? There's a sense in which this too, has its proper place within the pantheon of tribal instinct: somewhat like the reaction to parasites discovered in the home. But the truth is that the witch-hunt is usually an embarrassing farce of ritual exclusion, which is itself the fundamental tribal instinct – reliance on a histrionic form indicates its previous failure.

The healthy tribe does not need to hunt for witches, because they are already obvious, and already sufficiently persecuted by wicked children and sharp tongues. The healthy community wards off resentment with vitality: the continual celebration of the young, fertile, and victorious – along with a constant stream of mockery and party vibes whenever possible. The grandmothers are loved and the grandfathers honored, the girls are admired and the boys set loose on the world. The resentful hags, scheming old farts, and sourpusses of every kind retreat to the shadows on their own: a mad dance party is also a form of ritual exclusion.

- 286 -

The witch-hunt as we know it, is merely another *tactic of witches*: to inspire fear of the unknown, mistrust, and betrayal. The *uncanny reversal* is the signature of witchcraft: suddenly the sickliest and least desirable are in charge, suddenly a simpering sycophantic attitude wins, suddenly the skies are grey and the future dim... And the tribe ripens for the evangelist, the emergency tyrant, the health committee, the secret police, and moral posturing.

- 287 -

My work is not prescriptive, because you cannot prescribe health: the apotropaic powers of vitality must be natural or they are ineffective – everything else is the shambles of moral posturing, cute faces we make to each other in the feeble effort to conjure certainty from mutual deception. A good doctor *removes the obstacles to healing*, and then waits: Hippocrates was quite clear about this, despite all the distortions since. If you want edification, examples surround you: go to the largest public park of any medium-sized town in the Western United States on a clear summer weekend, and look for a humble *quinceañera*: healthy tribe is right under our noses, as natural as anything, as ordinary as daylight.

- 288 -

In the end, all I wish to advocate for is *health* and the wisdom of the body. But if I say these things so simply no one will know what I mean, or pretend not to and find excuses for distorting those words: and so I must *demonstrate* these essentials in a thousand ways, and perhaps spend most of my time boarding up the million and one pedantic detours and clever distortions – and still I will lose in the end and be willfully misunderstood by many and most. Only to a few then, will this tiny island paradise of clarity be granted: a mere foothold, a towrope in the water, an assuring smile. After all my words and elaborate dance, what do I pass on to my favored student but a firm handshake, a glint in the eye, and the possibility of enduring friendship?

HATE: THE DEVIL'S BUTTHOLE

- 289 -

The left provokes the right into acting out its own repressed impulses: that's a powerful formula, which is much older than "left and right" – most likely it is as old as "good and evil". What was it Zoroaster had his righteous god say to his evil twin?

> Neither our thoughts, nor commands, nor our understandings, nor our beliefs, nor our deeds, nor our consciences, nor our souls, are one.

> *Zend Avesta*, Yasna §45.2

- 290 -

There is a qualitative difference between the blustering explosive hatred of the right and the seeping vitriol of the left. When a political conservative gives himself over to hate, he is looking for a reprieve from his self-loathing: there is a *wishful and projective* quality to rightwing hate – it generally remains superficial, mere Ersatz, and "as if". He hates because it dispels the fog of his chronic confusion and sense of having been left behind: with a projective hate he finally knows who he is and what he wants. A white supremacist seeks shelter in his race hatred from his own lack of stable identity; a misogynist seeks elusive self-esteem from a disrespect of women; the ignorant man who boasts of his hatred for Mexican Americans will later mingle with them thoughtlessly and forget his slurs.

With the left, I find another order of animosity entirely – something both more archaic and perhaps more profoundly determinative of the human future: the seething hatred so characteristic of those who learn to turn weak social positions into strategic advantage, the boiling resentment of the avaricious yet mediocre, the accumulated frustration of civilization itself. I find something much more chilling and dangerous in the unconscious tactical malice of the "progressive": a much deeper thirst for violence lies hidden there, a thirst for police action, a thirst for anonymous atrocity, and the cleverness to carry it out with a *good conscience*. It is the *good conscience* of the progressive that is so dangerous: compared to the redfaced sputtering rightwing, who seem to act only by accepting their positions with a *bad* conscience, the left is many times more skilled in the fabrication of moral justification, moral disguise, moral *right*... The leftists are the artists of conscience and the conjurers of plausible deniability: it turns out that a life lived continually offloading frustration with the means available to the pointlessly educated, half-therapized, and sedentary urban bourgeoisie, results in an animal highly practiced in inventing reasons why they are never to blame, never responsible, and always already in the possession of a moral high ground. In urban modernity, any other tactic results in untenable guilt, paralytic anxiety, and crushing depression: from this perspective we almost begin sympathizing...

And perhaps we should in this case stand an unrelenting analysis of the truth, between our revulsion at the aesthetic totality of this vicious creature on one hand, and whatever fragment of compassion we are capable of on the other: because have we not also been this creature at one time? All of modern humanity is bound up in this tangle, for as long we continue to reinvest in the contortions of realized modernity. From this perspective the conservative convulsions are merely hiccups and belches and an attempt to flee.

In every distasteful compromise, in every calculating cowardice, in every moment of instinctual repression for the sake of safety and surety there is the potential for becoming more wretched – that is more "progressive": the moment we learn to make an enemy of our aggression and an ally of our ideological fantasies, is the moment we become more suitable for the world we have been crafting since 10,000 BC.

- 291 -

The political left is bleeding out its talented tenth, alienating its brightest youth, and forcing them into a no man's land where they stand much too nauseated to ever look left again, and yet still looking askance at the right and feeling more unwilling to offer uncritical loyalty to anyone than ever before – and yet we also feel that coherent political positions *are more necessary than ever before*: finally in our generation "rights" seem to mean something more than moral posturing, the facility of the U.S. constitution to *prevent despotism* suddenly means something, and what seems urgent is a renewed and genuine investigation into "the concept of the political"...

- 292 -

Progressive politics encourages and deepens the castration of instinctual life, replacing the rewards of family and tradition with the more volatile and dissipative gratifications of moral posturing and vicarious victimhood. This has the effect of accelerating the accumulation of *repressed aggression* – which is again what I see as ultimately determinative. In fact I'd say that progressive politics has the curious effect of simultaneously *permitting* egregious aggression while encouraging an atmosphere of ubiquitous frustration, as though no one were ever getting what they want despite incessant gratification.

When leftist thinking goes sour, when moral posturing and neutralized virtual rebellion no longer dissipate frustration fast enough, the system is pushed into a higher order parameter I term "ritual exclusion": a species of protofascism arises which we must learn to recognize. The big question: is this emergent fascism the inevitable logical conclusion of the liberal tradition, or only its degenerative offal? Yet as a psychologist, rather than analyze the problem from ideological grounds as everyone else does, I naturally gravitate towards what I consider ultimately determinative: the immediate and hidden psychology of political antagonism, or what I'd like to call *the taxonomy of hate*...

- 293 -

I see so many of my potential brothers and sisters warding off the perceived danger of an uncompromising misanthropy, with the solace of an imitative ethic of compassion. It may sooth your ragged soul, you may feel gloatingly superior for a moment, it may appear to be a prettier feeling than honest hate, and most importantly it may feel *sufficiently cruel* so as to sate your wrath – at least in twisting yourself up into a compassionate stance you have found an object for your violence – but it is not only a deferral and a detour, it is a quagmire from which you may never emerge

247

again. Your praxis of compassion will gradually shape you into a loathsome hypocrite: you will eventually become what you initially hated. Honest, responsible, good-natured hatred is beautiful and true – not merely necessary, not merely "Machiavellian", nor "Darwinian", nor anything to be taken lightly. Is the strength and power of the healthy human body somehow ugly? Is the history of the most successful predator of the last 100,000 years a "rightwing" story and thus a projection of self-loathing? Or is wrath one of the gods? Does Ares deserve Aphrodite, or should she belong to the resentful clever cripple? Sword or snare? The burning glance of contempt or the slow creeping revenge of the sanctimonious liar?

In modernity, summoning the *permission to hate* requires more integrity of self than the majority are capable of: the result is that one either foreswears hatred while practicing its darker arts unconsciously – leftwing; or one merely imitates attitudes of honest hatred while unconsciously projecting a self-loathing – rightwing.

- 294 -

The ground I'm treading here is dangerous: this is why no one with half a brain comes here. I'm well aware that I'm supposed to avoid it, that meditating atop a corpse whilst smeared in charnel ashes isn't considered kosher anymore... But hatred is not "goth", nor macabre, nor "maya": hostility is a living function of every organism. The suppression of hate is also the suppression of love: only when one does not know who one is and what one wants, is "universal love" possible – which I translate as "universal resentment". I find no one so incapable of *sincere affection*, as those who preach the elimination of hate.

- 295 -

All the most intelligent are *too clever* to tell the truth about aggression, hostility, and hate: they provoke the stupid laggards to say the obvious, so that they may claim the message is only motivated by stupidity and ignorance – all the while covertly gloating and dwelling upon every delicious detail. This is why someone like myself can seem so unusual: someone apparently stupid enough to say the forbidden and obvious, but smart enough to say it too well to ignore. I allow myself to be trapped, so that I may practice escaping.

In fact my work would probably stand a much better chance of "going viral", if I were less eager to demonstrate freedom of mind... I'm well aware that the sheen of erudition and poise repels the rightwing audience as much as my content turns away the left: the reactive crowd has learned to equate *ugliness with truth* and mistrusts anything else, while the politically correct have learned to equate *cosmopolitan polish* with an unassailable moral high ground and thirst for nothing else.

- 296 -

What should you hate? What is inimical to you. What weakens you, what hinders your growth, what you want less of in your world. Why are these words so dangerous? Because we are surrounded by neurotic, tribeless, desperate masses who despise themselves and therefore seek to project this loathsomeness into the nearest available target: hate is easily slandered in modernity, because almost no one is healthy enough to do anything but project self-loathing.

The most circumspect sense of responsibility is therefore required, in claiming the right to hatred with a *good conscience*. I would not advise this "Left Hand Path" to anyone who has not already passed through several incarnations of self-torture: the analysand, the meditation practitioner, the humanitarian, the compassionate one. Strangely enough, this is one of the few points at which I will advise the *praxis of compassion*: in selecting worthy enemies, in guiding one's hatred, in becoming qualified to know what you're aiming at. There are some of my readers who may sympathize with my work enough, to find traces of my own *compulsive compassion* everywhere in my psychology: but compulsive compassion is something one should be ashamed of, and seek to correct as a character flaw...

- 297 -

We freely hate spirits, ages, movements, ideologies, habits, traits, errors: one of the refinements along this path, is to understand how in any one personality, are to be found a loose combative parliament of contraries. Yet it's suspicious to say, "You are permitted to hate abstract entities, but never a real person." My first response is that a "person" does not really exist either: there are human bodies, human groups, and human feelings, but "person" is merely another word for "mask" – look it up.

Secondly, there are such "persons" so infected with a particular spirit, who so thoroughly embody an error of human maladaptation, that it becomes absurd *not to hate*. Yet I am also fully aware, perhaps more than I care to elaborate upon, how possible it is to find the redeemable in anyone: this is the point where you have to examine whether it isn't actually your *grotesque grandiosity* that makes you feel convinced that your petty little hostility is so dangerous and that your petty little theater of compassion might save the world. "My compassion for all sentient beings": I've heard this phrase verbatim from some of the most repulsive little bigots one can find in our world.

Finding our way back to a healthy, unashamed, mirthful laughing hostility: the phrase "fuck off" contains a dose of this health, doesn't it? It says, "You're not my responsibility and my hostility to you is therefore none of your business." I used to live in a small town of southern Germany, where the typical German bureaucratic pettiness was played out in such funny little rituals as their obscure rules about parking spaces and precise time allotments – I chose not to drive rather than deal with it: but I once was able to witness a delightful contrast, when such a pedantic German accosted what he assumed was a countryman with the usual "Schimpfkanonade" of scowling reproach concerning some breach of conduct – only to find out that this was actually an Italian couple, who thereafter offloaded upon this speechless man a bewildering torrent of Mediterranean hyperbole and wonderfully insulting gestures, who demonstrated for all the town the virtues of *unashamed healthy hostility*. "Vaffanculo" is how they say it in the sunny Italian hills, with that amazingly obscene flick of the wrist under the chin – and it's said so often that even this contraction is contracted further to just "vaffa"... If this doesn't make you smile and feel that life after all is worth living, and that humanity is after all not so bad – then I cannot help you.

- 298 -

Profanity is a deep and subtle art: one should probably undertake the earnest study of the Mediterranean forms of swearing in order to develop a lasting relish. It's not unlike winetasting: every curse has its own *terroir*.

Even a single word like "shit" has at least seven discernible senses. Yet as an American I'm always turning back to the *indomitable f-bomb*. Take the example of "fucking A" – one of my personal favorites but not something I can precisely explain: some say it's a piece of GI slang, for "fucking affirmative". Perhaps that's why I love it: it says, "my hostility and my affirmation can live as one".

- 299 -

"Vaffanculo" is a bold suggestion about which orifice to employ in intercourse: a common model for many of the most delightful insults – although also casting doubt upon your adversary's paternity or his mother's occupation is a common strategy. "Go fuck yourself", "sit and spin", or one of my favorites, "jump up my butt": what do these have in common? The *asshole* as primary locus of devaluation: shit comes out of it and the penis isn't supposed to go in it. But it's well known that children often consider their fecal matter a precious resource, going so far as to retain it and "lord over" it: I know one case of a bright little girl, who liked to stand over the toilet bowl and pretend to sell the recently deposited product to her loyal customers like a proud proprietor of a fine delicatessen. Shit as primordial ambivalent object: valuation and devaluation come from the same place, namely proximity to the optimal functioning of the body. The act of excretion is the template of devaluation, while the result of excretion also represents the healthy functioning and an artifact of that same body: what we deign to hate, is often something we have already honored. We *eat* our enemies: if you haven't digested him, you won't know him well enough to fight him. Thus the choice of enemy should be taken seriously, as long as you also take your honor seriously.

- 300 -

What I've just said also helps reveal the intimate relationship between *projection* and hate: this is the point where contemporary psychology becomes most dangerous to human health, because it teaches that *all hostility is projection*. Any behavior but domestic apathy and moral posturing is increasingly considered pathological: you are supposed to either channel your aggression into sanctioned rituals of *anonymous mass violence*, or repress it until it eats you alive, or act out explosively and become a target of moral outrage. Passive aggressive complicity as a prancing

Michael Pacher, "Saint Augustine and the devil", *Kirchenväteraltar*
c. 1471-75

bambino of political correctness, or depressive melodramatic self-destruction, or ineffectual domestic terrorism: those are the options available on this limited menu.

- 301 -

There is a convention in late medieval and baroque art, in which demons are depicted with a second face centered on the anus. Pieter Bruegel and Hieronymus Bosch elaborated upon this convention more than anyone else, and Bosch in particular seemed to understand its potential to express the *consequences of repression*: look how many of his priestly figures have the faces of pigs, how many of his sinners are folded up into an ouroboros of mouth to butt...

The asshole is *another mouth*, the butt is another face, the "evil" is another "good": it's actually common knowledge, as soon as one consults the context of the juvenile romantic novel, that "repressing a feeling only makes it stronger" – yet this common sense mysteriously disappears in the context of "negative" affect... Do not be deceived: no one is actually this stupid, but rather most are clever enough to *ignore the second face* – or rather keep a close eye on it, but never speak of it.

> ... daß die Verdrängung die Triebrepräsentanz nicht daran hindert, im Unbewußten fortzubestehen, sich weiter zu organisieren, Abkömmlinge zu bilden und Verbindungen anzuknüpfen. Die Verdrängung stört wirklich nur die Beziehung zu einem psychischen System, dem des Bewußten. [...] Sie wuchert dann sozusagen im Dunkeln und findet extreme Ausdrucksformen, welche, wenn sie dem Neurotiker übersetzt und vorgehalten werden, ihm nicht nur fremd erscheinen müssen, sondern ihn auch durch die Vorspiegelung einer außerordentlichen und gefährlichen Triebstärke schrecken.

> ... that repression does not hinder the instinctual representative from continuing to exist in the unconscious, from organizing itself further, putting out derivatives and establishing connections. Repression in fact interferes only with the relation of the instinctual representative to one psychical system, namely, to that of the conscious. [...] It proliferates in the dark, as it were, and takes on extreme forms of expression, which when they are translated and presented to the neurotic

Martin Schongauer, *The Temptation of St Anthony*
c. 1470–75

are not only bound to seem alien to him, but frighten him by giving him the picture of an extraordinary and dangerous strength of instinct.

Freud, *Die Verdrängung*, §I

Repressed content not only seeks expression via alternate channels – "acting out", hysteria, projection – it *seeks coherence*. This is the meaning of *la condition seconde*, the "split personality": given enough time and thoroughgoing repression, eventually what is repressed becomes *another person*. Everything in the psyche eventually organizes itself into a "persona", and because the prime coherence in primates is the *face*, it's inevitable to see *another face* in that locale of repression... In fact, one of the more subtle arts in reading the human creature, is the ability to glimpse this second face between the practiced grimaces and obsequious smiles: like stargazing, you must use "averted vision" and a peripheral attack. If you can catch the subject before he knows he's being witnessed, he will sometimes show you this face: it's the face he wears when he talks to himself.

In Michael Pacher's 15th century rendition of Saint Augustine and the devil, notice how the devil's primary face is partly obscured, so that we're left with the face of the saint and the assface of the devil: they are one spectrum, one analyzed rainbow of repression, in which the *most honest* face is the central face of *the devil who is being tricked* – a demon is by definition a canalization of blame, a leverage splitting good and evil. This is where *we* will end up: may we become ever sharper axeheads which split good and evil down to the roots where they join, where we may finally feel at home.

- 302 -

In discussing the uncanny, I have mentioned previously that Freud found that negation as such does not exist for dream formation. The most precise way of saying this, is that every valuation implies *the whole dimensional predicate* – ambivalence is the only stable signifying locus. But in dreams, there does seem to be an exceptional clause:

> In my view the contemptuous critical judgement, "it's only a dream", appears in a dream when the censorship, which is never quite asleep, feels that it has been taken unawares by a

dream which has already been allowed through. It is too late to suppress it, and accordingly the censorship uses these words to meet the anxiety or the distressing feeling aroused by it. The phrase is an example of *esprit d'escalier* on the part of the psychical censorship.

Die Traumdeutung, §VI.I

In so many of the medieval and baroque depictions of demons, the primary face remains a little unconvincing: it's often simply bestial and wild, as the demons surrounding Saint Anthony in Martin Schongauer's engraving. It's only when they give themselves permission to draw the assface, that something really hideous and uncanny appears. The demon's butthole is *doubly negated* – "it's only a dream"... This is something like how I feel about Donald Trump: he's not merely "rightwing", he's an *absurd caricature* of the right, such that he expresses the repressed content of the left. It was the left's obsession with this caricature, this bleary carnival afterimage of themselves, which granted him power.

- 303 -

The question becomes, whether there is any such thing as healthy hostility that is not a function of neurotic projection: but this is only treated as a serious question within the palace of absurdity that is human political posturing – ethologists do not wonder whether a predator is neurotic because it hunts. Obviously everyone already knows the answer: political correctness assumes as its *self-evident right*, the right to collectively justified violence. One must not be taken in by this pretense of ignorance and inquiry: it is only a hedging of bets, a cultivation of an aura of blamelessness, the shield of *plausible deniability*.

- 304 -

Hostility is always "projected": only true in the sense that aggressive affect is a resurgent function of the organism, which needs to find targets for the sake of reproduction, defense, and predation. But to imagine that all aggression is a symptom of malfunction or at best of "not knowing better", is nearly a direct inversion of the biological reality: almost every instinct in every life form, can be construed as "aggressive". Building a nest is aggressive, collecting seeds is aggressive, competing for mates is aggressive, and even photosynthesis is a *chemical attack* which transforms soil and habitat to the exclusion of many other lifeforms – only an *ad absurdum* can free us from the absurdity in which we are mired when we dither and blither with clasped hands and raised eyes about "aggression".

From an ethological point of view, if I were to provide a terminology to help us see *healthy instinct* rather than political jargon and the *fearful prophylactics against abandonment* which everyone else seems so eager to ingest:

⇁ *Aggression*: ethologically, this is most usefully applied at the infraspecies level. Competition for food, habitat, and mates: typically nonlethal, negotiating, but ubiquitous.

⇁ *Hostility*: most usefully applied to the predator-prey relationship. A predator does not "hate" his prey, he "loves" how it tastes – but in the moment of striking it dead he feels *hostility*: it must die, because it is his prey. There is also a kind of contempt possible in *interspecies* relations: the way wild horses have a contempt for domestic cows, or the way ravens seem to quietly look down on everything non-raven.

⇁ *Hate*: in the observation of animals, I only see something I might call hate in intertribal rivalries: for example, between canine packs or between competing tribes of raven. As tribal creatures adapted for an environment in which many hominid species once competed, it's highly likely that our capacity for hatred is evolved for *intertribal* and possibly *interhominid* rivalry.

- 305 -

Accepting the moniker "Left Hand" for this path, is not unproblematic: as though we were "sinister", "gauche", unteachable and everything slanderous said about the rightbrained. It's not unlike homosexuals calling each other "fag", or the way black men use the n-word affectionately. And now I've stumbled upon an interesting example: among the many varieties of profanity and abuse, the n-word is one I hesitate to utter – why? Because I'm a white man, because I've not been given permission to say it, because I feel the *impotent self-loathing of white men* in that word and it makes me shudder – yet we must also acknowledge the possibility if you cannot handle a slur with a good conscience, you are still susceptible to racism.

Freedom from imputations of ugly hatred alongside a freedom to be as potently aggressive as our nature demands: that's what we're after. *Knowing who you are* is necessary: knowing what you really feel, really think, and would do given the chance – true *tolerance* in the ancient sense requires nothing less than a power that has been tested many times. Hence the scarcity of this virtue and the ubiquity of its counterfeit amongst the powerless: the *repression and redirection of hatred*, rather than an integrated acknowledgment of one's own limitations.

The fortitude and shamanistic power to handle a slur as ugly as the n-word without succumbing to it, while transforming that spirit back into an affectionate teasing: possible, and yet many black men aren't quite capable of it... What I'm driving at is that hate cannot be outlawed, it can only be transformed and healed and directed wisely, because it too is an essential part of what it means to be a human being.

- 306 -

If you're still reading and have not resigned to moral outrage, you are to be congratulated. I'd like you to pause and pay attention to your own body: is there a tightness in the chest and throat, a tingling in the feet, a certain flushed feeling around the face, a rising nameless anxiety? Does it feel dangerous to continue? Can you feel the temptation to flee into a morally safe position? This is *the fear of abandonment*. Your tribal instincts are informing you that association with this voice is dangerous to your social status. Yet if you examine what I've said carefully, dissect its parts, you will find in it nothing ugly, nothing bigoted, and *nothing untrue*: what's dangerous about it, is the way I approach these problems with an *open mind*, without the customary flourishes and many prostrations and mutual assurances of immunity from blame – without the *pretense of answers*. Modernity is a *problem*: human maladaptation will not go away because of our fervent wishes, nor our repression, nor our willingness for deformity.

Once again I find it is my proud duty, to place myself in the line of fire: much of my vocation is to demonstrate the possibility of surviving moral censure without either losing faith in oneself, nor fleeing to the safety of a dogmatism. The imputations and insinuations of a repulsive motive which are inevitable as a response to what I've said, are motivated by at least several needs:

➞ The need to project unconscious bigotry: my intelligent prose makes me hardly an ideal target, but accurate description of a psychological symptom *will cause that symptom to appear* – an unconscious and systemically justified bigotry cannot afford the danger presented by clairvoyance, because the symptom quickly becomes unmanageable and difficult to hide – even from oneself.

➞ The need to quell potentially destructive vibrations of doubt within a fragile crystal of ideology, glued to prejudice, propped up by a fearful social greed. The *most desperately correct* cannot afford real questions, because they cannot afford to learn who they really are. Someone like myself must therefore be stupid, or a political pawn, or unthinkably pathological.

➞ The need to foreclose alternatives: the type of human creature most empowered by an atmosphere of perpetual social ostracization, political terror, and anonymous mass violence, cannot tolerate the possibility of an open-ended discourse. The *need for unqualified answers* is the protofascist's bread and butter.

- 307 -

"Fear of abandonment" may not immediately ring as true as it should, to those who have not yet grokked what I mean by "modernity": one of the first lessons to internalize, is that I do not treat modernity as a mere temporal envelope, but as a *threshold* of postagricultural civilizational realization. Any other approach betrays an inability to free oneself of the prejudice of historical progress: itself a symptom of modernity. In other words, we've been here before, and will be again: many years of brooding upon the meaning of the axial age and late antiquity has finally led me to understand that humanity is caught in something like a sputtering sine wave, driven between the resistances of maladaptation and the compressive force of civilizational advantage. That famous symptom called "alienation", which arises from the tribeless condition of realized modernity, lies right at the heart of the Foucaultian diagnosis...

- 308 -

The syndrome of modernity is to drift in a twilight between perpetual abandonment and an oppressive inclusion, to be both a hopelessly alienated and incomprehensible individual and a mere function of a fully analyzable mass. This is why Foucault is always talking about divisibility and modularity in modern systems: you are both a fragile inconsolable invalid and a disposable superfluity whose time has already come and gone.

- 309 -

You are already abandoned. The deferral of its enactment, is only contingent upon preventing anyone from noticing. You're not wearing any pants in this dream, but as long as you keep cool maybe no one will say anything.

Deferral of realized abandonment: keep this in mind, next time you are accused of a hate and bigotry which is not your own. What's being said, is: "You are endangering my tenuous inclusion, by exposing us both as fraudulent conformists." Just another exercise in the art of spiritual self-defense...

HATE: THE DEVIL'S BUTTHOLE

II.2

SPIRITUAL
SELF-DEFENSE
CURRICULUM

NEUTRALIZING MORAL CENSURE

- 310 -

This was the scenario: you're talking with a good friend. Someone you've known for years – someone you have loved, respected, and given your time to. You are relaxed and feeling grateful for your friendship. You're spending time together as you have many times before.

Then, the subject of COVID comes up. Taking the opportunity to air your irritation with the obtusity of the narrative, you say something like, "It was never deadly." Or, "Lockdowns do nothing but make it worse." Or, "I can't believe they're masking children." Or, "That experimental RNA crap isn't going in my kids."

And then it happens – your friend's face changes: the lips purse, the shoulders rise and tense, the neck goes stiff, the eyes become small, glassy and distant, the voice rises a few semitones, and they say something uncharacteristic and strangely formulaic: "We've all got to work together to *save lives.*" Or, "We all have to be *socially responsible* in this." Or, "I wouldn't want the blood of the unvaccinated on *my* hands."

You feel suddenly like you've just been pulled over by a belligerent cop, or accused of cheating during a math test, or had something you said at a dinner party construed as racist – you've been *mistaken for someone else,* but forcefully, willfully, almost knowingly.

Suddenly you're not connected to this person at all, and they seem so committed to their disapproving attitude that you're a little speechless. You even doubt yourself. Despite familiarity with the facts and your intellectual conviction, your nervous stomach, tight throat, and contracting vision makes you wonder whether they aren't right after all.

That look in the eye is not only disapproving and authoritative, it's predatory. You might feel for a moment like fried chicken under a heatlamp at a Chinese buffet. And although there's only one person looking at you, you

265

feel that maybe there's a whole crowd standing behind this person, looking at you with the same eyes. You feel trapped, desperately alone, angry, hopeless, and profoundly betrayed in a way you are not sure you can recover from – and from that moment the friendship is never the same and perhaps it ends.

This is moral censure. It is essentially human and happens every day with a slowly rotating cast of characters: race and gender being the most popular moral snares amongst the irreligious 21st century firstworld. But you're not actually racist or bigoted, so despite some uneasiness with shrill leftist politics, those forms of censure were easy to avoid previously. But about COVID you feel strongly, because it's so monumentally farcical and wrong: for the first time a direct confrontation with moral posturing becomes unavoidable.

- 311 -

What you're witnessing in this moment, is that the feeling of moral superiority and the safety of an unassailable moral high ground, is more gratifying to this person than any relationship to you will ever be. Moral sanctity quells anxiety in a way your affection never could. Finally they feel *assured* of their membership in the right group. That chronic nagging alienation which penetrates much deeper than you know, briefly vanishes: they become a We, a *voice of the We*.

- 312 -

In that moment, you are facing vastly powerful unconscious forces, against which any conscious effort stands no chance. Any appearance of rational argument is an illusion and a diversionary tactic. The fundamental question is *membership in the winning group*: by remaining strictly truthful in the midst of an emergent symbolic rite, you have placed yourself on the losing side. You must understand that you are being encircled and *marked for exclusion*: any defense you offer will be gathered as evidence of guilt. The only way out of the snare, is to accept your exclusion, and wonder to yourself whether it isn't a good thing to be excluded from that group after all: only when you feel assured of *some other invisible membership*, will their confidence waver.

⌐ Do not let the questions be framed for you.

⌐ Do not allow yourself to be pressured into providing simple answers to complex problems.

⌐ Do not feel obliged to produce comprehensive solutions as recompense for your incisive critique. It's not your responsibility to fix everyone's problem just because you reject a series of false and insipid answers.

⌐ Do not feel compelled to refute every accusation. Most accusations are red herrings and merely a diversionary ploy. Focus on what you know to be true, and elaborate on that basis.

- 313 -

I teach defense against moral censure for those who need it. However, I also teach the *exploitation* of moral censure for the sake of personal growth: there are no truths quite like the truths that emerge in the midst of a struggle for the moral high ground. Nasty dangerous lies are mixed with some of the most precious fragments of truth. When this creature is cornered, when his justifications are in peril, he will finally unsheathe his crooked daggers: the tip may be poisoned with lies, but the blade is sharpened with truths. This sharp edge is actually a treasure not worth passing up: being blamed as morally reprehensible is an opportunity to learn about your weaknesses and delusions. Many a false friend will in that moment unveil some observation he's kept hidden, some secret about your character you have not quite admitted to yourself: therefore while it's essential not to take him seriously, it's also unwise to discard all his censure as though it had no value. Those who merely dismiss what stings in an argument, will repeat the experience many times. What haunts you, could yet be an ally.

The problems is one of *untangling*: unfortunately there is no way to extract the worthwhile message from the ore of bluster and blame, but to work through each distortion in turn. This means nothing less than undergoing *your enemy's own undone emotional work*: an exhausting toil, the rewards of which are often enough a realization about oneself, which one *should have already known* - but we are fools about ourselves, without exception. In addition, the more generous hearts are *generous fools* who require half a lifetime to unlearn their generosity where it makes them fools.

The only good news is that the more you undertake this exhausting toil, the easier it becomes. *Doing the homework of lazy souls*: that's largely our fate, for as long as we are committed to the rewards of truthfulness. But don't be misled: the ability and commitment to tell the truth to oneself, will for a long time make you *weaker and more vulnerable* – hence its rarity. Not until you have refined your own perception, cleared out the accumulated underbrush of emotional counterformation, and gained the confidence that comes from years of indentured servitude to a world of committed neurosis, will this path begin to offer an advantage. One day your ability to tell the truth will be more valuable than the willingness to live a life of clever consoling lies: the power imbalance here is immense at first, and will seem hopeless. Moreover truthfulness is always a liability, because it will always greatly complicate the task of self-advocacy and make you careful, hesitant, and analytical – there's always more to learn. The real turning point comes when you feel you've had enough of learning and honesty and humility, and become ready for *your* hostility: refined, honest, clairvoyant hostility emitted by a compulsively compassionate soul, is one of the more beautiful tapestries of human psychology – and not easily defeated nor forgotten.

- 314 -

Even the average human creature, with his average bemuddled intelligence, is extremely adept at crafting the *barbed lure*: just enough truth to compel you, with a nasty hook embedded in the meat. The cleverness at work here is entirely unconscious and as ancient as the primate line at least: it is a function of the tribal instincts of peer competition for scarce resources, in which no means is too base or out of bounds. Among men, there is always the background of the hunting ritual in which male alliance counts more than any other bond – and therefore healthy men have a sense of fair play. Among women this does not prevail, and their competition is always potentially much more vicious: but modernity is such that we are all more or less tribeless women and incompetent men, and therefore the rules of honor play no role except in making some of us more stupid and vulnerable.

Make no mistake: your indentured servitude to your ideal of "truth", is quite sensible and obvious to the merest bystander. A glance at your face reveals this weakness to the tribal instincts of competition, and will therefore be used against you at the earliest opportunity: many social behaviors can be analyzed as forms of the *probing skirmish*, in which defenses are tested and weaknesses charted, gauged, and profiled. The more desperately ambitious types spend most of their energetic lives planning and preparing their next attack: that feeling you may occasionally have, that "everyone's talking about me the moment I leave the room", is not always mere paranoia. *Envy* is not a peripheral annoyance of social function: envy is what fuels at least half of all social behaviors. Nothing forms shallow friendship faster than a shared envy.

- 315 -

Refining and reviving *paranoid hypervigilance* is one of the more dangerous tasks ahead of us in this rare art, in which we repeatedly abandon and return to the deep wells of mistrust. Many cases of "social anxiety" amount to nothing but the *repressed hostility* of a previously healthy creature, grown exhausted, abused, and slowly convinced of the pathology of its responses. The healthiest course of recovery for some of the most socially anxious among us, is the cultivation of *unmitigated hostility*.

Nowhere in the terror-stricken atmosphere of moral panic which infuses 21st century academic psychology, in the preventative political posturing which quakingly expects banishment at the merest misstep, will you find the advice I just gave: I'm quite aware that I'm supposed to don a moral mien of condescending compassion at the sight of anxiety, and assure the victim that his paranoia is entirely misplaced. I'm quite aware also, that much of what modernity teaches, prepares us for *communal sacrifice*: the stronger natures serve no purpose, and the tribal instinct to purge outliers and strange variables, only grows more responsive. The threshold for the activation of rituals of exclusion drops steadily in response to the atmosphere of faithless tribelessness with which modernity is infused: the ambitious moral actor benefits from a nameless fear which justifies the "perpetual emergency" of moral authority. Once you know how to read, you will find that the message says: "Keep them anxious and blaming themselves." One of the most important insights of Foucault, is that nameless alienated anxiety is no mere unfortunate byproduct of realized modernity, it is the prerequisite to its optimal functioning. This "compassion" so lauded and fondled, this concern for the anxious, ill, and depressed, is also not merely disguise: it is the *reinforcing pathologization* of psychosomatic disease. Modernity must continually *neutralize the potential for empowerment within every disease* by redirecting blame into the body of the afflicted. The hospital is the school is the prison: psychosomatic disease must be institutionalized in order to become another useful modularity of systemic function – that's Foucaultian horror. But if we can manage to generate *internalized insight* out of what is otherwise merely intellectual discourse and bad faith mimicry, we have come away with something far more valuable than most expect from mere "thinking": the art of spiritual self-defense.

- 316 -

One of the greatest obstacles to a sensitive soul in developing the power of clarified hostility, is that many of us have a lot to prove – to ourselves. Some of us are afraid we cannot love. Some of us fear an incapacity for friendship. Some of us have learned to despise our own inhibition and reserve, such that we become intentionally sloppy and permissive in a bad imitation of generosity and fun. Some of us feel the need to punish ourselves for our superiority and self-deference. Some of us have just grown too weary of loneliness and will tolerate anything as reprieve.

In most cases, such exaggerated fears prove to be not only an absurd miscalculation, but a *positive inversion* of a repeated scenario of earlier trauma: strong children blame themselves for the limitations of their environment. She was very capable of love, but no one loved her when she needed it; he was an excellent friend, but there was no one to reciprocate it; his reserve was born of dignity and pride, but which isolated him and generated resentment – and so on.

It's rare for the truly inadequate and emotionally limited to *feel* limited: their neurosis is part of a socially adaptive package, which functions as long as the social contexts do not shift too rapidly. The arrival of an outlier, an exception, a prime specimen is what upsets them and makes them feel inadequate: therefore their dangerous unconscious malice, which works overtime and overnight...

Unfortunately there is no substitute for the acquisition of sufficient *bad experience*. A long meandering journey among the many varieties of ordinary betrayal, an education aboard the HMS Beagle of confusion and doubt, cannot be replaced. My kind of student must have *risked his self-respect* in the effort to gain it back: nothing less suffices for the establishment of a foundation of confidence deep enough to withstand the resistances ahead. Everything tells us to turn back: often enough it seems that anyone with a shred of worth is already permanently aligned with the agenda of universal compassion. We find only ugly bigotry as an alternative, and we learn to suppress our hostility *all the more* so that no one may find out how ugly it's growing there in the neglected dark. *Anxiety is a product of instinctual frustration*: this deceptively simple formula, which to an ethologist or veterinarian or dogpound clerk is self-evident, has become a strangely magic key to the unraveling of modern psychosomatic disease. But the further elaboration I've discovered runs thus: *anxiety inverts into persecution*.

Therefore what do I teach? *Prophylactic hostility* for those most targeted by this systemic anonymous persecution, which hovers on the horizon and remains fragmented only so long as no coalescing target appears. The COVID affair has taught me to trace the *seeds of fascism* deep in every minor fissure of civilizational maladaptation: in every sputtering beginning to the tribal instincts of ritual exclusion, in every social fragmentation which makes us modern folk so ridiculous and frequently out of place, in the many overlapping agendas and slowly crumbling institutions desperately seeking new ground and justification – *in the misery of the modern body*, are the seeds of fascism.

THE LEAGUE OF DIDACTIC WHITE BOYS

- 318 -

I recently took an ill-advised tour through the scribblings and pamphle-teering of my peers and rivals on Substack – the ranks of what I like to call the "League of Didactic White Boys". Many of them probably soft-ware engineers, data scientists, the kind of guy with a PhD in economics for no good reason – many of them clearly autodidacts, having spent a good part of their 20's gorging themselves on Wikipedia. They typically have decent historical awareness, a good grasp of the scientific method, a sense of humor – primarily employed to stave off the perpetual depres-sion and occasional waves of despair, varying levels of self-absorption, coupled with a crippling but intermittent awareness of personal insignificance and the improbability of possessing the "correct" answers. As a result, they have developed their intellect into a *formidable instrument of filibuster*: the deferral of anxiety and moral crisis via philosophical expository, analytic detour, and a shuffling of the cards of concurrent data and historical precedent until a satisfying tarot constellation is reached. They offer this up to you as entertainment, reprieve, enlightenment, hope, refreshment. But I must say I come away from their writing feeling much worse than I began. I feel their displaced anxiety. I feel how trapped they feel: their claustrophobia, their panic, their bitterness, their subdued rage, and above all, their *confusion*. What a bewildering confused world this 21st century is turning out to be. Go count the number of blogs pur-porting to *explain the madness*. – And am I any different? I'd like to think a fresh breeze blows through my words. I'll confess something: if I have a proclivity to any one species of fear, it's claustrophobia. I need the biggest sky possible. I need to feel as close to the stars as to the earth. I need to feel suspended between dust and annihilation in order to feel okay. I need to be reminded of my mortality on a regular basis. I must take risks, I must be outside in the wild with nonhuman creatures, between the unforgiving sun and the relentless squirming life evincing its indifference to my pres-ence or absence. I need to be held at a tenuous distance from the human world to feel sane. Therefore despite our similarities, I don't have a great degree of sympathy for most of the didactic white boys I encounter. I fault

273

them for their lack of courage. They make ideological excursions, they flirt with extremism, they try on various postures, and maybe allow themselves to finally become angry – but how many of them do anything differently with their body in space and time?

- 319 -

Generally I see four solutions to the creeping confusion of 21st century Euroamerican cultural decay, among the educated postliberal:

1.   Those with a background in science flee to statistics. Social science, and thus psychology, and thus the authority on all questions of why people are they way they are, is to be reduced to probability distribution. Again in this I see not much more than an amateur, uninspired, and exhausting form of divination. They shuffle the deck of facts until they get the reading they were looking for, and somewhere in that probability cloud is supposed to be an answer to "yes, but why?"...

2.   Flirtations with extremism. They begin this test: "How conservative can I become in my whiplash, and still respect myself and find justification for my views?" But as the centers of gratification and the dopamine pathways shift, from the *good boy* who mimics moral posturing as best he can, to the *bad boy* who delights in provocation, he finds that any degree of conservative extremism may suit him as long as it yields a sense of importance. At least he no longer feels ignored.

3.   Flirtations with religious apocrypha. An initially ironic exploration of early Christian and other Gnostic-Hermetic propaganda begins to become serious, as one acquires a taste for the certainty of the religious worldview. Most of these types were not raised under a religious regime, and thus the narcotic is novel. In fact, the only voice I found in my short survey which remotely reminded me of my own, was an ex-Mormon. He wants to be so "reasonable" and fair – and perhaps still is far too much a good boy. – A lesson to Bartholomy, if he's listening.

4.   An ever-deepening investment in an absurdist, cynical, black humor. Here I have the most sympathy, and here I find the most potential for healing – dangerous as an abiding, unrelenting cynicism can be. It's a poison I'm used to handling as an indispensable ingredient in my kind of health regimen. When I travel in the third world I make a point of

smoking the harsh local cigarettes and eating as much spicy food as I can handle, because it makes your skin less appetizing to the ambient mosquitoes. Is our cynicism a pesticide? Are we seeking to become less appetizing to parasitic ideology? Or are we merely seeking a sense of mastery at any cost, no matter how hopeless and desiccated we feel in the aftermath? At least by continually blackening our humor, lowering our expectations of fulfillment, and learning to live without hope, we gain back a sense of control. And truthfully maybe we were much too childish, pampered, and full of hopes to begin with. Maybe we're only discovering the proper orientation of a testosterone-infused mammal a little late in our life – maybe we're making up for being *uninitiated boys*. Even our pains are esoteric: we feel a crushing sense of responsibility, alongside a bewildering lack of agency. We want to be correct, we want to do it right, we want to lead responsibly and judiciously – all the while we want to unleash our pent up imagination and the funk we've been holding back too long. Finally we stop giving a damn and start saying what we mean: at this point people start paying attention, now that we no longer feel responsible, now that we're willing to go our own way alone. And so it is that every worthy voice in this little club, wanders off into some strange detour from which he'll clearly never return. I feel that I'm witnessing so many potential friends and beautiful enemies disappear over a horizon I have no interest in pursuing.

- 320 -

It's a strange lonely voyeuristic time, this age of the internet. A million peepholes for every decent conversation. A million passive identifications for every participation. Ten million mimicries for every originality. A hundred million nothings for every something. Again I find my healing in the dark – in the "blackout" that waits behind this electrical noise. If I am to wander a wasteland, let it be the wasteland of the stars. Just this moment, Venus is staring at me, chiding, beckoning. She is sexy, I'll admit. Governess of twilight. In her eerie white light I find the willingness to face this inevitable nihilism of a garbage world: I hate the internet for its ugliness, for the way it amplifies the worst of humanity and feeds our petty addictions, for the way it makes our bodies smaller and our minds overwrought – and yet I'm obviously just as dependent on it for communication as anyone else, and like everyone else I've learned to rummage it for trinkets and tools... But please understand me: what you're looking for cannot be found here. Therefore tread lightly my friends, this internet of dismay. If you must seek explanation, seek lightly.

- 321 -

In the morning light, an afterthought:

What are we doing? What compels us to philosophize, synthesize, and mythologize? If we insist that every response to stress is part of the core human adaptive package, then this urge to make sense of a world in the throes of cultural decay must also have its proper function, beyond "just getting by". My answer is clear: we're attempting to create the mythology of a new tribe. Not merely to plug the holes of a leaky lifeboat of personal neurosis – although this may get us started, we quickly find that these consolations serve to rally a following, and we learn to crave the social recognition.

We point to the chaos and confusion and say: "these are the wages of sin", or "thus the age of retribution begins" – look closer at these didactic white boys to see them each groping toward one of these prophetic formulae. But the most ancient, least colored by postaxial evangelical ennui, and thus most restorative and powerful justification of human tumult is: "such is the wheel of fate". Such is all life on this hairy globe. A deep tribal mythology does not merely tell a tall tale of how and why, but addresses what the human creature needs so badly: to rejoin the earthly family, to feel at home here, despite his nightmares of future and past, his fever-dreams of utopia and dystopia, his forever disintegrating tribe, the curse of his frail instincts and overwrought cleverness. The point of mythology is to turn cleverness against itself: to use neurotic entanglement to produce feelings of belonging, fulfillment, blessing. To make this over-heated expensive cranium do something other than get us into more trouble – the poet's craft largely consists of discovering as many mysteri-ous correspondences as possible, such that an overwhelming subterranean meaningfulness looms, sufficient to swallow whole all nihilistic fatigue. We want to live in a world knitted together by correspon-dences, like navigating a synaptic carpet, a world of shimmering mirror, a world in which every word speaks of the beginning and the end, in which everything has its place in the sacred circle of time, in which the hoop of life descends and ascends like the ecliptic of the sun, blessing us as the generations pass. That's the ancient vision we long for: that is the grand dream of the old man lodged deep in our ape heart, the one who sits blind in the darkest corner of the cave, smoking and chanting the songs of his fathers, he who makes us weep with the beauty and wisdom of this apenature.

REDEMPTION OF THE
TRIBAL CREATURE

- 322 -

O ur institutionally enrobed psychologists are so proud of their experimental apparatus – but when's the last time they *experimented with
experimentation?* Has anyone taken it upon themselves to prove the efficacy of their methods? The Stanford Prison Experiment seems to signal
the end of interesting social experimentation anywhere within a large
radius of academia: they didn't like what they found. Ever since, they've
been accumulating a mountain of wishful conclusions, hoping to bury
the disturbing vision under a crushing weight of mutually reinforcing
prejudice, faulty unconsidered method, and silent unspoken conspiratorial terror of political ostracization.

- 323 -

What are they so afraid of? What does the Stanford Prison Experiment
demonstrate? That we are indelibly tribal creatures; that our moral sentiments are shallow and vitiated, that we *don't know who we are*, until we are
tested. That the vast majority will fail the test of integrity: however, this
also means they will *pass* the test of tribal instinct. They will choose the
winning side, they will make accurate guesses about probable victories,
they will quickly and effortlessly realign their emotional investments and
discover rationalizations for any and all participation required to ensure
victory over "them". My work does not seek to denigrate the tribal creature: it only looks like a liar's game when contravening the shameful
clothing it was forced to wear up until that point – in other words, the
modern human being is a hypocrite because it's forced into too many
inarticulate, incomplete, and contradictory tribal contexts, not because
it's incapable of fidelity. Modern morality is largely *ashamed of itself*,
ashamed of humanity, ashamed of its essential hypocrisy and therefore
seeks grandiose compensations, calling them categorical, "universal" and
"the Good". The sycophantic modern human creature, cowering in a
corner of his cell, gathering information to be used against his friends,

consoles himself by believing that his intimate gossiping concern for everything and everyone is "compassion for all sentient life", rather than an informant's dragnet. "Inoffizieller Mitarbeiter" is what the East German Stasi used to call them, and according to their own records they generally numbered at about 200,000, or 1% of the population: but that's 1% of the total who are willing to *explicitly* cooperate in programs of oppression, rather than implicitly. That's 1% who are willing to take the risk of exposing their real motives *to themselves* – of learning who they are – so desperate is their thirst for the Punitive City. But it's *anonymity* and *plausible deniability* that is the safest and generally winning strategy in this game: tribal unrest, the crisis of treachery and betrayal which constitutes the modern tribeless condition, defines the Nash equilibrium we call "hypocrisy".

- 324 -

It's reported that Felix Dzerzhinsky, arguably the godfather of all 20th century secret police, once told Lenin that secret police work could only be accomplished by "saints or scoundrels ... but now the saints are running away from me and I am left with the scoundrels". But what is a saint in my terms? A *professional scoundrel*, a conman who has convinced more than half of *himself* and thus in a sense is *no mere liar* – which is why Dzerzhinsky was complaining about being left with the amateurs.

- 325 -

Keeping up the churning confusion of modernity, the punishing waves of alienation and nameless loss which creates novel opportunities for unique forms of power – such as coveted roles within the secret police – goes by other names: "permanent revolution" is what Trotsky would call it. Thus is the secret behind political posturing revealed: to the degree that one is a miserable but ambitious wretch, one delights in shallow political advocacy because it disrupts existing hierarchies and creates temporary power imbalances which can be exploited. Social media is largely the platform for a million and one wannabe politicians and dema-gogues: the middle and upper classes now raise their children as though they were already celebrities, encouraging the cultivation of virtual image at the earliest possible stage, so that they may be ready to compete in an increasingly virtual and reactionary social sphere...

- 326 -

But what we're witnessing in the Stanford Prison Experiment is not actually tribality, but tribal instincts *within the confines of civilizational scarcity*. One of the Foucaultian insights no one seems to have internalized, is that architecture not only expresses but *enacts* forms of coercion: it maps possible social configurations, subtly delimiting possible attitudes and outcomes. Human tribal instincts inside a cage should not be judged as though that's what they essentially are. I insist that a great deal of what's known as fascism, are the tribal instincts pushed to a critical threshold – an emergency protocol, not their healthy functioning.

No one asks what happens when you take the same impulses and *put them outside*, beyond the reach of modern architecture and artificial scarcity. There is the possibility that the Punitive City and prison behaviors represent an adaptive pattern: a prisoner in the *enemy camp*, the dissolving tribe. The women are willing to remarry, the men are willing to defect.

- 327 -

What do I mean by "phylopsychology"? Every group psychology I'm aware of, fails to take into account the fact that we are tribal animals, with functionally tribal responses. Ever since its inception in France and England in the early 19th century, sociology would rather ask why the human being fails to conform to the brutal but supposedly sublimely rational mediations of civilization, and in answer draw up a list of "cognitive biases" and outline novel educational opportunities for psychiatric torture, than take seriously the idea that we are already well-adapted for another context.

- 328 -

The architect of the original Stanford Prison Experiment, Philip Zimbardo, has had enough fortitude to faithfully stand by the results of his famous experiment. Yet he is also clearly not up to the *emotional challenge* of assimilating the lesson: he wants to wax tragically poetic about "how good people become evil". What's comical to my eye, is how even this mainline Marxist-Weberian sociological interpretation, oversteps what the majority are willing to accept: the postagricultural human race is primarily populated by the *peasant* type, who still needs to believe in a categorically demonstrable good and evil. The assertion, "I would never!" stands at the heart of all the blustering "refutation" of this experiment. Academic sociology and psychology has gone as far as making it formally impossible to repeat: they created a "standard of ethics" which forecloses *actual social experimentation* – thus what has taken place in these fields since, are 10,000 repetitions of *false experimentation*. With their sterile questionnaires and utterly riskless "experiments", they ask their participants to *pretend* to have a feeling, to *pretend* to have something at stake, to *pretend* to be acting socially – without establishing sufficient illusion to actually induce social behavior such as Zimbardo's experiment did: therefore what has been studied for decades now, is *the sociology of false sociality*. Which would make an interesting subject in itself, were it studied properly: every result of academic sociology and psychology should therefore be examined under the light of these questions: "How are the subjects falsifying a social response? What were the expectations of the researchers and how did the subjects sense and anticipate them? What does the falsification tell us about what we *wish* were true?"

- 329 -

I'll allow Zimbardo to speak for himself when describing the coping strategies of prisoners:

> Prisoners coped with their feelings of frustration and powerlessness in a variety of ways. At first, some prisoners rebelled or fought with the guards. Four prisoners reacted by breaking down emotionally as a way to escape the situation. One prisoner developed a psychosomatic rash over his entire body when he learned that his parole request had been turned down. Others tried to cope by being good prisoners, doing everything the guards wanted them to do.

from *www.prisonexp.org/conclusion*

In modernity you have a few choices:

- ⌐ Shallow symbolic rebellion
- ⌐ Crippling anxiety
- ⌐ Psychosomatic displacement

⌐ Complicity and authoritarian identification

Each of us dips into each of these strategies a little here and there, creating tapestries of denial and hysterical displacement with varying artistry. There is the rebel without a cause who later becomes an entrenched punitive conformist; there is the anxious wreck who covertly delights in lowering the quality of life for everyone else; there is the psychosomatic genius who protects himself with illness... Generally it is this last type whom I prefer: those who are capable of transformation of psychic pain into physical, are also capable of the reverse – something generally overlooked in the analysis of what is called "shamanism". Psychosomatic phenomena is relatively the norm in the human species: the difference is a matter of degree and imagination. The human being is sick: thus it is that spiritual practice is properly termed "making medicine"...

- 330 -

The informant who compulsively collects compromising information about his friends, also tends to be prone to *compulsive yet genuine intimacy*. But this type is to the same degree prone to fantasies of inferiority and unresolved Oedipal tension: which is later reinterpreted as an instance of abuse and therefore works to generate a narrative of reprehensibility. When the context shifts and he finds himself in a better position of power, he will employ that accumulated resentment in combination with the information gathered from within that intimacy to seek revenge. In other words, he will gladly betray his own capacity for friendship for a reprieve from the repetition of inferiority: the charming if slightly cloying little boy is replaced by the venomous sycophant and gossip. This is an increasingly common type, as it fits like a hand within the glove of the metrosexual identity strategy: *the cultivation of an aura harmlessness*, conscientious choice, and everything well-considered and *intentional* not only serves as protection from blame, but the ideal cover from which to launch self-righteous attacks upon one's friends and neighbors when the time comes.

- 331 -

It's telling that "game theory" resorts so often to the *prison scenario* for adequate plausibility, and then attempts to explain social dynamics with that same poverty of choice. The truth is that there is an evil bouquet of distortion strategies available to apekind, but the most interesting ones emerge only under conditions of extreme stress, perversity, and civilizational excess. In modern relationships, these are some of the more common *fleurs du mal*:

⇁ *Willful misunderstanding*: a great many ploys depend on the pretense not to understand, in order to confuse the issue, defray inquiry, and redirect the dialogue into more profitable channels.

⇁ *Moral posturing as lure*: by seeming to advocate for something one does not actually believe, it's possible to evoke the articulation of ugly truths from one's opponent, in order to ascribe the ugliness to him. It's important to realize that moral posturing always has at least two functions: not only to safeguard one's position within a group hysteria, but to disown and allocate what has thereby been displaced. A great deal of moral posturing is performed in the *hope* of evoking disgust.

⇁ *Inflammatory red herring*: bringing up a topic known to be irrelevant, but concerning which the opponent has unresolved feelings. The acquisition of emotional highground rather than moral.

⇁ *Erasure*: it's always possible not to hear. Through the power of repression, anything sufficiently unworkable in conscious terms can be eliminated to the degree that the one who spoke it feels that it did not happen. Ever had words disappear as soon as they left your mouth? Or the feeling of evacuated lungs? Ever noticed the group silently agree to ignore something even before it happens?

⇁ *Pretense of wisdom*: it's commonplace to pretend to have put more thought into decisions than one has. Among the unhappy majority, it's usual to pretend to have *resolved* for compromises rather than merely falling ass backwards.

⇁ *The bait and switch*: the "switch" involves alternation between a fatigued nihilistic irony, and a histrionic moralizing posture. This is a composite of the previous strategies and is therefore more advanced, but highly common among the educated urbanite: to become flippant in the presence of sincerity and serious in response to the mockery of moral pretense. The flippancy is ubiquitous and the default response: it serves to continually weaken access to sincerity and innocence such that truth begins to appear impossible. However, this nihilism does not make its full appearance until someone has committed to the advocacy of one of those unwanted truths: the goal is not to defeat the opponent per se, but to ensure the suppression of that truth by associating it with naivete and stupidity – as though maturity lies in assuming an ironic and apathetic attitude towards the essentials. However, should any of the dissociative fictions which line this world of bitterness be challenged – the notion of universal human equality, for example – what appears is an equally vicious, and *cynical*, moral posturing. A target has been discovered for the much-needed discharge of illwill and contempt: there is often much more *ungainly delight* at work in moral censure than any threatened fear.

- 332 -

> During the parole hearings we also witnessed an unexpected metamorphosis of our prison consultant as he adopted the role of head of the Parole Board. He literally became the most hated authoritarian official imaginable, so much so that when it was over he felt sick at who he had become – his own tormentor who had previously rejected his annual parole requests for 16 years when he was a prisoner.

As a rule, the human creature will unconsciously ally itself with the *worst offender within the limits of social acceptance*: identification with tacit perpetration is the norm, not the exception. What do they win? Firstly, the certain relief that they themselves are not the target: as long as someone is stupid enough to play victim, they are safe. A mapped trajectory of punishment and blame is always desirable. Secondly, because identification with the perpetrator allows the safest possible offloading of their own aggression: they can at least watch the carnage from a safe distance. And thirdly, because even if the perpetrator should eventually misstep, they still have taken no risk and only need shift to a moralizing stance concerning the "discovery" of wrongdoing – in fact the recrimination permits of more chances to gain in status through moral posturing.

Thus, we get feigned ignorance, the cultivation of blamelessness, the readiness for betrayal, preparations for sudden opportunities for status improvement, incessant calculations of the perceived social value of any one agent, and a constant vigilance concerning the trajectory of group consensus.

This wait-and-see strategy is by far the most common, because it is the least risky. But it is called by other names: tact, prudence, tolerance, and especially *compassion*. "Compassion for all, at all times": translated properly this reads, "Vigilance, espionage, and labile loyalties for all, at all times".

- 333 -

Lessons from Abu Ghraib:

⌐ Women are just as likely and able to commit torture as men.

⌐ The pattern is as follows: the stupid little people commit the deeds, the authorities wink. Thus is blame sufficiently diffused: the perpetrators are typically former victims repeating a history of abuse; while the authorities are people of protected status fully accustomed to complicitude, hypocrisy, and skillful *ex post facto* moral reasoning. No one is to blame, everyone is guilty.

⌐ The worst offenders are always underachievers, overlooked wannabes, chronic losers, and ambitious police and paramilitary. There is a long chain of implicit systemic violence at work in these "scandals": they are merely the *last* element in a long displacement of violence and the accumulated humiliations of civilization. Only at the very tail end, in an isolated prison on the other side of the world in a chaotic newly occupied country, does the repression finally lift: and we witness what has accumulated in the human collective.

- 334 -

Everything which one of us does is the responsibility and response of every one of us: this is a worthwhile perspective, and I believe that you will not be able to digest and assimilate the long history of atrocities until you learn to accept the force of its truth. *We are all responsible*: there is one human psyche, and it is capable of everything of the worst as much as everything of the best. Until you accept this axiom, you will remain trapped within the moral illusion, unable to tell the truth, and have no access to the equally valid assertion of our *universal innocence*. There is no other final redemption and liberation of the human creature.

What is the meaning of the prison? As metaphor, as symptom, as expression of genetic and historical forces?

The essence of sociality. What is social? The wide-eyed obsequious answer we generally hear, is "cooperation". The prison teaches something else: the essence of sociality is *infraspecies exploitation selectively repressed*, which generates hierarchies of dominance for the optimization of group function. In other words, cooperation is *a coincident byproduct of inhibition* due to competition between roughly equivalent agencies: establish an imbalance of power, and this constant competitive thirst for dominance will percolate out from the corresponding willingness to be dominated. We are all potentially warden and inmate. The ape is both *greedy* and *fearful*: he wants power and will delight in it at the first opportunity no matter how petty and shortsighted, but he also fears exclusion through moral censure and thus learns to hide his schemes and wait for the right moment. Character and ethical integrity are rare because they are not adaptive for social life: what does "character" mean but the inability and unwillingness to adapt to novel social imbalances of power? Integrity is an expensive liability which rarely pays. Poverty and isolation are generally its fruits: one must therefore learn to delight in these things, if one is to possess the rare gem of autonomous self-respect.

In the prison environment, repression lifts and we see human sociality for what it always was in virtual statespace. Which also means, our hypervigilance and misanthropy were after all not so misplaced, and must also be part of that adaptive tribal optimum – a skeptical wary witness in the mix, a knowing grin, an impatient sigh. Fear not therefore: we are already armed with the knowledge and instinct to defend against the excesses of the unholy ape. It may seem a contradiction to say on the one hand, "Human tribality should not be judged while imprisoned", and on the other hand to say, "The essence of sociality is hereby revealed": but I say it nonetheless. The tribe is actually the most humane form of sociality, because it is a functional compromise between the indifference of the flock and the *punitive normalcy* of the colony: there is a discernible scale of social function, wherein many of the apex predators sit in the middle. But the hymenopteran insect colony is termed "eusocial", because of the prejudices of modernity: maximum sociality and "the Good" have been considered synonymous for some time and formulated as such since at least the English utilitarians... Actually everything edifying and decent

287

about social life, everything which makes travel, conversation, and friendship worthwhile, is its *unrealized* and *imperfect* nature: freedom and dignity lies in imperfection, improvisation, and the futilities which demand disciplined creativity – in other words, *the spirit of nomadism.*

- 336 -

What are the historical manifestations of the gestalt called "prison"? I see one in the past, and the other in the future.

¬ *Slavery.* To the precise degree that a species is social, it is capable of enslavement: thus ants enslave. Some species of Hymenoptera cannot survive in any way other than by enslaving another species. This is also the meaning of agriculture and husbandry, and why again the ants are capable of it. Slavery is not some unique human evil, it lies at the heart of the problem of the organic: how does an organism acquire predominant power at an emergent level of competition? *Predation and slavery* – which are only the initial and final expressions of the same function. This is the point at which my own biosemiotics diverges from the driveling hopes of academe and the likes of Thomas Sebeok.

¬ *Realized modernity.* Modernity strives to distribute the roles of master and slave equitably among us all: the institution and spirit of slavery has not been abolished, it has been dismantled and reassembled elsewhere. I consider the work of Foucault invaluable: and yet few seem to be able to read him honestly, and look rather to mine it for the ammunition of political posturing – they would rather seem to join the fight against "the man", than discover the fight within their own beliefs and motives. Why can't they stand him? Because they lack the emotional strength to endure the insight: one must possess a large hidden reserve of *meaningfulness* to endure the cold hard stare of modernity such as it peeks through Foucault.

- 337 -

I will have much more to say concerning the Punitive City.

But allow me a phylopsychological digression. The purpose of the *beauty response* in men, is not only to judge the reproductive fitness of a female at

288

a glance, but the *capacity to be seduced*. But sufficient seduction for sexual reproduction is easy – a few shortlived hormonal responses are all that's required. The exaggerated aesthetic faculty of the human male is something more: to seduce him into tribal life and tribal loyalties. The tortured male, torn between violence and peace: women have been conditioned to find this type most attractive of all.

Why do I rely so heavily on the resurgent sense of beauty in my rhetoric? Why does it seem so important to constantly point the way back to a redemption? As though I were to leave traces behind us as we venture further into a wilderness. Because we have reason to be doubly afraid: afraid because our hearts are children and easily tremble, and afraid because the wildernesses of modernity are actually worse than that of our ancestors. More brutal, more nightmarish, more panoptic, more *personally impersonal* and thus worthy of paranoia: Foucault should be read in small doses and digested thoroughly, in order to internalize the importance of his work... His overly erudite French excesses of style don't actually do his insights justice – the scope of what he's talking about is not generally clear because he insists on such detailed analysis... Leave it therefore to a poet of terror, who seeks to make a sharp vision of modernity clearer: this is why I have need of so many rhetorical downbeats, in which our emotional endurance can catch up and expand. It is *emotional* intelligence and strength we're after: raw intellect is cheap, explicit logic is easy. The unconscious implicit logic, the invisible architecture of the breathing human world, the transgenomic factors seeking expression through humanity itself: we are so sure that our civilization has conquered nature, but it is very likely that all civilizational forces are merely a competitive form of life seeking to exploit *us*. The realization of modernity is this debt falling due: a technologically dominant future is very likely to be merely the next recursive plane of a very old war within the confines of life itself. "The bentback bow": too many assume that "life" is necessarily some unary force, and forget that its essence is competition and exploitation – there are not only many species of life, but many *species of the alive*.

THE TINY ABACUS

- 338 -

What do Nietzsche and I have in common? I'm a big Romantic dummy who required half his life to figure out what everyone else is up to. I'm fundamentally a poet who has turned psychologist only by necessity. I have a big juicy heart that refused to learn, until it had been not merely disappointed but kicked repeatedly from every angle: not until my "qi hardened" as Confucius says about turning 40, did I become ready to learn *mistrust*. I finally learned *not* to expect great things of humanity, *not* to look up to anyone, *not* to dream the biggest dream I could in their honor. It took me half my life to stop giving *honor* where there is none. But once I did, I had learned to control not just my admiration but my contempt, and with mistrust I had finally learned the *long stare*: where once I couldn't help myself from painting over the scene as though it were canvas, now I look into the grain and dream my dreams within the fibers. Where I once had only insight as a form of depression and indigestion, I developed insight as a means of dissection: what was once blind worship has become open-eyed vivisection.

- 339 -

What sets me apart is my overflowing heart: *gratitude and wrath* are as common with me as boredom and loneliness are with everyone else. Finally understanding this has required about 40 years of confusion on my part: a genuinely big and bloody heart is rare. It's been something I take for granted.

Without wrath there is no sweet gratitude. Without heartfelt hate there can be no superabundant love. Without violence there is no freedom. Everything else is mediocrity, confusion of ends and means, confusion of heart and fist, disorder in the home, abuse of the eternal child, unforgivable cowardice, betrayal most foul, a poisoning of the collective well, the agenda of the weak, the repulsive nihilism of those who cannot love nor hate, in whom every breath is a commingling of resentment and anxious desire.

One will either know this already and be relieved to have heard it formulated, or one will recoil in horror and hold it up as evidence of degenerate immorality.

- 340 -

Why is it that I have so much to say? Why do I seem to find inadequacy and contradiction everywhere? One could try on the hypothesis, that I've chosen the most contrarian perspective *in order to have something to say*. But then again, perhaps *being contrary* is the healthiest response, and therefore both the urgency of my message and the message itself, are conditioned by the real motive: *get healthy*, at any cost.

- 341 -

Cassandra syndrome: to know, to see, and be not believed. I know what it is to be alone in one's vision, and to be isolated by a gift. My gift isolates. It necessarily refines the taste for solitude: we learn to turn solitude into another wellspring of insight, which isolates yet more.

A prophecy of doom, a bad diagnosis, a scornful mien: we're permitted to ask, why all the gloom? What do our bad diagnoses do for us? Not merely reassign blame – we're too proud for that obvious arbitrage. We are if anything *too sincere*: our sincerity is our badge and shield – with it we earn the right to our scorn. We are willing to go down with the ship, we are willing to share blame: we do not see conspiracy – we see fate, illness, error.

Our sincerity gives us away: it's not merely that we want to punish and see punished, rather we want to be transformed and transported by the merciless. We want truth to swing a flaming sword through the mob. We seek revenge through truth: to be so aligned that no matter what the result, we will be satisfied. Even a proof of the *existence* of truth and its consequences would satisfy us... Most of apekind is quietly sure of the opposite: that nothing but "society" has consequence, and therefore value, and therefore truth. To see this covert *nihilistic* element in apekind punished for its sins, for its playacting, for its posturing...

- 342 -

The psychology of the smallminded. The ubiquitous hidden sociology of pettiness: that I seem to be the first qualified psychologist to examine the reality and ubiquity of *petty scheming*, preemptive calculation, and social maneuvering. That once your eyes are opened, you find it everywhere. That the proportion of this kind of scheming decreases relative to the quantum of excess vitality and vigor: the young and healthy are generous because they have *so much to waste.* The old and barren, the strategically weak, the beancounting majority who feel compelled to track every slight and advantage: the commonality of this behavior has been overlooked and denied for much too long.

Why have the psychologists and philosophers perpetuated this lie concerning human nature? Firstly, because they are often just as petty as the rest, if not more so. They love to speak of "transcendence" and "the absolute" to the same degree that they live timidly. Kant and Hegel are the angelic mastheads of the dyspeptic voyage to *anywhere but here.* Secondly, because exposing the commonality of wretched character risks the inevitable counterargument: that it is *I* who am petty, that I only see what I am, that I cannot help but blame humanity for my limitations. Or even that the analysis may somehow encourage the behavior: thus is born a slanderous adjective like "Machiavellian". That somehow, we "dark philosophers" are not aware or capable of the sycophantic fables of altruism, civilizational progress, and social reform with which everyone else is so besotted. That *we* are the miserable wretches, who cannot find "the Good", who seek therefore to imprecate humanity for our failure to dream and hope.

But I employ a revised hermeneutic when dealing with *the ideal*: to the degree that one worships and flatters an ideal, one has failed to grow and mature. When they speak of their compassion, the goodness of human nature, the improvement of mankind – I don't see aspiration, nor do I see gullibility, I see *dangerous flattery.* Obsequious preemptive positioning, furtive glancing mimicry, hoping not to be noticed with one hand even while straining for attention with the other: the greedy scheming ape, the fearful rodent-heart, the nervous wide-eyed vigilance of the nocturnal insect-devouring tarsier, our ancestor. The Chinese have a nice idiom for pettiness, 打小算盤, which means "to work the tiny abacus": I have discovered this tiny abacus at last, in the hands of everyone - in my own hands far too often. What took so much imagination and bad experience to realize, is not only the determinative scope of this behavior, and not only the longstanding conspiracy in hiding its influence, but the concomitant *shamelessness*: I could not imagine calculating social advantage so habitually and ruthlessly without *unbearable shame*... Therefore we talk ourselves out of the realization: "But if he were so petty, he couldn't live with himself. I must be missing something. It's me who needs to grow up..." And indeed this mendacious generosity must grow up: into withholding, into coldness, into *justice*. To merely allow the consequences of the unequal distribution of virtue to unfold, to prevent the impulse to conceal and repair the gap, to allow the *shame* of the inadequacies of one's neighbors to parade in our eyes, to watch them writhe in discomfort under our unremitting gaze – to allow *the justice of inequality* to run its blade across the flabby fantasies of humankind. We must turn a naïve eager heroism into a harder kind of pride – a pride strong enough to handle the mockery we will also need. Apekind generally does not behave well until it's mocked. We must learn to be as proud of our unforgiveness as we are of our sense of humor about this ridiculous, grotesque, all-too-human tragedy.

- 343 -

To be a modern human being is to be a damaged half-adult encompassing an exhausted and confused child. I have my intellectual prowess, my psychological laserbeam, my sublime transforming laughter, and my bleeding heart of passion: but let no one imagine I wish to pretend this represents any "ideal". We are broken, we are permanent convalescents, we are at best no longer a sad story but a story of incremental redemption – but not an innocent bloom, not a fully unfolded fractalic ramification of strength and beauty, not a creature at home in the world, with blazing unhesitating eyes. We are permanently homeless, and only by embracing nomadism to the bone do we become worthy of a second look.

In my case, I have learned to be grateful for my "böser Blick": without that excess ballast of bad experiences my ship would never have remained upright. I would never have learned to see the human race for what it is, never learned to catch it red-handed and in the light of a flashbulb. As quick a study as I am, it nonetheless required a long string of heartbreak before I finally resolved to *learn from every experience* and trust my first response, no matter what the result: overcoming the best wishes of an overflowing heart is like teaching an especially stupid child... Take my word for it.

Finally a wickedness to match the material at hand. The squeamish unwillingness to acknowledge the essential pettiness of human nature is what the majority of the human race counts on to get by. But the answers generally get much worse than that! Several layers deep into the discovery of cognitive dissonance and hypocrisy, like mucking out an old barn, one unlearns disgust and dismay and finds it all funny again: apenature must be funny, else we're doomed. Dismay is actually near the end of a long series of responses to all the bad news. First comes depression, then rage, then the vacillation between contempt and compassion, then grey-hearted dismay... And of course we may traverse this series in a single moment. But years later, after many traversals, we learn to race to the end where neutrality and a knowing grin waits, and find even a *wicked amusement* is possible without losing touch with good taste. A sense of burgeoning freedom alongside a much more refined sense of duty: to have finally learned to be selective in taking up a cause rather than hastily self-sacrificing, to know the difference between obligation and responsibility, to know where and how to be effective, to know what the heart really wants. "Telling the truth" is only the first stage, near to confession and adolescent self-absorption. But *being* the creature that creates an atmosphere of insight: that requires joyful wickedness, that requires bad experience, that requires the restless eye of the psychologist.

II.3

RITUAL EXCLUSION

THE BASAL TRIBAL
INSTINCT

- 344 -

I n this essay is buried an answer the question: what do I mean by "ritual exclusion"? I first used the term when describing the Chinese glyphs 非 and 罪, which demonstrates that ancient connection between crime, banishment, and nonexistence... It was the ubiquity and plainness of this assumption in ancient thinking which first led me to see something under our collective nose: this is an *instinct* we share. And therefore to begin, we must ask another question: *what is instinct?*

WHAT IS INSTINCT?

- 345 -

> It will be universally admitted that instincts are as important as corporeal structure for the welfare of each species, under its present conditions of life.
>
> Darwin, *On The Origin of Species*, ch. VII

But this is no longer universally admitted: biology is increasingly determined to find everything "in the genes", and if not there, "in the brain".

In psychology and sociology, the hostility to the concept *instinct* has never been greater. The word is treated as though it were hopelessly anachronistic. When a purely "organic" etiology cannot be conjured, as a last resort we say "ontogenetic behavioral program".

Ethology is largely a dead science. The slow death of the fundamental natural sciences parallels the death of psychology: 21st century life science hangs suspended, having severed its roots to the skillset which brought us here. Every ambitious psychology of the 21st century wants to portray itself as a frontier of neurology, with nothing whatever to do especially with Freud, the humanities, and simple observation.

The idea that behavior can be rigorously studied at the level of natural observation, is terribly out of fashion. Moreover the idea that the human creature and its societies can be studied in precisely the same way, is even more out of fashion: that this study lacks statistics will be reason enough for dismissal. I am not unaware of the resistance, when I speak of *human instinct*: I insist that no other term need be invented, for we must confront this resistance directly and trace its distortions.

- 346 -

> It is tempting to ponder this over-emphasis on studies of causa-
> tion. I believe that it is partly due to the fact that, as the
> development of physics and chemistry has shown, knowledge
> of the causes underlying natural events provides us with the
> power to manipulate these events and 'bully them into sub-
> servience'. It is perhaps for this reason that Man, and
> particularly urban Man, is inclined even in his biological
> studies to ape physics, and so to contribute to the satisfaction of
> his urge to conquer nature.

> Nikolaas Tinbergen, *The Study of Instinct*, 1969 Preface, p.x

Why the suppression of the science of instinct? Because instinct repre-
sents a lifeform's *resistance to distortion*. Its inherent intelligence, that which needs no teaching, that which outperforms all supplementary learning, that which does not need nor want civilization. The resistance to studies of instinct, and particularly the idea of innate *human instinct*, can be traced to the need to dominate, erode, and warp the human biosphere into whatever arbitrary shape civilizational forces demand. Our laboratories seek to humiliate animal intelligence, torture it, berate it for its nakedness: look carefully at B.F. Skinner to see this urge exposed – the sit-
uation has not improved, only become more crafty. Our laboratories cook up chemical castrations for the children: look carefully at the history of autism, the history of lobotomy, the history of drugs like thalidomide, and extrapolate the longterm effects of histrionic pandemic lockdowns. "For your own good": this is what the circus says to its animals, the prison to its inmates, the psychiatrist to the child as he scribbles another prescription of Prozac...

- 347 -

It requires a great deal of humility, patience, and imagination to properly study instinct at the total organic level – I recall a fragment of a story from Tinbergen, describing a baby seagull crawling into his shabby windswept blind to get warm under his crouching body... To grok the "state of adaptedness", as he says, requires the kind of passionate, wholehearted science of mind and body which grows scarcer, the more mere statistical agglutination is foisted upon the student as the only possible answer, the more science becomes *the administrations of what a computer can discover for us*, the more the human body becomes an appendage of a technocracy which seeks its futurity by entwining itself deeper into that body, becoming more invisible the more it dominates...

- 348 -

The situation in the 21st century, is that any psychology which does not ground itself in the ethological fundamentals is worthless drivel: either one ends up promoting vague, fashionable, animistic "syndromes" such as the psychiatrists do; or droning on about Upanishadic fantasies like "objectless prelinguistic desire" as the worst psychoanalysts do. *We are animal*: now is the time to take this realization more seriously than ever before. Psychology has been until now, and continues to be, the "story of the soul", just as its name translates: the problem is not so much this idea, as it is with the postaxial degradation of the definition of "soul". *Psyche* used to mean "living essence", and not "consciousness" nor "mind" nor "human person": it means that which *animates*, that which is constituted by animation, that which is irreducible from *the living whole*.

- 349 -

It's been slowly dawning on me, the more I attempt to reconstruct the functional sociology of the Pleistocene epoch: everything which previously seemed arbitrary, disappointing, thoughtless, messy, and careless in preagricultural nomadic life can be viewed as the natural ease of a creature in its home. The profundity and deep rationality is present *all the more*: its presence makes it possible to be at ease, and the ease invites it. It struck me as I was listening to the songs of the Baka Pygmies of Cameroon. There's a recording of children swimming, drumming on the water and singing, casually demonstrating a mastery of polyphony and polyrhythm that eludes almost all of us: this weaving of talk and song, play and ceremony, jokes and admonition, is the original mode of acculturation – if you listen carefully to the ceremonial songs, you'll find that even the babies have learned to *cough in polyrhythm*. The deep social rationality is there, *human instinct* is there: in the midst of song as communication, in the midst of story as authority, in the call-and-response, in the formation of tribe-as-family, in *the ceremony of ceremony*...

> Hunters and gatherers, most of all, appear deceptively simple and straightforward in terms of their social organization, yet that appearance is far from being true. What is true, perhaps, is that the result of a typical hunting-and-gathering organization is a simple and effective system of human relationships, and this is what so strongly appeals to many of those who have worked with them.
>
> Colin Turnbull, *The Mountain People*, I.31

- 350 -

My contention is that instinct can and *must* be conceived as *behavioral algorithm*. The usual features of algorithms apply: a diachronic progression, hierarchical structuring, well-defined parameters, feedback channels, optimization routines, functional redundancy, definite finalizing conditions, and so on. It's the complex science of answering a simple question: "How do we achieve a consistent result from variable conditions?" To imagine that metaphysical vagaries like "intention" are the only recourse, is to betray an inability to see the *deep rationality* which characterizes instinct: not the chatty *raisonner* which with modernity is so impressed, but the supreme functionality of the organic.

There is no "mind-body problem": the mind is a function of the body – one of many. Everything which characterizes a well-functioning mind is a characteristic of a well-functioning body: efficiency, ease, fast switching, modularity, diurnal rhythm, hierarchically arranged products of synthesis, well-defined criteria of defense, aim-directed aggression, and so on.

But we have not yet overcome the agency-matter problem: our best guess is that the organic is living agency emergent from the fallback of dead matter pushed to criticality. Function, agency, intent, and *anima* are there-fore roughly synonymous: Aristotle's much-too-clever coinage in ἐντελέχεια (*entelecheaia*) is worth reviving for a moment, even if just to admire the old bastard's talent as a theoretical biologist if not a philoso-pher. In this dorky portmanteau Aristotle has managed to communicate for once something of his better intuition: that what lives strives for full expression, wholeness, its own "telos". It merely remains to us moderns to attempt to define in terms we can accept, what a "whole" might be...

THE MARRIAGE OF PSYCHOANALYSIS AND ETHOLOGY

- 351 -

I have something to point out, which I have never heard a psychoanalyst say, nor read in any literature concerning animal behavior: when Tinber-gen discovered something he called "displacement" in his animals, he was rediscovering what Freud had also called displacement – as *Verschiebung* is properly translated. For example, when a goose is frustrated in his attempts to mate, he will peck furiously at the ground: the insight is that this pecking is merely an adjacent and easily aroused instinct, and receives as it were the excess energy which seeks expression. The further insight is that this displacement of the act, immediately becomes a sym-bolic communication – everyone knows what it means, especially the geese.

Tinbergen observed the same in creatures as overlooked as a 5cm fish, during his famous study of the mating ritual of the stickleback: when frustrated in their attempts to attack another male, and especially at the *borders* of their own territory, when the urge to flee frustrates the urge to fight, these little fish will suddenly dig a nest in the sand – an instinct belonging to a later phase of the mating sequence, but with a low activa-tion threshold and plenty of "room" for the original aggression to find outlet. As a consequence, this furious digging has become a threat display and already partially ritualized – that is, it's become symbolic communi-cation by virtue of being adjacent to the original and cheap to activate.

It's possible Tinbergen was aware of the Freudian idea, but it's much more likely that he was merely following Konrad Lorenz's thinking to its conclusions: Lorenz's model of instinct was influenced by some of the same early Germanic neurology as Freud. Now it's easy enough to criticize the terms "instinctual energy", "psychic investment", or "object choice" as much too vague and ungrounded in physiology, but when dealing with holistic behavior we have no choice but to begin with *precise descriptive vocabulary*, and wait for confirmation of the mechanics. To attempt a premature physiological correspondence is to commit an error of superstition, and is in fact much less scientific: neither Freud nor Tinbergen committed this error. Psychology is nothing but the art of precise description at the most synthetic levels of organic complexity: this is why it requires that curious mixture of stubborn technicality and relentless imagination. Many hours of careful observation, terse stubborn theory, a sense of knowing precisely what one means, and most importantly, carefully outlining what we do not know: this is what I look for, and what I rarely find.

In the end what I have to contribute here is very simple, and is more of a corrective history than a theory:

1. As Tinbergen's work shows, displacement is necessary in any meaningful theory of instinct.

2. Tinbergen's conception of displacement is precisely analogous to the Freudian conception, and much more than mere coincidence. Tinbergen's successful experiments demonstrate the validity of the approach.

3. Symbolic communication is *not* derived from the advantages which might accrue in cooperative behavior – as is always assumed – but from instinctual displacement. In other words, *communication is a consequence of frustration.* Cooperative behavior enhanced by communication is a much later addition: the threat is much older than the greeting.

4. Therefore a working theory of repression and displacement, which Freud first developed, is indispensable in ethology, and therefore anthro-

pology, and therefore psychology, and therefore philosophy in the 21st century. But the suppression of the Freudian discovery is no mere historical accident nor a whim of fashion, and will likely only become more intense in the years to come.

- 354 -

Good theory is always simple: sometimes so simple that it begins to disappear into what you already knew. Repression and displacement is to psychology what F=ma is to physics: something every nervous system already knows and uses daily, else we could not walk. But the good teacher knows how to take a simple accepted principle and exploit its consequences to their limit: only by demonstrating the mechanics again and again, can we learn *consciously* what we all know unconsciously. This is the art of psychology.

- 355 -

I should also add that psychoanalysts have utterly failed to develop this theory in the way it deserved: "displacement" is not even commonly spoken of, only "transference" – but this misses the fundamental relation with repression. Freud himself failed his earlier work: his later theorizing belongs among 19th century mediocre philosophers, something on the order of Schelling or Fichte.

Why? Partly because the theory is so deceptively simple. Partly because "ego defenses" and chartable symptomatologies seem so much more relevant. Partly because appreciating the depth of this discovery requires a brilliance capable of keeping up with the young and ambitious Freud.

But there's much more at stake. Why have psychoanalysts consistently emphasized his weakest formulations, his most reifying fictions, his most egoically oriented perspectives? But I've already answered: because even in the midst of the burning light of analysis, there has been far too much acquiescence to expectation – the farcical overemphasis of the Oedipal conflict was what both the fans and critics wanted. Because analysis has given way to consolation. Because finding gratification in such a powerfully humble theory requires an *arid mind*, a love of desert air which perhaps only arises in those with a chronic fecundity, a spirit which wants emptiness as the space in which to create.

- 356 -

Tinbergen's work helped me realize something: *repression is the prerequisite to sociality*. It's not in the dance between male and female, despite the mutual urgency of the task – spawning does not spawn the society, as so many species demonstrate. It's in the *peer conflict*, at the boundaries between competitive instincts, where frustration demands novel solutions.

Repression is the ability of a social animal to suppress and defer certain behaviors according to the temporal and social context in which it finds its best advantage: displacement breeds the symbolic act, which is the bread and butter of all society.

This can be temporary: as in the case of an adolescent who must repress his sexuality until the culturally appropriate moment. Or it can be semi-permanent: as in the case of a civilized man who has learned to repress his urge to physical violence no matter the intensity of his feelings.

Displacement, not "cooperation": complementary functioning is not the essence of sociality. There is no cooperative instinct in the beginning, merely displacement behavior which may lead to adaptive gains, which are then secondarily reinforced. This dry technical description hides something extremely important and relevant to the human future: an increase of society is an increase of frustration. Moreover everything we mean by "neurotic" is a consequence of displacement behavior: one does strange little things in place of the original thing. Irrationality in the animal only appears when instinctual frustration exceeds the adaptive displacement paths, and it requires many hundreds of generations for such displacements to become natural, instinctive, and painless again. The human race is well along in the exploration of maximum possible tolerance of instinctual frustration, and thus neurotic displacement and psychosomatic illness are fated to only increase until something breaks.

- 357 -

The kind of neurosis with which modernity is shot through, was already in place in order to deal with the frictions of tribality: repression, displacement, symbolic substitution, everything which enables neurotic solutions to impossible problems – but which in a tribal context allows for success because it coaxes rational behavior out of a frustrated creature, by largely offloading the unadaptive component into an irrational sinkhole which nonetheless has very rational consequences: animism, sympathetic magic, taboo, the realm of the gods and the dead.

Modern neurosis is therefore also as adaptive as can be expected: a tribal animal adapting to civilization. Actually it's admirable how well we function in our squirming cities and cramped chunnels to nowhere and everywhere.

- 358 -

It's possible that Freudian mechanics are entirely derivable from *game theory in a tribal context*: displacement, repression, overdetermination, and every neurotic distortion are strategies for dealing with momentarily unadaptive instinct in a semi-cooperative group. A table of needs plotted against probabilistic risk estimates, made extradimensional with every additional future group trajectory, and again multiplied by every estimate of the likely strategies of one's rivals and half-friends, until we reach a compounded n-dimensional space which only the massive human forebrain is capable of compiling, as though it wished to outdo the ancient 4-dimensional calculus of the cerebellum... And we begin to understand why this creature thinks so much.

- 359 -

As long as I'm here, there's another important correction to make:

> Ebensowenig kennen die Ubw-Vorgänge eine Rücksicht auf die Realität. Sie sind dem Lustprinzip unterworfen; ihr Schicksal hängt nur davon ab, wie stark sie sind, und ob sie die Anforderungen der Lust-Unlustregulierung erfüllen.

The unconscious processes recognize no connection with reality. They are subject to the pleasure principle; their fate depends only upon how strong they are and whether they fulfill the demands of the pleasure-unpleasure formulation.

Das Unbewußte, V

This is Freud at his least insightful – and tellingly – most philosophical. He's always wrong when he fumbles with his "pleasure principle".

Unconscious process is not merely a blind machine for discharging drives in wishful directions: it is designed to *create niches* and *exploit opportunities* and *prepare for eventualities*. One of the principal failures of my dear Freud, was his failure to understand the adaptive function of dreaming: not merely *Wunscherfüllung*, but wishcrafting. To dream is to assimilate experience, to mine it for solutions to the insoluble, and to rehearse those solutions.

Freud never attempted to see the total psyche *as adaptive* – unfortunately his work was handicapped by that English-industrialist's assumption that *the organic is stupid* – merely bovine, merely blind, merely discharging like a vivisected frog: an assumption which still sits in the driver's seat of neuroscience.

Primary process is adaptive: its job is to choose instinctual targets, to navigate environmental barriers, to create and exploit opportunities, to dream solutions. How does a bird build a nest? It *dreams* a nest: it sees a nest where there is only a crook in a branch, and everything afterward is only realizing that vision. "No connection with reality" is a mistake, although in a Nietzschean sense it could be on the right track: animals *make* reality. We *recreate* reality. Unconscious primary process shuffles the deck, plays with symbols and problems, rearranges the crystal for the sake of discovering novel advantageous configurations: the issue with neurotic solutions is not that unconscious process and instinct in general demonstrates so much independence from the total "Umwelt" of potential sensory data – not that we *desire* rather than perceive – but that our environments are no longer as receptive to those neurotic solutions as they were in the past. A bird that hallucinates a nest on a windmill could just as easily be construed as "neurotic".

For far too long psychologists have only sought illness and error while carefully avoiding personal implication. In modernity everything is illness and error, and yet to understand any of those errors we must understand their original adaptive value. Every quality of the human being must be transposed to a tribal hunting niche before it can be rightly interpreted.

BABBLING COMES FIRST

- 360 -

Ein Trieb kann nie Objekt des Bewusstseins werden, nur die Vorstellung, die ihn repräsentiert. Er kann aber auch im Unbewusstsein nicht anders als durch die Vorstellung repräsentiert sein.

A drive can never become the object of consciousness, only the projection which represents it. Neither can it be represented in unconsciousness as anything but a projection.

Das Unbewusste, §III

Instinctual behavior demands symbolic operant algorithms – otherwise known as the prerequisite to linguistic thought. "This shall serve for that": instinctual behavior means nothing else.

But it's *displacement* that makes the symbol possible: because symbolization is nothing other than the eclipse of one hidden thing by a more visible thing, a syntactic relationship which distorts and obscures. The immediate present object "stands for" the virtual instinctual object: which means the present object is both obscured and charged with alien significance, and that the never-experienced instinctual object is both revealed and hidden by this substitution. How do we detect displacement in daily practice? How do we know when someone's up to something deserving of analysis? By detecting an alien significance, an intensity of feeling that seems out of place: this is the crux of all good psychologizing. It's likely that this *misplaced feeling* is the urform of both instinct on the one hand – down the path of increasing investment in a singular response to a singular sign – and symbolic communication on the other hand – down the path of increasing the lability of response to the point that it becomes almost moot. To communicate is to trade in cheap displaced behavior: thus growling, chirping, fluttering, and every energetically cheap displaced behavior which serves to indicate something much more expensive.

Transference, "cathexis", the symbolic relation and *culture itself* follow from the mechanic of displacement: as though simply by overflowing and half-malfunctioning, the instinctual urge stumbles upon the linguistic faculty.

- 361 -

If instinct requires the symbol, and the symbol requires displacement, it follows that instinct requires displacement: despite the fact that it was the frustration of instinct which seemed to invent it. This suggests that instinct cannot exist without a minimum of deferral. Instinct is constituted by *waiting for the right time*: the reflex is easy enough to inherit, the calibration of the trigger is probably much more difficult.

- 362 -

Yet it's also true that displacement from one instinctual vector to another seems to occur via symbolic affinity: it's not merely the low cost of activation, but the *similarity of the aim and means* which selects a given behavior as the displaced target. The man who spits when he's angry; the woman who chews her lip when she's aroused; the child who hits himself rather than someone else... But we're looking into the heart of the origin of the symbolic, and we should not expect a neat conceptual hierarchy. Most likely, this is all a chicken-and-egg complex, and it's senseless to speak of either a historical or logical "origin" for something like instinctual behavior. These are at some niveau one and the same:

- ⇁ Repression
- ⇁ Displacement
- ⇁ Symbolic communication
- ⇁ Instinctual targeting

Tinbergen says the same concerning the emergence of all complex instincts: it's not assembled piece by piece in ordinal fashion, but rather begins as a fragmented atemporal soup of the final behavior, which is only gradually parsed and arranged through repetition – we babble first, imitating the totality and tone, long before we articulate. In other words, this is a case of "dependent coarising".

- 363 -

Freud discovered another clue: just as we cannot become conscious of instinct itself, repression works only upon the *image* of the object, its containment by symbol, rather than acting upon the "drive" itself. There seems to be no other means of defusing instinctual behavior once it's initiated.

> Wir haben behauptet, daß bei der Verdrängung eine Trennung des Affekts von seiner Vorstellung stattfindet, worauf beide ihren gesonderten Schicksalen entgegengehen. Das ist deskriptiv unbestreitbar; der wirkliche Vorgang aber ist in der Regel, daß ein Affekt so lange nicht zustande kommt, bis nicht der Durchbruch zu einer neuen Vertretung im System Bw gelungen ist.

> We have asserted that in repression, affect and image are divided, whereby both encounter their unique fate. In the descriptive sense, this is incontrovertible; but generally the real process is that an affect does not occur until the emergence of a new representative within the conscious system.

> *Das Unbewußte,* §III

We often don't know what we feel until an excuse arises. Lesson: *feelings are not the cause of behavior*, but merely the behavioral modulator. That we believe we do things because of how we *feel*, is just the success of that priming function they are supposed to serve.

- 364 -

We distinguish between inhibition and repression: we understand that repression is nothing but a specially visible case of that instinctual inhibition which it's safe to assume rules at almost any time. Any given instinct spends most of its lifecycle in suspension.

Repression is *retroactive inhibition*: it occurs when an instinct has already been triggered, but is frustrated in its course and seeks other paths – thus repression and displacement are only terms for the beginning and end of the same process.

The essential difference between inhibition and repression therefore would be: repression is conceived to act upon the *symbolic*, a kind of secondary inhibition designed to abort and redirect instinctual process in the presence of too much frustration and risk. This is why repression rises with sociality: complicated intraspecies relations entail abortive and half-realized instinctual responses, and thus the ability to make use of them.

HIERARCHY OF INSTINCT

- 365 -

The attempt to correct evolutionary psychology, and thus all relevant psychology today, requires a viable theory of instinct – one in which any and all distortions have in some respect their adaptive value: no matter how sick and strange we become, we endure.

Since long before Freud, before William James, before Charcot, before the idiocy of John Locke and the brilliance of Hume, since perhaps Socrates and Democritus, psychology has been bogged down by the stupidity of a theory of pleasure-and-pain: as though the animal were merely blindly reactive, pingponging from pain to pleasure, without any deeper instinctual rationale. If this were remotely true, life would never have begun, nor persisted, nor blossomed. Pleasure and pain are epiphenomena at best, and should be understood just like every other affect: as priming feedback, attenuator or accelerator, but not at all the "goal" nor the driving force nor the final word. They are not even essentially distinct.

So allow me a simple corrective theory – again so simple as to be painfully obvious: repression and displacement are driven and organized by a *hierarchy of instinct*. Some behaviors are more important than others, and thus inhibition is born. Some behaviors are essential and yet the cost of any single execution is trivial, and thus displacement is possible. Some behaviors are easily triggered but costly to finish, and thus repression begins.

- 366 -

Repression indicates a hierarchy of instinct which mobilizes unconscious behavioral calculus: although we're talking about risk mitigation, in successful repression the affect of fear is absent – it does the creature no good to be afraid of a consequence which has been avoided. Due to the enormous confusion here, it's worth emphasizing that repression is the prioritization of a *basal layer* behavioral routine, and not the fulfillment of a "higher" moral ideal: we are good boys and girls because we need social status to ensure maximum reproductive success, not because we are God's children. Actually Freud was on the right track in his formulation of the "Überich", it's just that most of his followers ignored the engineering: the superego is mostly a locus of *unconscious* social calculation, a symbolic means to risk mitigation within behavioral combinatorics.

The conscious rationale for good social behavior, when there is any, may take the shape of an introjected parental figure, but its compulsion is derived from fundamental needs: the acquisition of resource, securing genetic lines, tribal power. What is repressed is generally predictable: sexual consummation or aggression. Fucking and killing constitutes most of what we want to do and cannot.

- 367 -

Repression initiates the immediate search for alternate discharge channels: "spreading activation" and network exploration should be apt metaphors. Repression does not become recognizable as such, until the search for alternate routes has already begun: as psychologists, we detect repression when we detect distortion in the semantic field – something's off, the rhythm is clunky, the neural timing is sour.

Likewise displacement always occurs via a *lower priority* channel: displacement is the search protocol among lower priority routines for a low-risk discharge. The *shittiness* of neurotic behavior is due to this low instinctual priority: scratching, chewing, tics and transient spasms, neck muscle activation, bowel maintenance, little white lies and tiny factual distortions, minuscule vocal modulation, a fleeting grimace, flickering in the eyes – all easily triggered, easily justified, easily communicated, and thus potential displacement vectors.

- 368 -

Repression gains its power and invisibility due to the origination of the first impulse in high priority routines: a discharge must be found.

Displacement gains its humor and genius due to its localization in lower priority routines – genius provisionally defined as the reconciliation of many competing needs into a coherent response. Shakespearian multivalence is the coordination between parallel routines. Displacement, artistry, poetry, neurosis, comedy, and dreaming itself are thus intimately connected.

WHAT IS RITUAL?

- 369 -

We're now in a better position to understand what *ritual exclusion* might mean.

What is ritual? It is *instinct emptied of content*. Ritual retains the form of instinct but the aim is plastic. One of the core human adaptations is to have weakened instinctual coherence past the point any other animal would normally survive, while strengthening the instinct for ritual, symbol, and displacement: our ability to adapt to almost any ecology under almost any form of stress requiring almost any technological package, is due to an extremely high tolerance for frustration, and thus symbolic displacement, and thus ritualized learned behavior. We've turned frustration and maladaptation into advantage: we're adapted to the state of maladaptation.

- 370 -

How are Freudian mechanics necessary for understanding what I call "ritual exclusion"? Why is repression and displacement necessary? Firstly because I insist on a viable theory of human instinct. Secondly because to understand what "ritual" could mean, we must understand instinct not only as a form of pure compulsion, but as intimately bound in the process of symbolic communication. We call it "ritual" because it is a behavioral set which is both more and less than it seems: less because human ritual includes much symbolic excess – typically organized under its moral justification, its metaphysical origin, its magical goal – and much more than it seems because *ritual is realized in side-effects*. We accomplish many things through neurotic extravagance, preparations for the impossible, delusions of grandeur and fears of insignificance: half of civilization runs on these ingredients. The ritual of exclusion is not to be found at all if one is not accustomed to looking in *displaced vectors* and under rugs of repression: in fact because this instinctual response is a result of frustrated tribal living and attendant anxiety, it can hardly take any other form. But this is part of why it works: else "plausible deniability" wouldn't provide the risk-mitigation necessary for a tribal creature under stress. In other words its not possible nor desirable for the human creature to be aware of its creation of criteria of exclusion when it really needs them: only the comfortable, healthy, assured tribe can afford to admit what it's up to. A Freudian grasp of repression and the return of the repressed is therefore indispensable in observing us, as modern tribeless folk, behave tribally despite ourselves: and suddenly why this has never been successfully hypothesized makes sense.

- 371 -

Since we're returning to old masters of neglected fields, allow me to properly introduce Konrad Lorenz, the leader of what should have been a long line of 20th century ethologists. Lorenz analyzed instinct into two components:

→ *Erbkoordination*: literally "inherited coordination", the innate response gestalt. What is generally observed as the instinctual act.

→ *Taxiskomponente*: the "taxis", the guidance system, the stimulus response factor.

Combining Lorenz's terms with Tinbergen's findings, we arrive at the following schema. Every instinct can be analyzed into:

1. *Sign receptor*: the ability to scan for and recognize the sign stimulus. Would involve a continuous scanning routine, a recognition function, and an output signal sent to the threshold.

2. *Release threshold*: a complex quantitative summation of qualitatively heterogeneous input, determined by relevant factors including time since last discharge, health, hormones, stress, and social primers. Is variable as a result, and upon activation an initiation signal sent to the response gestalt.

3. *Response gestalt*: the *Erbkoordination*. A coherent, *co-ordinated* set of responses. Could be conceived as a *directed acyclic graph*, which means each point is visitable singly but ends by pointing along the series toward a definite terminus – which would explain the meaning of play.

4. *Guidance system*: the *Taxiskomponente*. A complete instinct with its own rules, which may be initiated prior or posterior to its superordinate instinct, for aiming and correction respectively. This implies a recursively structured set.

Instinct must answer these questions:

⇁ When: sign receptor + threshold, what Tinbergen calls the "innate releasing mechanism".

⇁ How: response gestalt, the observable instinct itself.

⇁ Where: taxis sign receptor + taxis threshold + taxis response.

Therefore instinct may be *recursively structured*. In pseudocode:

```
def instinct(sign, threshold, response, taxis):
    if sign and threshold:
        return response(taxis)
    else:
        return instinct(
                taxis.sign,
                taxis.threshold,
                taxis.response,
                taxis.taxis)
```

- 372 -

If ritual exclusion is an instinct, it must have:

1. Sign receptor: that the tribe is in trouble, thus dysfunctionality, depression, anxiety, infertility. Hysteria was not interpreted as the "wandering womb" for no reason. An ability *to read the signs of collective dysfunction* is implied in any definition of a social animal. The tribal creature assesses tribal health.

2. Variable threshold: the responsiveness to these same factors at both the individual and group level, mostly conditioned by frustration. In practice this becomes a variable readiness for collective violence mitigated by the need for plausible deniability.

3. Taxis: assessment of the value of any one member to the tribe (envy), assessment of the likelihood of personal exclusion (loneliness), the ability to anticipate group consensus and thus the ability to maximize status passively (conformity), the ability to exploit hierarchical instability and thus to maximize status actively (posturing), the ability to display multiple conflicting attitudes depending on context (hypocrisy), the ability to alter alliances in response to shifting consensus (betrayal), the ability to display preemptive hostility to disqualified outliers in order to protect group status (bigotry), the ability to ostracize outliers once consensus passes threshold (anonymous mass violence).

4. Response gestalt: the ritual itself. The actual moment of exclusion is perhaps minimal, and depends mostly on the capacity for betrayal and *anonymity*: in other words, shallow alliance and cognitive dissonance are necessary preparatory work. The final act of ritual violence is powered by the accumulated aggression of instinctual frustration expressed in a thousand small ways. Who actually "does" it, is negligible: nobody and everybody casts the first stone.

Most of what I call "ritual exclusion" is actually the *negative tropotaxis of abandonment*: group exclusion effectuates itself largely through the *preparatory identification* phase. This is what makes modern identification schemes so dangerous. This is the sinister potential of the phrases, "May I see your papers?" and "You'll have to come with us": this ritual hides and distributes violence across many perfectly "humane" stages, from identification to detention to internment up to the very last moment and beyond to the autopsy – the violence is buried so deep in the bureaucratic machinery that it no longer exists... This is what Kafka recorded more vividly and plausibly than anyone else, including Orwell.

The compatibility of the ancient tribal means of justice – where no one in particular decides the sentence and no one in particular carries it out – with the most modern forms of architectural oppression, is probably the most fateful resonance of our past with our future. *Plausible deniability* rules the skittish band of apes and the calculating anonymous mass of the obedient.

- 373 -

It's possible to parse the components of instinct into "appetitive and consummatory":

→ Appetitive behavior: the search function initiated at a superordinate level – plastic, adaptable, ubiquitous.

→ Consummatory behavior: the final concrete function – static and strictly ordered.

An animal spends most of his waking life *searching*. Exploratory "appetitive" behavior characterizes the early and superordinated stages of instinct: instinctual behavior is hierarchically and recursively structured, but at every step down the behavior becomes more concrete and less plastic.

Most of ritual is preparation: I've known this since my first traditional sweat-lodge, but not known what to do with it. But human ritual is itself a simulacrum of instinctual behavior: an *instinctual mimicry of instinct*. The same primate capacity for mimicry, which makes us so capable of learning, sociality, and camouflaged hunting, is exploited to generate *substitutive behavioral coherence* through symbolic ritual. A human ritual has an emptied structure of instinct, but with its aim and means plastic. A kind of reversal of generality has taken place: by freeing the concreteness of the consummatory act, and placing concrete behavior at the beginning, the human race works its symbolic magic: *the appetitive behavior achieves the aim*, while the consummatory act becomes abstract, magical, imaginary. We trick ourselves into behaving functionally, by placing imaginary powers at the end of a series of functional social behaviors supposedly justified by those imaginary reasons. Most of human ritual achieves concrete social functionality *as a side-effect*: tribal cohesion, unambiguous membership, and stabilized hierarchy is realized invisibly, while we address those angry gods, those heavens and hells, curses and taboos, currencies and debts, shames and glories...

- 374 -

The functions of taboo:

⌐ To keep protocols separate, discreet, organized. Tribal life has a tendency to become an unending parade of petty toil without real peace.

⌐ To maintain an atmosphere of respect and seriousness regarding the essential activities of livelihood: tribal life has a tendency to become saturated with mockery, chatter, impudent familiarity.

⌐ To allow unconscious valences to work themselves out in their own time. To give breathing room to the sacred and dangerous – such as the killing of a bear, or the death of a comrade. Tribal life has a tendency to become cluttered with the mundane occupancies of women's work: many of the rules are designed to give the hunter a break at home after an intense hunt, or to allow the ceremonial corrections time and space to adjust unconscious priorities.

⌐ To give women a break from their work: most of the taboos surrounding menstruation seem designed to allow women a rest, while avoiding the emotional complications of PMS.

- 375 -

Taboo operates primarily through the collective displacement of aggression, and is correctly considered the urform of the conscience: taboo was for at least a couple hundred thousand years the primary social glue and lawful delimiter. It stands for everything beyond the tribe which necessitates the frustration of living in one: it is therefore hated, feared, and bargained with.

Listen to Tinbergen again, discussing the "Innate Releasing Mechanism" (IRM):

> Now the striking thing about social releasers is that they corre-spond exactly to the IRM they act upon. They send out little more than just the simple sign stimuli which are required to stimulate the corresponding IRM. It is as if social releasers are adapted to the properties of the IRM.
>
> *The Study of Instinct*, p.56

The meaning of sociality: exploitation of instinctual sign stimuli at the intraspecies level. Sociality is *subsequent* and parasitic. The ridiculous excesses of social signaling are inevitable because it's fundamentally an abuse of another contract: an arms race between the social signal and the innate releaser, which leads to peacocks, antlers, and whalesong.

But sociality takes on a life of its own: granted that social behavior is inherently exploitative, this exploitation soon confers conditional advantages leading to group selection, which initiates a new plane of competition and cybernetic control. The beginning of social behavior is *getting what you want from the group*, but the longterm consequence to the species is that eventually the group *gets what it wants from you*.

This is all merely preliminary outline. However, it's not merely ungrounded theory: Tinbergen's discovery of the supernormal sign stim-ulus should have proven the validity of this line of thinking – but in the years since, it's been abandoned along with the entire field of ethology. There are much shinier toys with sinister profit margins than the study of animal behavior. The nearest analogue comes from robotics, namely "subsumption architecture"... But again that approach is the long road, and the developments in AI since the 1980s have demonstrated a clear preference for highly impoverished digital domains – a computer that acts like a human using a computer we consider more impressive than a computer that acts like a human using a body.

THE CRISIS CULT

- 378 -

Rather than speak of "ritual exclusion", I could have used the term "crisis cult". In his tirelessly researched, overly ambitious masterwork *The Ghost Dance*, the psychoanalytic anthropologist Weston La Barre set out to show that all forms of religion find their origin in the *crisis cult*:

> "Born in stress, sacred culture is nourished endlessly by new stresses."
>
> p.223

This text contains perhaps 100 pages of examples drawn from every major culture and nearly every historical era demonstrating the same pattern. We learn that the Ghost Dance movement of the 1890s was not at all unique but merely the last of dozens of other similar apocalyptic revivals among Native Americans spanning back to the 1500s in Peru. In every instance, the promise was the elimination of the white race and the restoration of the old ways. But the pattern is even more widespread: La Barre finds examples in Greece, Rome, India, England – anywhere and any time the human creature is under extreme stress, usually precipitated by cultural deterioration and rapid change. A Quaker, a Rastafarian, a Nazi, and a Chinese Red Guard – it sounds like the beginning of an elaborate joke, and perhaps it is. They all share these features:

⌐ The end of the world as we know it and the dawn of a new age.

⌐ A profound urgency addressing itself to the collective anxiety of a people.

⌐ An ability to unite disparate groups. Many of the North American movements united tribes which had never before considered themselves allied. The Ghost Dance even spread to the Mormons of Utah, who interpreted it in the language of their own apocalypse.

⌐ A deeply syncretic, revisionist doctrine: almost invariably these cults are radically futuristic where livelihood and *unconscious moral expectations*

dominate – the dissolution of the family, gender equality, and the abandonment of tradition is a common theme – while simultaneously
appropriating diverse conservative signs and symbols. They promise
restoration through revolution, wholeness through penance, a healing
through severance and abstention, a belonging through exclusion. They
typically seek to appropriate *the means and power of the cultural threat*,
while promising the elimination of that threat.

- 379 -

But like the work of Julian Jaynes, this book is simultaneously valid,
unjustly neglected, and yet too riddled with the limitations of the author
to recommend unqualified. He never once speaks of hysteria, nor can he
see the *social function* of this response pattern: but I believe these failings
are no accident due to the fickle history of ideas, nor merely the failings of
an unimaginative little man. A book like this is useful for us not only for
the evidence amassed in our favor, but almost more so for the evidence of
the resistance to the obvious: for years on end, a capable scholar studied
cults designed *to create novel criteria of exclusion for recreating the tribe*, more
obviously and overtly than any other historical pattern, and yet all he
could learn was that their metaphysics is false, the motivation is anxiety,
and the means neurotic – but he never understood the goal. Like every
other psychologist of our time, when asked to interpret anything interesting, he can only see sad futile neurosis and regression – never what this
regression accomplishes. There is a profound failing to understand all
behavior as functional, one way or another: perhaps at great expense,
perhaps ringed with grandiose failures, perhaps sustained only by outlandish cost to tradition and livelihood – but in their wake come new
forms of belonging, *new transient tribes*. The Ghost Dance and related
movements even articulated these goals explicitly, since in that case the
healthy tribe was only a generation or two away – and yet no one as yet
has hypothesized that such mass hysteria might be an adaptive response
for just that purpose.

A "religion" is a tribal simulacrum fit for the anonymity of modernity as
left behind by a crisis cult: thus far we agree. But this is only halfway, and
by emphasizing metaphysical delusions and unresolved ego regression, it
leaves the modern intellectual in essentially the same secure position,
safe from "religion": and thus the cargo cults of our own time remain
safely unanalyzed. As long as cult behavior wears the guise of the political

and scientific, it remains immune from this critique, because the human creature does not want to follow me to this insight: *membership is established by exclusion*. The goal of cult behavior and any novel form of belonging, is the formation of criteria of exclusion: once this is understood, what's called mass hysteria, what's called fascism, what's called communism, and what's called cult, all coalesce into a single recognizable instinct – ritual exclusion.

- 380 -

It's not a lack of Darwinian thinking that prevents someone like La Barre from seeing the social function within mass hysteria, it's *ordinary unconscious nihilism*: to suppose that anything other than comfortable "adult" conformity is merely useless neurotic regression, to see only pathetic isolated dysfunction as the alternative to punctual drudgery, ulcerated coping, and resigned resentment – is not only the typical psychiatrist's point of view but the secret conviction of every convert of modernity. This is a nihilist, not because he doesn't believe in the god of the cults, but because he has never given leave to the perspective that every response of the human creature, in all conditions of stress, has its value. Homo sapiens the *supreme adaptor*: not a drop less admiration is required to appreciate the full extent to which we are in fact hopelessly neurotic, because our neurosis itself is *so well adapted*.

- 381 -

Religious behavior is not so much genuinely adaptive behavior as it is symptom formation; to understand this, let the reader reflect, not on his own "true religion", but on some exotic alien or primitive religion he knows about. Are we not permitted to doubt that the sacrifice of children to Moloch was good for Phoenician society? That the tens of thousands of human sacrificial skulls in aboriginal Mexico City actually secured the Aztec state?

The Ghost Dance, p.20

The answer which seems so obvious to me, is that human sacrifice always lies at the root of state security; and that infanticide may very well stabilize a population, which is why we practice *prenatal* infanticide. I find it much more remarkable how common it is to *sacrifice a faith in deeper human rationality* to the heathen idol of moral posturing: another reason why universal literacy is such a bad idea, since the first thing the ape does with his learning is to prove why he doesn't need to learn from anything.

- 382 -

Religion as a partially effective tranquilizer for the instinct of tribal formation: it does not actually solve the underlying problem, but requires rather the constant dosage of a narcotic which *simulates* tribal belonging and ritual exclusion: religious movements, fascism, mass hysteria, moral posturing, cultic behavior all merely address the *symptoms* of a fractured tribe and the signaling pathways of threatened fitness. In a tribal context they would no doubt be effective, in civilization they are merely vestigial fragments of the same fundamental instinct. The crisis cult is effective in so far as it addresses alienation, nameless anxiety, contagious xenophobia, moral panic. But it's ineffective in that it does relatively nothing to secure genetic descent: thus the need for constant reapplication, "revival", episodic "faith", demonstrations, trials, ideological war, the discovery of heterodoxy.

Vestigial tribal instinct in the midst of a civilizational ecology: dysfunctional, hypertrophic, fragmentary – in other words, an instinct seeking a more adaptive form through exaggeration and excursion – in other words, *mutation*.

The human being is delusional because its instincts are seeking to mutate. Unconscious distortion, neurosis, and acculturation is a kind of evolutionary hack applied to temporarily fix the problem of mutilated and outdated instinct. Our capacity for symbolic displacement, which produces the capacity for cognitive distortion and hallucinated agencies, which in turn produces the capacity to function in the midst of high levels of frustration and instinctual weakening, has been exploited to the maximum breaking point in modernity.

At the nomadic level, it's already visible: hallucinated agencies in the form of spirits; elaborate mythologies and ritual; strict taboo which contains and justifies tribal order.

At the ancient level, it has already grown exponentially: a hallucinated canon of gods; many rituals of propitiation; an expansion of apotropaic magic as anxiety grows; an increase in the reliance on divination.

At the late ancient level, the cracks are showing: hallucinated gods no longer convince; the oracles cease to function; old gods die rapidly; new cult fevers take hold; some take refuge in a redoubled rationality, some in nihilism; the search for a universal religion begins.

At the modern level, the levee has burst and the flood of illness begins: chronic illness and psychosomatic disease become the norm; anxiety is ubiquitous; instinctual frustration past the redline; outbreaks of hysteria increasingly common; fascist counterreactions; recruitment of science for the sake of new religious orders...

- 383 -

Moral behavior is the *dance of membership*: the qualifying test, the antennal sweep, the *shibboleth*. "Do you lisp like us?"

The need for inclusion is driven not only by personal alienation, but *the prevention of wasted investment*. A mother who realizes the child is unviable: abandonment. A mother who realizes her actions are promoting the children of her rivals: invention of trials, witch-hunts, contests. The tribe is fractured, disorganized, with unclear lines of descent and priority, in which energetic investment cannot take place rationally, and thus inclusive fitness cannot function efficiently: instinct for expulsion, for a ceremonial house cleaning, for a tribe-wide expulsion. Hysteria is the emergency protocol of the ovaries whose investments are threatened.

What I suddenly understand is that ritual exclusion is not only about securing membership for oneself, but perhaps more importantly for securing the delicate conditions which make *inclusive fitness* possible: the future of one's genes in the midst of group living – whether that means abandonment of current investments, expulsion of distant or unrelated members, or the hierarchical instability enabling sudden gains in status.

Male politics constitute the familiar profile: secure access to fertile females, secure access to marketable resources, consolidate visible alliances, weaken rivals, identify enemies, stage winnable conflicts, collect trophies.

But in crisis, it's female politics that dominate: secure lines of descent, secure access to essential resources, restructure hierarchies via histrionic appeal. Why else should the crisis cult have such a noticeably feminine character: this is true in postaxial religion, mass hysteria, and the witch-hunt. Most males if anything benefit from a more chaotic tribe: more chances for sneaky fathering strategies, the rise of the beta male...

The woman has precious few investment windows. Pregnancy is risky, childrearing is expensive. The prevalence of miscarriage in modernity has yet to be explained satisfactorily: hysteria and moral fevers could be constructively construed as *cultural miscarriage*. The destabilization of hierarchy, marriage law, and resource allocation represents a chance for dramatic improvement in circumstances and therefore a last bet for the ovaries.

One of the more significant stories I heard amidst the COVID panic, was the tale of a woman whose middle-aged husband slowly died from preventable heart attack: as she witnessed the event unfold over a few hours, listening to his deathrattle in the next room, she told herself she couldn't go to the hospital because of COVID, nor even call for help. She publicized her story as tragic, but I read it otherwise: she was boasting of how she found a means to justifiably remove the obstacle of a well-insured but deeply boring husband...

- 384 -

What does it mean, that in Weston La Barre I find another example of a psychoanalyst who *failed to study hysteria*? These Anglo-American psychologists never got further than "ego development", and thus never actually learned anything about unconscious mechanics. In everything they want to see Oedipal regression, and cannot ever point to simple dynamics like repression and displacement. In the end they aren't much better than Jungians, because all they can do is return to the same tired archetype.

For example, in discussing a clearcut case of mass hysteria in Papua New Guinea, the "Vailala Madness" of 1919, he misses the opportunity to study hysterical contagion: the much-abused natives had pseudoepileptic fits en masse – speaking in tongues, quivering, moaning, rigid and frantic by turn. Firstly it's worth noting that there essentially was no cult ideology, no metaphysics, no promise: these all came later in the form of a magic boat full of yams and the disappearance of whites. In this case the symbolic content is so fluid and weak, that the essence of repressed aggression appears in its *purer neural form*: this is classic hysteria. But what's really educational is what they called it: *iki haveve*, "belly-don't-know" – the belly being the seat of knowledge and wisdom. The Papuan theory of *repression and displacement*: the belly doesn't know what or why, but we do it anyway.

Note also that there is no other better explanation for the common cultic presence of a radical *morality of nonviolence*. Shouldn't it arouse our suspicion, when a people as thoroughly warlike as the Sioux of the late 19th century embrace wholeheartedly a pacifist doctrine? The explicit teaching of Wovoka, the last of the Ghost Dance prophets, was the distillation of postaxial morality: "Do no harm". Thus its typical juxtaposition with apocalyptic tales of supreme revenge and progressive futurism: hysterical displacement not only arises from repressed aggression, it *invests* in a condition of repression as a sustaining feedback – thus it is that mass hysteria is not merely a neurotic accident but a *functional instinct*. "The white race shall be wiped from the face of the earth"; "the capitalist pigs will burn"; "the infidel will be brought to ruin"; "the unvaccinated will be identified"... In every case "progressive politics" is only a polite name for displaced anonymous violence.

- 385 -

> Behind each God is only a paranoid messiah, the shaman and false wonderworker; he has somehow retained everyman's infantile omnipotence.
>
> *The Ghost Dance*, p.19

La Barre is not necessarily wrong in his profile of the shaman, as a regressed paranoid putting his neurosis to work with culturally sanctioned means to the acquisition of social power. However, this actually has very little to do with mass hysteria: except insofar as a *placeholder charlatan* is generally required for the maintenance of a sufficiently supple fiction. In the examination of the crisis cult, we should notice that its first instigator is almost invariably some nobody, a chronic loser with little left to lose, risking it all in his next scheme – almost every "seer" of the late dance movements among Native Americans was, upon closer inspection, merely a lazy pretender looking for the ultimate dodge – never a medicine man of the old caliber. Joseph Smith the serial conman; Adolf Hitler the shiftless bohemian; Saul of Tarsus the carpet dealer... Cultic formation is incompatible with responsible leadership, and the instincts at play will resist it: hysterical displacement requires an atmosphere of *social farce*, such that the lonely Führer and narcissistic prophet supposedly at the heart of the thing has merely been recruited from a pool of the bereft, implicitly trained to mouth the right nonsense, and fully used up by the end.

- 386 -

So far I've mostly avoided any discussion of the term "fascism" which would treat it as a limited historical phenomenon, and most emphatically avoided any purely "political" treatment, because I seek to define both terms much more anthropologically, psychologically, and with a historical envelope many times greater than is generally used: the fascist movements of the 20th century are merely a convenient example, merely a distinct and recent outbreak. I'll only stop to point out a couple features:

→ In all manifestations of what is typically called political fascism, the group began as radical leftists. In Italy this was especially clear: the movement had its ideological roots in Marxism and various forms of revolutionary socialism.

→ *Fascio* means "bundle", and was used as loosely as "union" or "party". What's worth noting, is that in every case – whether it's in Italy, Germany, Russia, or China – the fascist pattern was discovered and exploited because a small group was willing to do or say or think whatever necessary to achieve power faster than their many rivals in the midst of an atmosphere of national confusion. In every case, they each gradually discovered that the fundamental appeal of any "rivoluzione" had nothing whatever to do with its intellectual content, that any doctrine was as good as another, as long as it addressed modern alienation, modern confusion, modern *tribelessness*: what was important was that one belonged to a "bundle", that one had purpose, that one gained the right to violence against one's neighbors – that one became briefly and partially *tribal*.

Amongst my little pile of evidence, I submit a piece of some of the most beloved American television. I'm referring to *The Andy Griffith Show*, Episode 17 of Season 2, "The Jinx". The episode opens with Barney and a small group of men hanging around the barbershop. They accuse a certain man, Henry, of being such an unlucky presence as to qualify as a "jinx". He's demure, clearly not popular nor witty, perhaps an old bachelor or widower, and thus socially vulnerable. When Andy asserts it's all nonsense, Barney insists that luck and the hexing influence are "scientific fact" and employs terminology suitable to the time, like "atmospheric rays". Eventually Henry almost believes it himself, and in any case decides to leave town because of the stigma. The guys are disturbed to hear this, but the key moment comes immediately afterward: Andy confronts the group and forces them to admit that despite all their previous insistence, they *never actually believed it*. The belief they demonstrated was purely a means of ostracization.

The reason I bring all this up, is because it can be extremely difficult to demonstrate the degree to which *belief is defined by disbelief*: yet it's also such common knowledge, that it readily appears within the psychological acumen of a CBS television show of the 1960s – and what's most important to note is that all of this was therefore considered well within the comfortable understanding of the average American dope. Barney's pretense of science is apt: superstition, the scapegoat function, and *cargo cult scientificality* occur together. (Remember the witchtrial scene in "Monty Python's The Holy Grail".) Why? Because knowledge is a form of social power, and social power is what's at stake: all pretense of certainty, conviction, and "fact" are superseded by the necessity of discovering and maintaining a sufficient object of blame.

I find it a little uncanny that the writers of this episode unconsciously understood well enough what they were drawing upon, to also refer to the ceremony of *ostrakizein*: the episode is supposed to find its happy ending when the town conspires together to fake a prize drawing, in which Henry is rigged to win. Notice that the ritual means of preventing this outlier from leaving the community, is to *mark him again*: a "winner" is doubly excluded, just as a king is – Frazer was correct about that much. The excluded one which no one shall exclude: *homo sacer*, to give a nod to Agamben...

THE DARKEST HEART OF CIVILIZATION

- 388 -

It may be misleading to call it a "ritual". It would be a mistake to imagine that what's involved is any more elaborate than the *ritual of sex*: there is flirtation, suggestion, innuendo, the involvement of powerful body language, scent, eye contact; followed by foreplay, resistance, exploration, negotiation; and finally consummation and all those wonderful instinctual postures... So when I say that "everyone already understands the ritual of exclusion", I mean it in precisely the way that everyone already "understands" the ritual of sex, or the ritual of the communal meal, or the ritual of speech. These are human instincts, with beginnings, middles, and ends; with inherent tensions, inherent satisfactions, inherent significations and inherent structure. They have relatively simple aims but extremely complex means, and thus they are endlessly adaptive and responsive to time and place. They are in every culture essentially the same and yet always a little different. They can be drawn out into fantastically elaborate deferrals and sublimations involving hundreds of participants and many years; or they can be compressed and abbreviated into a hasty minute; and they can always be suggested, hinted at and invoked with subsecond flickerings in the midst of any other human activity.

Therefore to insist as I do that the *ritual of exclusion* belongs to this canon of core human behavior, something experienced and performed daily, hinted and negotiated inside every relationship, is both easy and extremely difficult. We're in danger of either believing it's too ordinary to matter or too farfetched to be valid. If I point out a thousand commonplace occurrences the reader may believe it harmless; if I stick to the big historical shocks the reader may dismiss the evidence as irrelevant to himself. To show the human creature his own *instinct for the formation of tribe*, is more difficult than revealing the ritual of sex, even in the most repressed culture: because essential to the ritual of exclusion is *plausible deniability*, anonymity, the invocation of justice. Sex may be strictly contained within the bounds of marriage and repressed beyond recall, but it does not need the name of "justice" to function. The resistance to the awareness of this instinct is therefore also part of that instinct: to become aware of it threatens its efficient function, which threatens the cohesion of tribe and thus the existence of the group itself. "They have ears so that they may not hear": in the Lacanian sense, this means that the facility to understand and respond to a symbol also precludes any other interpretive play with that symbol – otherwise it would not be "instinct".

- 389 -

Whether it was an individual or a group of individuals who committed some offense against any of the neighboring peoples, the rest of the Ik turned on their own with a remarkable and rare show of unanimity, a measure of the great value placed on this inter-tribal relationship. [...] A good example was when one-eyed Jana was setting off across the hills, not far from Pirre, and came across a stray goat. He promptly killed it, took it to where he hoped he would escape notice, cut it up and cooked it. By the time the Dodos herdsman who was looking for the stray goat found him, he had been joined by Atum, Lokeléa, Kauar, Lokbo'ok, Lomer and a few others, and the goat had been all but eaten. The usual excuses – that it had been found already dead, nobody knew to whom it belonged, and so forth – were *not* made. As soon as the Dodos appeared, Lomer, who had been keeping watch, gave the alarm. Atum and the others sprang to their feet, swallowing the last morsels, and turned on Jana, chasing him and shouting, "dzuuam, dzuuam, dzuuam!" (Thief, thief, thief!") They caught him and thrashed him soundly and then threw him at the feet of the Dodos, telling him to take Jana to the Police Post and have him sent to Kaabong to be tried.

Colin Turnbull, *The Mountain People*, p.176

There is the ritual of exclusion, naked, a little ridiculous but amply expressed: notice that the one-eyed victim is already marked with inferiority; notice that the ritual finds expression in relation to another tribe; notice that it has the power to temporarily unite an otherwise fractious and bickering people; notice that the episode has the quality of a farce with serious consequences.

It is this simple, this silly, this ubiquitous, this easily understood, this profoundly rooted in human nature and thus something that the future will reckon with many times yet. Indeed it seems that one of the symptoms of peak modernity is an overwhelming concern with exclusion: thus "toler-ance", thus "equality", thus "identity". The weaker the circles of family and tribe, the more urgently invoked this instinct, and the more zealous the moral posturing. Yet just as one first eats the stolen goat and then fingers the thief, the deliciously ironic modern twist is to center this moral posturing around *the crime of exclusion: intolerant, elitist, racist, sexist* are the charges of those who desperately need the criteria of exclusion to remain safely within the realm of moral farce. What's more, every traditional circle and ancient criterion of tribe is found to be so hostile to the program of moralized hysteria, that it's attacked as inherently criminal: and as a result, modern alienation and tribelessness deepens further, which fuels that hysterical displacement finding expression in moral pos-turing... And thus modernity crests and crashes, sustained by enormous expenditures of hysterical energy, seeking its fuller form in feedback and critical excitation paths, only to fall away again exhausted, leaving its mark on history, our institutions, our law, our body, our collective health.

- 390 -

So how does the theory of displacement supplement the theory of ritual exclusion? It's quite simple:

⇁   Granted that the human being is a tribal animal, it must have instincts which produce this social organization. The uniformity of anthropologi-cal evidence concerning our past as tribal hunters – at the absolute minimum of 400,000 years with a more likely span of 2 million – should tell us that our instincts for tribe must be strong. These instincts may be a loose assemblage, they may be difficult to identify apart from cultural inheritance, but when isolated from the continual pressure of postagri-cultural civilization, that we tend to form recognizable tribes of 50 to 100 individuals is indisputable.

⇁   Granted that displacement behavior is an important function of instinctual life, it follows that these same tribal instincts must also exist in displaced forms. Furthermore it follows that these displacements are likely to have been already folded back into an adaptive response: a frus-trated instinct is put to work in restoring the environment and resolving competition such that the original aim can be fulfilled.

"Ritual exclusion" as I've named it, is this displacement: a frustrated tribal instinct seeks to regain homeostasis by restoring the conditions in which a tribe can exist – while exploiting the instability for a promotion in personal status. Thus cult, thus religion, thus political farce, thus the universality of the scheming alarmist, the twofaced evangelist, the shrill activist: in every sizable group at almost any time, someone will have taken this position or have prepared the way to take it. Sit at the edges of a playground and watch the kids form tribal alliances, tribal strategies, tribal means to collective ends and collective means to personal ends.

- 391 -

The logic of dreams and "primary process", which seems so miraculous and otherworldly when examined in psychoanalytic terms, transposed to the instinctual domain becomes simply displacement behavior and the search for low-risk discharge channels. The linguistic faculty and the ability to handle instinctual frustration are at the earliest stage one and the same. Therefore what seems uncanny and special about this human unconsciousness, can be recognized in something as humble as the way a stickleback digs a nest as a sign of his frustrated aggression – like an angry dad mowing the lawn.

Everything remarkable about primary process is therefore what has been in place for untold millennia as the ancestral animal's ability to find and *create* a receptive niche fitting the instinctual pattern. An animal goes out into the world loaded with keys searching for the lock. What seems amazing to us in our dreams and the Freudian analysis of neurosis, is just the inexhaustible creativity of instinctual process itself. We didn't invent displacement, nor the symbol, nor neurotic distortion, nor the dream – because we did not invent instinct.

- 392 -

The final contention is that ritual exclusion is *the basal tribal instinct.* It's what makes the baboon troop organize itself into concentric circles; it's what Japanese snow monkeys are drawing on when they decide who inherits the privilege of the hot springs; it's the reason for sports fans, neckbearded subreddits, cosplay, and dressing up for church. It's part of the optimal healthy functioning of our species, with as much as right to exist as sex and friendship. It's not something which can be suppressed nor eliminated from the primate character. It's not "the root of evil". But it is problematic in modernity – much more so than mere personal aggression: because when repressed and irradiated by the invincible alienation of modernity, the formation of tribe undergoes its most frightening metamorphosis, drawing on that part of the ancient instinct most amenable to civilization – namely *plausible deniability*, becoming finally that anonymous mass violence which constitutes the darkest heart of what civilization is and can be.

- 393 -

The formation of tribe is also much more fundamental than any supposed human moral character: one can witness the emergence of this realization in my last book. Even guilt and the conscience trace their origin to group status and the frustration induced by social conformity: every postaxial psychology which wants to trace the origin of "the Good" to the atomic individual conscience, as best epitomized by that gravy-laden British philosophizing in the likes of John Stuart Mill, Jeremy Bentham, and Richard Dawkins, has been merely the posthoc revisions and polite deceptions of a helplessly upsidedown creature – or an assbackward ass to put it less mildly. Individual conscience is nothing but the internalized conflicts of the immediate group and wider culture: it's a measure of the frustration of aggression, which itself is a measure of sociality, which is for us a measure of our departure from the tribal adaptive optimum. *Every social contact entails frustration*: the tribal compromise is the halfway point, the most functional statespace attractor in a broad field of possibilities for midsize predatory vertebrates, which accounts for its commonality across so many species beyond the primates. In fact, primates are relatively new to that adaptation, which might also account for why it seems unsteady in us: were we canine, or cetacean, we might not have so much trouble with tribe.

- 394 -

Allow me to clarify. Is ritual exclusion:

⟶ The basal tribal instinct,

⁻ The displaced form of tribal instinct,

⁻ Or the consequence of the displaced and frustrated forms of many other competing instincts, which produce tribe as a side effect?

The ethological evidence points to the last and most complicated answer: according to Tinbergen, there is no "social instinct" per se, only the resultant social forms in the wake of other instinctual processes. Animals seek out others of their kind, in the vicinity of which they perform their instinctual behaviors: there is a difference in perspective there that's more than pedantic.

Therefore to call ritual exclusion the "basal tribal instinct" is after all only a shorthand, as theory always is.

- 395 -

I catch myself wanting to "prove" my thesis – as though that were possible! As though history weren't crawling with examples of ritual exclusion, as though we didn't already understand its shape, as though each of us hadn't already participated many times, and most importantly: as though assembling an airtight case would do anything but make this book tedious... Every worthwhile thesis of the humanities stumbles when it wants to prove itself. We pick examples, we demonstrate the depth and ramifications of our theory, we gather historical precedent, we cash in our erudition, and we hope that the remainder of rhetoric is sufficient to persuade the sympathetic and infuriate the opposition. Every serious opposition to a thesis like this was decided *long* in advance for reasons *deep* in unconscious reasoning among people *far* gone from our way of seeing and being: soft science is often more profoundly political than politics itself.

- 396 -

What remains to be shown, is that what I call "ritual exclusion" is a *resurgent tribal protocol* discernible at the preagricultural nomadic strata and which shows upper harmonic reflections in postagricultural civilization. What makes this plausible is the idea that ritual exclusion is itself an emergent order parameter within the tribal nomadic modality: tribes don't behave like this most of the time, only when under extreme duress. Of course it's possible to construe postagricultural civilization itself as an emergent order of a once tribal nomadic species undergoing the constraints of a runaway predatory success. Civilization drags the protocols of tribality with it, adapting what it can to the new situation: therefore *mass* ritual exclusion is a kind of second degree order parameter emergent in the new paradigm. This is not as exotic as it sounds, since for example, the chiefdom and the nationstate are themselves second and third degree reflections of the tribe, whereas the soldier is the selectively hypertrophic reflection of the warrior-hunter, and so on. The difference between the perspective I'm outlining here and the usual romantic historicizing of humankind's development away from endogenous nomadism, is that these societal structures are not considered inherently rational nor irrational, nor self-evident, nor conditioned solely as progressions to the present – as all political science has assumed up to now. They are emergent patterns, conditioned by human instinct undergoing *progressive distortion*. Although it must be simultaneously admitted that most of the series is highly *functional*, even if entailing a large cost of maladaptive friction: feudalism for example, probably being one of the most stable and longlived postagricultural modalities. But modernity is a *critical threshold*, a phase transition in which latent tribal protocols are revived and put back into service. In fact there is a kind of chaotic state-switching in realized modernity which acts as an additional feedback pushing the system toward novel channels of dissipation: the frustration generates mass panic which generates mass policing which generates more frustration. These crises will continue as long as modernity continues to seek realization: the closer we come to a humanity united in its homogeneous alienation and frustration, the more prepared the substrate is to generate novel forms of mass psychology. The last time this happened was late antiquity: a prefigurement of our own time occurred, eroded and destroyed the classical world, generated postaxial proselytizing religions, and then ebbed as the Eurasian world gradually settled into a stable feudalism. It may seem ridiculously grandiose – and perhaps it is – but the sketch I've just given would seem to indicate that this process will repeat many times yet until something changes in the human constitution such that we can make a transition to whatever comes after modernity. That process I would expect to require at least another 10,000 years.

THE BRUTALITY OF
CLOWNWORLD

I always feel when I meet people that I am lower than all, and
that they all take me for a buffoon. So I say: "Let me really play
the buffoon. I am not afraid of your opinion, for you are every
one of you worse than I am."

Dostoyevsky, *The Brothers Karamazov*, §II.2

- 397 -

S exual dimorphism is at least 600 million years old. The story of male
and female is so ancient that it predates the colonization of land by
marine life, reaching back to that point before there was even a clear distinction between animal and plant. In fact, most of the terrestrial plants
with which humanity is familiar, utilize the related strategy of heterogen-
esis. To imagine that we could subvert such an ancient force at the very
root of genetic power and the diversity of life since the Cambrian explosion, something shared between marijuana, butterflies, and jellyfish, with
merely a few years of ridiculous moral posturing and political powermongering, is so ridiculous as to be not worth mentioning. – So much for the
serious consideration of transgender rhetoric.

- 398 -

The real causes of the transgender movement are this:

⟶ The quest for an unassailable moral high ground.

⟶ A protected status which gives leave to behave badly while acquiring
social power.

➐ An identity so redundantly fortified by prestige and the histrionic display of self-realization, that it promises to banish the eternal nameless anxiety with which modernity is shot through.

The 21st century transgender movement is not about sex, and it's barely about gender. It's only about gender insofar as *gender is the weakest link* in the chain of identifiers conditioning the urban, sedentary, enfeebled body of the 21st century. Gender is the easiest point of provocation, the locale at which it's possible to stage a farcical revolution, in order to gain the gratifications of moral posturing: to pretend to be something one is not, and can never be, and then demand to be identified as such by all the world, is still sufficiently provocative to produce the illusion that one is fighting for something worth having – namely personal freedom. But all one is really doing, is baiting common sense with irritating nonsense, such that one can appear to have persecutors and enemies, such that the stage can be set for the drama of victimhood. Now one has a part worth acting out: a thousand times more socially rewarding and personally gratifying than the half-anonymous drudgery of being just-another-shmuck in a sea of shmucks – however brief this gratifying episode may last. I see very little discussion of the long aftermath: the many years after the medieval brutality of genital mutilation, after the initial shock and awe has worn away and one has run out of neighbors and friends to alienate and scold... Especially among those under 25 the longterm story must often be very ugly and sad. To encourage confused young people to transform their bodies into biological impossibilities ripe for the curio cabinet of vicarious exploitation, to leverage the *healthy response of confusion and anxiety in youth* for the production of political mascots in service of myopic and transitory social gain, strikes me as monstrously exploitative.

The brutality of transgender politics is almost equal to the cruelty of those ancient warlords who enjoyed the entertainment afforded by the castrated and disfigured. To call it "clownworld" is more true than we want to know. The origin of the "clown" is rooted deep in some of the ugliest traditions of *mutilation as entertainment.* "But we're not laughing." – But aren't you smirking? And don't you delight in the ironic cruelty of baiting what remains of human instinct, of watching the stupider half of humanity roil in outrage and bewilderment, as the smarter half winks to one another, knowing that when the fun is over the clowns will be shut away into the same dark corner where we keep child celebrities, botched plastic surgeries, old porn stars, and other discarded human biomass.

- 399 -

Is this a little dark for you? I tell you I see into the ape-heart and I know its secrets. I'm not fooled by its sanctimoniously puckered lips and feigned surprise: the wickedness and cruelty of our ancestors will find a path to daylight – not despite the moral pretenses but precisely because of them. Morality is the disguise one assumes immediately before performing something one does not otherwise have the stomach for. That's what it means to be "apesick": to be caught between one's urges to act like an ape, and one's disgust at the subterfuge required to follow that instinct. It slowly dawns on this creature what he is: the nausea of self-awareness.

- 400 -

Arguably one the reasons for the development of meditative discipline among hermits, is its effectiveness in dealing with *the nausea of self-aware-ness*. "How can I be defined by that, when I'm capable of witnessing it and feeling such repulsion?" And thus begins the ascetic quest to create a stable identity out of critique and contempt. Therefore allow me to abuse one of their most famous formulae, and say *thou art that*. What empowers the perspective I embody, is precisely the tension between critique and identification: all psychology begins and ends with self-knowledge. The ape does not want to be what he is, and in seeking the solution in disguise, posture, pathos, rhetoric, advocacy, reason, and critique, he *becomes ape*.

- 401 -

A neurosis is a containment field of personal power: a guardian spirit which once protected you against something worse than the heavy cost of neurotic behavior. Thus every neurotic entanglement is a steep contract you signed in a moment of desperation. Making shady deals with twisted spirits for the sake of protection: unfortunately that's the norm in a modern childhood, and almost no one buys their way out of that deal. What does it require? Such a spirit cannot be frightened away, wished away, nor commanded: that's precisely what qualified it as guardian. It must be *appeased*: there is always a sense in which even the most ridicu-lous neurotic distortion was, is, and will be correct. "Everything's bullshit anyway"; "no one can be trusted"; "no one really cares"; "I'll never be happy": these are all self-fulfilling prophesies, the fundamental validity of which can't exactly be disproven in even the best case. *Fake it til you make it* doesn't work with neurotic contracts: no matter how much evidence piles up in the opposing category, the conviction will remain. The neurotic spirit must be allowed a place at your table: it must be fed a little blood now and then, honored, named. After all, it is your first faithful friend: the depression he created was a warm blanket you shared together. You cannot ever leave him behind, else he will curse everything you do: he must be allowed to be correct, he must be allowed a little sacrifice of optimism, he must be allowed to shade your eyes from stupid wishfulness. There is a place for doom and gloom, there is a place for the worst, there is a sacred seat for violence and horror and a bitter end: that was the meaning of the ancient practice of sacrifice, a commonality in every culture of the world. Blood, sacred blood spilled right at the heart of the contract with life – the old ways said there was no greater mystery. Our private neuroses, our all-too-personal skirmishes with darkness, our needlessly ashamed thirst for the worst which inevitably finds its way to expression in every relationship, every squandered opportunity, every brutally flattened expectation which makes the general character of modernity seem so bleak and pointless: aren't we looking for a return to the sacred relation with death and loss? Isn't the "anxiety epidemic" a symptom of a body aching for the sobriety of pain? Aren't the endless consolation schemes and heavily medicated suppression apparati a stopped-up steamvalve that only builds the pressure?

I see both a growing acceptance of debilitating anxiety and a growing shame surrounding the thirst for the worst: it's no accident that the movies of the 21st century seem to become ever more adolescent, divorced from reality, and yet overstimulating and absurdly violent. Both cloyingly escapist and naïvely pessimistic: the "John Wick" series as example... The proliferation of the *comic book* point of view: the deferral of adulthood and its sense of responsibility for the world *as we find it* – and not as we wish it were. The proliferation of moral posturing and ridiculous politicizing belongs here also: all of it is merely *as-if* social positioning, which seeks to mine strategic advantage out of absurd fantasies no one actually believes. The great insight, which takes years to internalize, is that the ape will *gladly feign stupidity* as long as it's socially advantageous. No one actually believes that sexual dimorphism isn't an important genetic fact, for example: already the smarter actors are backing out of the extreme transgender rhetoric, seeking an unexhausted lode of moral authority...

There is my dark vision laid bare: can you stand it? He is my guardian spirit. He's right in this case: or at least, hearing his voice and following his logic is worthwhile, because no one else will go down that dark road with a cheerful knowing grin – but somehow he can. He looks at such things and laughs: the ape makes him laugh, despite how deeply he feels wounded by its wretchedness and how much he longs to admire it again. But not until he's been heard, in every gory detail, and every bit of mendacious cowardice before the truth of our situation is exposed, will he sit down and allow the overflowing heart of the singing poet to take over. So it is that the two sing together in my best moments, telling tales of tragedy and comedy, making all eyes weep like Odysseus in the house of Nausicäa...

- 402 -

Only rarely is this contemporary transgender movement concerned with anything like the mysterious power of the *heyoka*: that would require far too much personal excellence, solitude, spiritual cultivation, mojo, verve – in other words it could never apply to the mediocre majority of anxious modernity so desperate for a safe harbor. The aggression of a man united with the biological priority of a woman: a recipe for rare social power which requires a rare character. Unfortunately the current transgender fascination has almost nothing to do with the cultivation of outlandish character, and everything to do with an abuse of social contract for pathetic aims. The traditional allowance made for the sacred clown demanded that he orient his antics toward the communal wellbeing, that he become *more responsible* for everyone's sanity and health even as he threatened its norms and expectations, that he represent faithfully the thunderbeings and their power of change – but one cannot obtain this kind of power without a genuinely idiosyncratic orientation – in other words, one has to really be a strange twisted creature that's found its way toward the light and not merely a sad spectacle of imitative desperation. I fault the transgender movement not for its perversity, but its *lack of glorious perversity*: the trans population is ever more tame, invaded by dull moral actors and pedantic genderless bores the queens and queers of the 1980s would have mocked into oblivion if just for their bad taste in shoes.

- 403 -

装わぬ人の世を，人の美しさを，人の醜さを，この眼でしかと
見た。

The human world without pretense, human beauty and
ugliness, with this very eye I've seen it.

The Hidden Fortress

Again and again, Kurosawa asks this question: is humanity redeemable?
What's the balance of beauty and ugliness? Is human nature more cruel,
cowardly, and greedy than it is noble, kind, and generous? And most of
the time, he succeeds in edifying us – he shows us the worst only to contrast the best. In the hands of the artist humanity becomes an object of
informed love and pity, clarified hatred and contempt – and through his
eyes even that hatefulness becomes something we are willing to swallow
again and again... An artist may be essentially a seducer, but to be
seduced willingly and without regret is not such a bitter fate. Yet all this
only proves is that *Kurosawa* is redeemable: the rest of humanity *through
the eyes of the rest of humanity* is unlikely to be anything worthwhile!

- 404 -

When are people redeemable? When they're looking out for themselves,
when they're looking for a good time, when they're tribal and channeling
their intelligence through instinct: the hustler, the hottie, the moshpit bro
– these types are at least drawing upon *fully rational* sources of behavioral
calculation. In comparison, the cargo cult scientificality of self-conscious
late modernity, the lisping pretense to rational motive, the pathetic disguises of a fundamentally anxious creature, is all rather laughable, no?
Isn't it about time we stop taking it seriously, when an obviously desperate
but socially clever wretch takes up another posture of scientific *reason-
ableness*? Shouldn't we be quicker to spot this clown? Shouldn't it strike us
as a bad joke when another pointlessly educated dope wants praise for
boldly assuming a riskless compromise?

- 405 -

I consider the clown to be one of the most difficult archetypes of humanity. Unraveling it for myself has required the assemblage of highly diverse

psychological firepower – my indirect circular approach serves me best when addressing what we believe we already understand. At first glance, it seems easy enough to formulate: *the exaggeration of the ridiculous for the sake of social advantage*. Often the clown is simply someone for whom there is no other form of attention.

But this immediately demands a communal definition of the ridiculous, which implies that what is parodied is what the community already knows about itself. And if a society is willing to pay something in exchange, what is the service rendered?

- 406 -

We should ask a professional clown. Allow me to introduce the most articulate and enigmatic clown I know of: Jacques Lacan. I've previously compared him to that famous character from *commedia dell'arte*, that *Pulcinella*: the wily amoral protagonist, somewhat like Coyote trickster, or 孫悟空, the Monkey King from 西遊記, *Journey to the West*, or any of the dangerous old shamans of our collective past, who fooled us, inspired us, led us astray, and probably helped stitch together a feeble sanity to get us over the next icebridge, past another winter, into another generation.

- 407 -

It's probably much too complementary to say that Lacan is "the psychologist of subjectivity". Where does he really shine? Where is he not merely promoting his primped Hegelian foppery, but speaking *from experience*? When he speaks of *seduction*. Lacan, the psychologist of seduction. A theory of perversion, a theory of sexy annihilation, a theory of dominance, of endless titillation – that's what he always meant and what was understood by *désir*. Psychoanalytic metaphysics through the eyes of a sexual predator: fascinating, but not liberating.

- 408 -

Why Lacan? Because his incessant talk of "the Other" clandestinely satisfies our engorged conscience and its consequences:

⇁ By hardly speaking of anything but "Other", we seem therefore to be satisfying the demands of altruism.

⇁ By constantly discovering how gravitationally repulsive true alterity is, we are excused from our failure to practice what we preach.

⇁ By constantly discovering how annihilated and "subjected" subjectivity is, we feel understood and becalmed by a paternalistic master who makes of our embarrassing personal failures a tale of impossible universal woe.

⇁ By narrowing psychology exclusively to the scope of "self and other", "imaginary and symbolic", Lacanian thinking arms and outfits the raging yet idle narcissism of the average over-and-under-educated urban pedestrian.

With Lacan we get back the right to Spinozan systematization-procrastination and the seemingly rigorous yet largely fantastic Hegelian habit of binary thinking: in other words, philosophy as irrelevant indoor unviable system-building and vacuous talk, just like we always wanted it to be.

- 409 -

The real admirable skill of philosophers as I find them, is to have created intellectually stimulating puzzles and *ontological forms of rebellion*, without ever disturbing a single brick of the edifice of our morality and means of life: to make philosophy into nothing more than *well-mannered procrastination*.

- 410 -

There is no healing power in Lacan. Lacanian teaching seems to make a mild neurotic into a much sicker but much more fascinating creature: *self-interest is confused for self-respect*. But maybe we prefer a "venomous flower" to a just another grimacing would-be butler? I've known such cases of Lacanian conversion, all too personally: what seems to liberate them partially, is *the backdoor out of moral paralysis*. Lacanian thinking does not confront but circumvents questions of how to live, even unconsciously undermines their relevance: everything becomes a question of seduction, of repulsion and attraction, of revelation and subterfuge, of information and disinformation, of beginning over again from an imaginary beginning, and thus *never beginning at all*. To impart a sense of a fresh start, of a beautiful ignorance, of an exciting new cloud of unknowing: perhaps that's more healing than we realize? I fault it for its lack of honest confrontation and eternal procrastination – but perhaps for a time, a youthful season, this kind of autumn of fugitive love is exactly what's needed?

- 411 -

Lacanian thinking is largely Hegelian idealism under new guises: a grandiose dialectic of self and other, the subject as constituted by a mysterious interiorization, an eternally unfolding logic at the very heart of consciousness... Largely fantastic and unreal – but mesmerizing. Most students simply cannot tell that very little of it is applicable to reality: it has the charm of an articulate calculus of psychoanalysis, or the innards of that ultimate anti-metaphysics.

Even if Lacan were right about everything he says about subjectivity, it might still be irrelevant. Is this advanced study suitable to spiritual masters who have conquered everything but the essential fabrications of subjectivity itself? Or is it the *pseudologia fantastica* of a supreme showman and artist of illusion, giving us what we want? A carnival ride of the soul? Would thoroughly understanding Lacan actually lead to greater freedom and self-mastery? Or would we only continue to stand in awe of his magic? Does he seek to liberate, or *intoxicate*?

- 412 -

Lacan talks endlessly of "desire" – but what no one ever says about it, is that this desire is always only neurotic and erotic. Only a deferral, a sleight of hand, a pursuit of mirage, a mindfuck. Lacan never talks about wanting and doing in the real world because he seems not to be familiar with it: perhaps he dresses himself, perhaps he nibbles a croissant, perhaps he prepares his toilette – but someone else builds his shelter, someone else cooks the food, someone else carts away his various messes. Nowhere in any of this fashionable psychology is the analysis of what it takes to *do* something big and real and difficult: the tension of yearning, the breakthrough of vision, summoning the courage to try, assessment of resources, preparation of material, assembling of parts, the recklessness required to begin, endurance of minor failure and oversight, repetition, the long will to see it through, the patience for the drawn out end, the polishing stage, inevitable disappointment, learning to move on and begin again.

How telling must it be, that Lacan did not seem to have the endurance to write books, but preferred to merely *talk endlessly*?

Lacan seems not to be able to analyze even his own realized ambition as preeminent psychoanalyst of Paris: what did it really take to get there? Was it all along a seductive game of neurotic deferral? Or did it take some *cojones* and more than a little reckless scorn? Where is the analysis of healthy youthful scorn? At least half of what is really accomplished in this world is powered as much by *contempt* as "desire".

- 413 -

Il y a pourtant une autre formule, qui, si elle ne démontre pas mieux son efficace, ce n'est peut-être que pour n'être pas articulable, mais ça ne veut pas dire qu'elle ne soit pas articulée, c'est « *Je te desire, même si je ne le sais pas* ». Partout où elle réussit, toute inarticulable qu'elle soit, à se faire entendre, celle-là, je vous l'assure, est irrésistible. Et pourquoi? Je ne vous laisserai pas ceci à l'etat de devinette. Si ceci était dicible, qu'est-ce que je dirais par là? Je dis à l'autre que, le désirant sans le savoir sans doute, toujours sans le savoir, je le prends pour l'objet à moi-même inconnu de mon désir, c'est-à-dire, dans notre conception à nous du désir, que je l'identifie, que je t'identifie, toi à qui je parle, toi-même, à l'objet qui te manque à toi-même. C'est-à-dire que par ce circuit, où je suis obligé pour atteindre l'objet de mon désir, j'accomplis justement pour lui ce qu'il cherche.

There is another formula, which if it does not demonstrate any better its effectiveness, it is perhaps only because it is not articulatable, but that does not mean that it is not articulated. It is, *"I desire you, even if I do not know it"*. Wherever it succeeds, however inarticulatable it may be in making itself heard, this one, I assure you, is irresistible. And why? I will not leave this as a riddle for you. If this were sayable, what would I be saying by it? I would be saying to the other that by desiring him without knowing it, still without knowing it, I take him as the object of my desire unknown to myself, namely in our conception of desire that I identify him, that I identify you, you to whom I am speaking, you yourself, as the object which is lacking to yourself. Namely that by this circuit that I have to take to reach the object of my desire, I accomplish precisely for him what he is looking for.

Séminaire X: L'Angoisse, §II

I've figured it out: Lacan modeled his teaching based on what he learned as an analyst: you only need to appear enigmatic, aloof, and not one but ten steps ahead at all costs – and the patient will do all the real work. Do not encourage clarity: employ the power of misunderstanding, of sudden reversals and revelations, of the unexpected. Lacan understood the power of *perversity* to inspire a sense of freedom and the illusion of exponential personal growth. He understood the power of *seeming to be what the other wants*. Cogency, empathy, and explanation are antithetical to fostering this illusion: the idea is to remain out of reach, yet so near. In fact sometimes so much more near than one ever expected – cheeks grazing.

Lacan *did* understand neurotic desire: this much must be granted. He is practically the prophet of intellectual seduction. But does any of this have any healing power? Or is it only an impressive narcotic – and a narcotic only for the hopelessly neurotic? Is its seductive power dependent on neurosis and does it therefore encourage and deepen the neurotic condition? Does Lacan secretly whisper in our ear that there is no escape from the ouroboros of eros? Is Lacanian thinking in the final analysis only another poisoncraft to be appreciated from a safe distance?

I would add that if one employed psychology only to seduce intelligent young women looking for the intersection of the intellectual and the sexual – one could find no better master. But to lure earnest young men into this labyrinth, to encourage this eternal swirl of the elusive, this indulgent dance of veils that does not yield to suppertime, this heady perfumery of the intellect – I cannot but find this deeply irresponsible.

- 414 -

I don't think Lacan at first, or ever, knew how or why his teachings were so compelling. To have known it would have broken the spell. I think he stumbled or intuited his way toward his seduction technique: I think he knew how to read an audience.

It's not Lacan himself I find objectionable. In fact there is a certain amoral atmosphere about him I appreciate. He mocks perhaps more than he teaches. I can sympathize with the delicate exigencies and risks of embitterment the *stage performer* must navigate: flirtation with hatred of the audience is not merely a degeneracy among rock stars but a necessity for all profound actors. Marlon Brando once said that acting was an occupation unfit for a real man. One is faced with either despising oneself for the falsification, or despising them for believing it, or finding a precarious beyond in the role of the mocking fool.

One can see that Lacan's charm has at times worked on me, also: as a "metrosexual" I was in the past more at risk of infatuation. But I've become much more wary: it's the way the icon of Lacan is used, that nauseates. *Lacan the dildo...*

- 415 -

L'animal – vous dis-je – efface ses traces et fait de fausses traces. Fait-il pour autant, des signifiants? Il y a une chose que l'animal ne fait pas: il ne fait pas de traces fausses pour nous faire croire qu'elles sont fausses. Il ne nous fait pas de traces faussement fausses, si je puis dire, ce qui est un comportement, je ne dirai pas essentiellement humain, mais justement essentiellement signifiant. C'est là qu'est la limite. Vous m'entendez bien : des traces faites pour qu'on les croie fausses et qui sont néanmoins les traces de mon vrai passage, et c'est ce que je veux dire en disant que là se présentifie un sujet, quand une trace a été faite pour qu'on la prenne pour une fausse trace, là nous savons qu'il y a, comme tel, un sujet parlant, et là nous savons qu'il y a un sujet comme cause et la notion même de la cause n'a aucun autre support que celui-là.

The animal effaces his traces and makes false traces. Does he for all that make signifiers? There is one thing that the animal does not do: he does not make false traces in order to make us believe that they are false. He does not make falsely false traces, which is a behaviour, that I would not say is essentially human, but essentially signifying. That's where the limit is. Understand me: traces made so that one believes them to be false and which are nevertheless the traces of my true passing – and this is what I mean by saying that here a subject is presentified. When a trace has been made in order that one should take it to be a false trace, then we know that there is a speaking subject as such, and we know then that there is a subject as cause and the very notion of cause has no other support than this.

Séminaire X: L'Angoisse, §V

Because I live in the high desert of North America, in the warm months I must be vigilant when walking through the brush: rattlesnakes are always in the back of my mind. There are periods when I encounter one daily. In the meantime I've learned something important about camouflage. Camouflaged shape and color can be more of a *signal* than is realized: it is sometimes the *unsign*, the false deadend, the preparatory inducement to false negative.

Would it be so difficult for a rattlesnake to produce a more subtle and less diagrammatic coloration? Moths and grasshoppers achieve this – as does the praying mantis, to pick a predator. Or is the crisp geometry of their patterns designed not to hide precisely, but to *induce excess hallucination in the search function*? Think about the jagged black diamonds on a pale background: doesn't this look suspiciously like the errors and artifacts of the visual cortex? What I have found through the last few years of anxious experimentation, is that trying to find a rattlesnake slowly makes you worse at recognizing it, because you have been infected by a hallucinatory gestalt. I have at times looked directly at one without seeing it, before it suddenly decided to reveal itself. Rattlesnakes hide between layers of neuronal signal processing, disguised as errata.

Why tiger stripes? Partly to break form and blend with leafy shadows, but also because they mesmerize, because they induce mild trance in the midst of a terror ripe for trance. Therefore much predatory camouflage does not merely conceal, but inspires *preliminary hallucination* in the search for it – and thus sufficient false positives to induce doubt: when the moment finally arrives, you hesitate.

But it was Lacan who gave me the additional clue, despite his ignorance of ethology. In spotting a hypnoid camouflage you have spotted a *falsely false trace.*

- 416 -

La trace faussement fausse: this is also *the mask of irony*. The primary means of confession in modernity is to reveal oneself through mockery of what one is, seeking to erase its traces even while exploiting its position. The clown says: "Because I wear the clownface, I am less clown than you." Consider the arrogance of those comedians whose career hinges on emphasizing their own neurosis: Louis C.K., for example.

This is the typical strategy of the openly neurotic and half-therapized: to achieve an unassailable position as simultaneously compassionate enough to see dysfunction in everyone, yet reserve the right to bad behavior as long as it can be diagnosed. Yet another reason why the proliferation of psychotherapy tends to only *deepen neurotic investment*...

The real purpose of intellectual sophistication in the modern subject is *smoke and mirrors*. To set up so many false positives along the way, so many *parodies of neurosis*, that the real neurosis remains hidden among the arsenal and one begins to believe that all traces are false: that there is no human nature. That we are thus "free": this is the meaning of French post-structuralism and postmodernity generally – hence the conspicuous usage of "post-". The final triumph is to hide the shameful secret in plain sight: to seem to be proud of one's weakness, to even convince two thirds of oneself that one is proud of it, to build a personality around this pretense! That is the urban intellectual manchild perfected.

- 417 -

To make compulsive insincerity a strategic advantage. To feign irony so frequently that sincerity merely seems like bad taste or poor acting. To disguise profound serious nihilism with a shallow cosmopolitan nihilism: imitative cynicism as a social maneuver. To induce misrecognition via a saturation of the signal of falseness: thus to hide in plain sight. To exhaust the native sense for bullshit by total collusion and barraging of the communicative channel, so that one may sneak right in the front door. A premature and purely mimicked irony concerning oneself which induces the nausea of a world of as-if, whose function is to blunt the power of recognition by preceding it with falsely false names.

The normative state with us is to be a liar thoroughly in form and essence, yet so well conformed to the time and place, that one is mistaken for "more genuine than genuine". One could just as easily analyze Jerry Seinfeld this way, as Socrates: modernity is not "new", and the pretense to novelty is only a symptom of degeneracy.

- 418 -

Das »Geträumte« des Traumes soll wiederum entwertet, seiner Realität beraubt werden; was nach dem Erwachen aus dem »Traum im Traume« weiter geträumt wird, das will der Traumwunsch an die Stelle der ausgelöschten Realität setzen.

What is "dreamt" in the dream is devalued and robbed of its reality. What is dreamt in a dream after waking from the "dream within a dream" is what the dream-wish seeks to put in the place of an obliterated reality.

Freud, *Die Traumdeutung*, §VI.C

I'm beginning to understand that the dream and mechanisms of the dream, can and should be employed to understand *social behavior*: all purely social behavior is *as if*. This is not necessarily to disparage sociality, only to point out why it is so susceptible to economies of deception: to see it any other way, is to risk disparaging everything about the human creature which is *irresistibly genuine*.

Therefore what happens when an essentially fictional behavioral set contains an avowed element of fiction? *Truth appears*. This is the meaning of "in vino veritas", the "play within a play", and why I consider television and the circus to be such valuable sociological sources: under the aegis of fiction and the protection of apparent negation, we begin to tell the truth.

- 419 -

So how do I watch for rattlesnakes? By practicing *alertness without consciousness*. The solution is to attenuate apperception at the center and rely on peripheral resolution, at all costs avoiding preemptive visualization. Don't think about it, don't prepare, only keep the perceptual surface clean of debris: I usually react to a snake before I have become conscious of it. The lesson for us is this: the falsely false trace relies on an excess of consciousness to succeed. The ironic clown requires an audience which *wants to believe it already knows*: there is a profound and disturbing connection between the scientific revolution and the proliferation of ironic actors, as the Greek renaissance demonstrated so well – Socrates was only another hipster-sophist pretending not to know...

- 420 -

What does Lacan represent? *The freedom of the mask.* The freedom of someone who has discovered he is too clever to be caught, that his gift of unflappable gab can get him out of any jam, and that by acting masterly he becomes master. It's extremely telling that Noam Chomsky called him a "conscious charlatan": does anyone else sense envy in that phrase? Is he telling us it's against the rules to be *conscious* about one's farce? That is indeed the sense Lacan gives us: his game is so obvious, so upfront that we convince ourselves it can't possibly be the truth: Lacan hides in plain sight. The purloined letter in Lacanian teaching reads: *it's all bullshit.* But the fact that he gets away with it, that everyone loves it, that the audience applauds and sits with open mouths scribbling his every word – that's the real lesson in studying Lacan: *all the world's a stage.*

- 421 -

He's thrilled to be fooling us all on multiple levels: too many levels to have been conscious of. Chomsky was wrong again, as always: Lacan was the ultimate *unconscious* charlatan. To the degree that he was conscious of it, was only mask, mockery, deflection – which is why someone like Chomsky feels so insulted.

- 422 -

It's unfortunate that Lacan was so irresponsible with his insights. For example, he was right to point us psychologists toward projective geometry: it's one of the crucial aspects of the method of the masters to understand that in the morphology of psychic phenomena, some relationships are *invariant*, others are not. Nietzschean thinking often revolves around this insight, and takes delight in shifting perspectives in order to watch the play of variance – in order to eventually hint at what *does not change.*

Entwining pure math with psychoanalysis is just too tantalizing. But Lacan lacked not only the intellectual conscience, but the assiduousness to see it through. And this is not all that prevented Lacan from reaching serious depth: as is typical of the latin lover, his levity extends only so far as his vanity permits. He cannot afford to ever admit to being a *goof.* The result is a nonchalance which is a mask for how terribly seriously he takes himself.

- 423 -

I believe that with "la faussement fausse trace" I've drawn out the best and worst of Lacan in a single stroke. I also feel I've fulfilled my obligation to him by demonstrating both his genius and his deviousness. Lacan himself is the purloined letter of postmodern philosophy: he is exactly what you hope he isn't. And in the tension between your better judgment and your desire, he reveals your weakness. That *you* feel exposed and in risk of coming up short, is only the same tired gag of every fashionmonger and friseur. "You're nobody without these trinkets": nearly every success in postmodern philosophy has been predicated on conspicuous consumption. Which explains why Lacan is so popular with art students and film critics, and so unpopular with establishment psychiatry: the psychiatrists didn't want sexy bullshit they can't keep up with, they wanted a dullard's taxonomy. To bore your rivals out of the competition, to secure authority and the illusion of knowledge through impenetrable dullwittedness... To the precise degree that psychoanalysis was able to become dull, it has been absorbed by establishment psychiatry.

- 424 -

Lacan is the pinnacle of the French style in psychology: one must appreciate how much that style owed to the novelists and playwrights to understand the statement. His fluency in unconscious mechanics, the ease by which he deals with the uncanny, the way he is able to convincingly paint anxiety, paranoia, and seeming-to-be...

But Lacan lacks an intellectual conscience: this also cannot be denied. The most flattering way of accounting for this lack, is to say that he had to sacrifice our expectation of coherence in service of what is not necessarily very intelligible and certainly not *expected*. He says this more or less somewhere: "why should we expect the truth to be intelligible?"

Lacan has in the end only accelerated the decline of psychoanalysis. Like a belligerent rightwing commentator confirming the prejudices of the left, he confirms what the stodgy reluctant psychiatrist wanted to believe about the whole of the field: that it was fashionable nonsense from the beginning. Klein, Bion, Lacan, and not to even begin to mention Jung – not only failures to continue the discipline of Freudian thinking, but effective examples of why this discipline cannot succeed on any scale.

But with these failures I've come to understand something about this "soft science" which is not commonly known. Physics and mathematics are usually regarded as the finest expressions of science: but are we ready to admit that these are the fields in which the scientific attitude requires the *least* emotional maturity? *Psychology is the toughest test of the scientific spirit*: no other project of knowledge forces you to gamble your self-respect, your worldview, your loves and hates, your sanity. In no other science are you so at risk of becoming a clown.

- 425 -

Allow me to demonstrate again what a *hostile takeover of evolutionary psychology* might look like. What's the origin of this unique primate ability to laugh? Firstly, it's important to dwell on the image of monkeys in the trees, screeching and gesturing at you from above: you understand what they mean by this. Consider the squirrel who won't stop chattering at you when you come too close to its cache: what do you feel? Irritation, a little embarrassment maybe – annoyingly witnessed. Laughter is the arboreal technique for dealing with threat: to make a fuss, sound the alarm, emphasizing distance and unreachability, so that superior firepower feels diminished or at least irritated enough to leave. The important factor distinguishing it from a simple alarm call, such as prairie dogs or chickens make, is this factor of irritation through unreachability: "You can't get me, and I know you want to". In other words, because taunting deters leopards, we developed laughter. Therefore who is the clown and why is he universally granted a place of ambivalent honor? Is he the first one to laugh, or is he the one who causes us to laugh, making us feel safe again? Is he the parody of a threat – the threat of self-awareness, *the threat of the mirror*? By containing, exaggerating, and mocking our potential for self-consciousness, the community feels relieved: the leopard of exposed ape-nature has retreated again... Which would mean that the real function of comedy is to *suppress self-recognition*. An abject fool even the lowest slob can feel superior to: one could learn something by measuring the average social distance any audience wants between itself and its clowns – close enough to know people like that, but far enough that the thought, "he's better than me" never occurs. Does the successful sitcom need to toy with identification of the average loser just long enough to discharge self-recognition? Or is merely shining the spotlight on the mediocre enough to pique vanity, and thus forestall any awakening? This gets filed under everything I wish sociology actually was.

- 426 -

The clown's relationship to ritual exclusion: instigator, lure, or scapegoat? Perhaps all of them at once. But it's certain that the clown satisfies the need to find someone within the group to exclude: the clown is almost a parody of ritual exclusion, as though for the edification and sanity of the community. Look carefully at *Emmett Kelly*: the hobo, the sad loner, the ne'er-do-well. He not only knew what a post-depression era crowd wanted to see mocked, he understood something more about the function of clowning. In his most famous bit, he would stand dejected in the center ring with a broom, and act as though it were his job to *sweep up the spot-light*. The lazy loser who just wants to escape notice, pursued and plagued by attention. He tries to splatter it, scatter it, and diminish it, but it sneaks after him – which especially seemed to delight the crowd. Eventually he sweeps it under the rug: identification and exclusion has been deferred... We can't doubt that in the most direct and universally appealing forms of comedy, the indelible logic of apenature appears: a shadowplay like this is much more ingenious than it may seem.

- 427 -

It's certain that the clownface was originally designed to make facial expressions more visible at a distance, just as most early forms of makeup in showbusiness. But immediately something else is invoked: the face of

357

the ape ancestor, with his big expressive lips, his ringed eyes, his upturned nose. The clown is what Homo sapiens knows it is and needs to pretend it is not. This was clearly also involved in *blackface*: the "minstrel show" as one of the uglier examples of ritual exclusion – or its parodic discharge.

- 428 -

Why is the mime universally hated by good taste? Because it's an abuse of the clown-contract: the mime proceeds in the direction of the clown, and at the last moment wants to be taken seriously. He wants the recompense of a comedian, but rather than laugh at his parody he asks us to invest all the more: he only thrives where a sufficient baseline irony already exists, where good comedy is impossible anyway – in other words, among the insufferable.

- 429 -

Why is the clown so often ugly? Because he seeks a position lower than the average. Because when creating something everyone can laugh at, free of envy, ugliness helps.

- 430 -

Why is the clown frightening? In the "whiteface" type especially, there are echoes of the social predator. Whenever a stunted, twisted reject chooses to occupy himself with children, the community should beware. Whenever undeveloped adults attempt to relate to kids, the result is always the same: they parody stupidity and limitation, rather than drawing on innocence and potential – *Mr. Rogers* and "Barney" versus *Sesame Street* and Jim Henson generally. But the clown proper has nothing to do with children: it's about the failures of adult life, the sad absurdities they are subject to, and their need to feel at least better than the worst. That children are afraid of clowns is to be expected: subjecting them to it is only a cruel whim, an insult to childhood as some kind of preemptive failure. The clown as *failed child*: now we've tunneled back into the heart of ape cruelty, and discovered what it finds entertaining.

- 431 -

Here I turn again to anthropological testimony. I would like to recommend Colin Turnbull's classic, *The Mountain People*: as emotionally difficult a piece of anthropology as they come. Whereas he was blamed for idealizing the Pygmies in his previous work, here he's been accused of demonizing: the Ik people he did not love – in fact they taught him to unlearn love. If the Pygmies showed him innocent goodness, the Ik showed him *innocent malice*. He confronted the reality of a dying tribe, as many anthropologists have: but what was perhaps unique was the recency and suddenness of the transition from nomadic hunters to sedentary villagers. The result was a disruption and displacement of morality which is rarely so visible.

> So we gave her more food and made her eat and drink all we could, put her stick in her hand and pointed her the way she wanted to be pointed, and she suddenly cried. Thinking she was afraid or wanted us to go with her, I asked, and she said no; she was crying, she said, because all of a sudden we had reminded her that there had been a time when people had helped each other, when people had been kind and good. Still crying, she set off.

> The Ik up to this point had been tolerant of my activities, but all this was too much, combined with the fact that my colleague established a dispensary where he treated old people as well as young, but gave food only to the old. Openly critical of this waste of effort and food and medicine, the Ik said that what we were doing was wrong. Food and medicine were for the living, not the dead. But the old continued to come, the few who were left, not in the hopes of being kept alive, but so that they could go off quietly and die a little more comfortably. Then I thought of Lo'ono – that incredibly wrinkled old face, the sightless eyes peering as though they could still, with a struggle, see, and then those sudden, frightening tears of anguish at a memory that had been better forgotten. And I thought of other old people who had joined in the merriment when they had been teased, knocked over or had a precious morsel of food taken from their mouths. They knew that it was silly of them to expect to go on living, and, having watched others, they knew that the spectacle really was quite funny. So they joined in the laughter. Perhaps if we had left Lo'ono, she would have died laughing, happy that she was at least providing her children with amuse-

ment. But what did we do? We prolonged her misery for no more than a few brief days, for although Longoli did let her into his compound, he took her food and gave her neither food nor water. Even worse, we reminded her of when things had been different, of days when children had cared for parents and parents for children. She was already dead, and we made her unhappy as well. At the time I was sure we were right, doing the only "human" thing. In a way we *were* – we were making life more comfortable for ourselves, confirming our own sense of superiority. But now I wonder. In the end I had a greater respect for the Ik, and I wonder if their way was not right, if I too should not have stood with the little crowd at the top of the *oror* and laughed as Lo'ono flapped about like a withered old tortoise on its back, then left her to die, perhaps laughing at herself, instead of crying.

The Mountain People, p.228

- 432 -

One must have courage to read *The Mountain People* with an open mind, and even more so an open heart. It's quite palpable and even familiar, what Turnbull felt in those years: it's the disappointment and bitterness of our worst moments, when life seems like a cruel joke played out for no one – when we suspect that we have been the *chump* all along, and that nothing was ever going to turn out differently than this final indifferent contempt. For most of us, only a scathing lifelong affliction of neurosis will ever teach us to feel this way: that no one cares, that even you cannot afford to care, that not only are you alone because no one else will be with you, but because you have abandoned yourself also...

> [...] the quest for morality seemed increasingly pointless. It was yet another luxury that we find convenient and agreeable and that has become conventional when we can afford it, but which, in times of stress, can and should be shucked off, like religion and belief and law and family and all sorts of other appendages that become hindrances at such times.
>
> p.230

Turnbull found out how shallow human virtue is, that familial bond and loyalty are luxuries, that the human creature makes accurate calculations of personal advantage at every turn, and will exploit every opportunity to seek the slightest gain. He found out that morality is a shadow puppetry, because the human being can live without it, because when it is no longer advantageous, it is shed entirely rather than adroitly shifted in a politically safer direction. His book is a chronicle of a *forcible disillusionment* with the human character: it would never have happened to a such a nice and well-meaning man without such extreme and prolonged exposure to a tribe at the edge of annihilation.

But we are mistaken to say: "Here is human nature revealed", as though an emergency protocol sufficiently expressed the entirety. The human nature we're looking for is not a core essence of selfishness which resists some other virtuous force called altruism – there is no tidy binary relation between "altruism and selfishness" as has been propagated by sneaky priests hoping to inspire malleable stupidity in the wake of that teaching. Rather what we're looking at is a layered series of functional modes, each with their adaptive value: a chain of metastabilities along several dimensions stretching from stress to ease and back again. Cruelty to kindness, violence to peace, loyalty to treachery, lies to truth: each have their place, their function, their time, their reason for being. And each will negotiate with the other to achieve expression in any moment: every gesture, every word, every emotion is a compromise with everything the human creature has evolved to be ready for. What the Ik were forced to become, is what humanity has been forced to become many times before: to capitalize on the worst of apenature in order to ensure another day and another chance. If they are devious, cold, and vicious it is because *these are virtues* in the canon of ape behavior: it's their *genuine innocent happiness* in the midst of cruelty that seemed to disturb Turnbull the most – that laughter could be so sweet when inspired by pain and death. But mocking laughter is almost a "metavirtue" accompanying all others: it's a sign that the ape believes in itself and its future. There is no essential bond between innocent laughter and moral innocence: that's a vertiginous lesson cutting right into the heart of apenature.

Therefore what's most instructive about this book to me, is not so much the Ik themselves but to watch Turnbull spiral and divest himself of his illusions. Piece by piece, he learns to find the part of himself reflected in the cruelty and indifference of the Ik. The ledgerbook of his soul shrinks by the day, as he concedes more and more territory to an exposed moral posturing and finds himself more honest but seemingly less substantial than before: moral outrage is a swelling, a bluff which conceals lack of resolve. So much of what people fear in a supramoral perspective is that *nothing will remain*: but this is only the fear of a balloon-spirit, a gasbag, and the reality is that so much more subtlety and sweet emotional valence lies waiting in the aftermath of the grotesque posturing of moral defenses. There's also no essential enmity between cold calculation and gentle affection: a successful hardass can afford such delicacies.

- 433 -

The beautiful human, like the beautiful body, seems to be a myth perpetuated by the game of self-deceit, at which humans are so singularly adept. In fact, after even a few months with the Ik one is tempted to think that if there is such a thing as a basic human quality, self-deception it is.

p.33

It is ugly because one expected to find something else. One expected to find a pantomime of the social virtues: a *good people* will respect your fears, your fragile ego, your sense of fairness, your sentiments and consolations. A *bad people* will reveal the shallow and transitory nature of your own virtues, and laugh at you for them.

- 434 -

Even *reciprocal altruism*, that overfed brat of anthropology, doesn't survive the experience:

These are not expressions of the foolish belief that altruism is both possible and desirable; they are weapons, sharp and aggressive, which can be put to divers uses. [...] The object, of course, is to build up a whole series of obligations so that in times of crisis you have a number of debts you can recall, and with luck one of them may be repaid.

p.146

But this is merely the unconscious social calculations which the human creature performs at all times, in all circumstances: here it's merely naked.

The Ik are merely *more naked* than humanity usually is: their greed, their pettiness, their vicious delights, their incessant scheming, their shallow emotion, their transitory alliances – these are usually the "foibles" our storytellers and psychologists go to great pains to reveal in the everyman, peeling back the many layers of flattering clothes. These vices are usually the crux of a gaudy morality play, or the butt of a racist joke, or just the more obvious sins of a wretched gossiping old woman, or a greedy old fart, or a spoilt child: but to find it at the heart of everything a society is, to suspect as Turnbull seems to, that these calculations are in fact *the definition of sociality itself* – that is a brave first step, and yet also *still too naïve.* Cynicism is the naïveté of the disappointed. It's the interplay between flattering costume and ugly motive that defines human sociality still more: without the polite lies and deferential mutual deception, it would not be human society. And who's to say that our beautiful illusions don't have just as much validity? When we dance in concert and mime the rituals of a virtue we don't possess, don't we come almost as close to the possession of those virtues as to the dispossession of them?

Therefore it's not so much "altruism" which the Ik have been forced to abandon under stress, but *vanity.* The most adept social maneuverers are always on the lookout for those two most reliable handles of primate psychology: greed and vanity. If it were only greed at play, there would be no recourse in negotiation and the stalemate would result too often: the salesman must have something else to appeal to. The ape also needs *social greed* alongside his impeccable material greed to function as a group: in other words, it's the foible of vanity that makes us good neighbors.

- 435 -

Turnbull summarizes the Ik childhood:

> [...] that is the *rite de passage,* the destruction of that fragile bond called friendship. When this has happened to you three or four times you are ready for the world, knowing friendship for the joke it is.

p.137

But this is just *ghetto logic* – this short ride "from the bullied and beaten to the bully and beater". It seems clear to me that he could have done the same study in the worst neighborhood of 1980s Detroit, or 1930s Shanghai, or Soviet Moscow, or a supermax prison in Alabama. Turnbull's book is after all only the record of a remarkably brave but still very naïve *clean boy* coming to grips with some hard truths, in his own scholarly, heavily moralized way – something Bartholomy would know about. He makes a few feeble attempts at academic detachment, but has too much honesty in concert with so much violent exposure to sustain it: he admits the defeat of his conscience, his worldview, his prejudices. It is the process of this defeat which is interesting and instructive.

- 436 -

It's clear that in a more embedded historical context Turnbull's study would not have cornered his moralizing naïveté so effectively: it's always possible to blame "society", or the institution, or economics, or whatever other name one finds convenient. And in the case of the Ik we blame politics and hunger: but there was something about their situation perched on their mountain, largely autonomous, almost enjoying their own slow demise, refusing to learn another solution that cut into Turnbull's tender heart and showed him "all the bestiality I ever want to see".

- 437 -

It's important to remember that Turnbull was an Oxford-educated British boy: suddenly all the shock-and-awe and the drawn out self-absorbed moralizing makes more sense. If he had been an American of the mid 20th century, perhaps Brooklyn-born, he might have attempted instead to jive with the Ik – to already be that cool, unconcerned, a true realist. And we would have lost this useful confrontation between Western cultivated naïveté and instinctual necessity.

- 438 -

While they still retain the quaint old-fashioned notion that man should share with his fellows, they place the individual good above all else and almost demand that each get away with as much as he can without his fellows knowing.

p.101

364

Its likely that even at the height of their functional nomadic days, Turnbull would have found the morality of the Ik difficult to accept: they clearly possessed the harsh pride of the hunter and the political cunning of the nomad. It seems that by being thrust directly into sedentary life, this naked pride of the hunter found itself most compatible with the shameless exploitation of the village lout: and thus the Ik began hunting each other. The cold heart toward the young and old that once kept their lineages strong enough to handle the herds of the African steppe, now seemed merely cruel and thoughtless.

- 439 -

And as is clear from the preface composed in the aftermath, he found a way to escape his own insight – scathed, wiser, but again foolishly wishful where his wisdom could not grow:

> In spite of it all, and contrary to the first tidal wave of disillusionment, it has added to my respect for humanity and my hope that we who have been civilized into such empty beliefs as the essential beauty and goodness of humanity may discover ourselves before it is too late.

- 440 -

All that remains to the Ik is mockery, derision, the misfortune of others. The finest and most unique weapon of apenature remains to the end: without laughter, the human race could not have convinced itself to press through the unimaginable bottlenecks of the last 2 million years. What I'm terming "clownworld" is therefore only a resurgence of this core adaptive strategy in the midst of cultural decay: to find someone more ridiculous than oneself, to *manufacture* someone – an angry dwarf, a mutilated child, a sanctimonious eunuch, a half-man half-woman sacrificial object, carried aloft to the highest temple... Praise and glory are prelude to that communal sacrifice which justifies and perpetuates even the most corrupt and dissatisfied social sphere.

- 441 -

That the human race is a making a fool of itself is no accident and not merely a result of its social desperation. Just as I see calculated risk mitigation in gullibility and willful stupidity, so in the grotesque clownfaces of moral posturing I see a deeper unconscious stratagem. Not only to make the world uglier, and thus flatter, and thus more navigable, and not only to induce the atmosphere of farce such that the terms of social negotiation remain safely within one's powers of imitation, but also to draw out disgust and dismay from those in whom *aesthetics retains the compulsion of instinct* – in order to identify, isolate, and target them. The nausea induced by the moral clown is part of the targeting system of anonymous mass violence. They exaggerate precisely those traits they know you cannot stand: partly as a form of short-term revenge, but more profoundly in the hopes of eliminating all destabilizing forms of clarity and beauty. This is one of the deeper motivations for the epidemic of obesity, for aggressive cultivated ugliness, and general slovenliness in the lower classes – alongside the hyperbolic demonstrations of morality in the upper classes: they seek to know *who cannot withstand ugliness*. This isn't a particularly new arrangement, and I could probably have made the same observations in postrevolutionary France, as Stendhal did.

- 442 -

When surprised by an unexpected scrutiny, people often behave *worse* than usual – not merely as an expression of nerves and self-sabotage, but as a means of regaining control. When people feel judged for their wretchedness, they often seek to provoke *yet more* disgust in order to find a commonality at the lowest possible level. At the moment you feel infected, they say: "You are no different."

- 443 -

And we have to admit, there's an entanglement between our attitude of superiority and their cultivated ugliness: who's the clown? Who's confused about essential human nature? By splitting and projecting its extremes, we have made the problem seem insoluble: one side judges moral posturing for its ugliness and hypocrisy but requires its haughty mien; the other mocks the judge but would like his right to rule. And both get what they want at the cost of their better judgment: the result is the well-known arrangement wherein the unconscionable hypocrite achieves rule by deepening his cynicism into nihilism, while the conscientious objector achieves haughty critique by repressing his moral skepticism and risking hypocrisy – and around we go, blurring one into the other.

- 444 -

He looked me straight in the eye as he carefully said, "They are burning a man for incest." I think he was looking for some kind of reaction that he could exploit, but I merely felt a mild interest and asked if they would burn him dead.

p.262

The connection between clownworld and the Ik: they're hoping to catch you in a moment of genuine moral outrage, so that they may laugh at your naïveté, your credulity, and maybe your hypocrisy. By spending the currency of self-contradiction so blatantly, by exposing his own hypocrisy so flagrantly, the clown hopes to evoke moral outrage – to find a point of compulsion, which is a point of weakness. Anything non-negotiable is a point of weakness in social terms: *morality is always laughable* – this has never been far from awareness in human history, despite appearances.

- 445 -

It's long been my intuition that hidden in the clown is a form of wisdom which defeats all others. That the clown represents the end of wisdom, or its penultimate. There the problem of desire is supposedly overcome. Desire within the project of knowledge always threatened to reduce every discovery to wishful conclusion, vanity, premature enlightenment. By seeming to resign to foolishness, the holy fool obtains that which was not his to begin with. When I was on Mount Athos in my early twenties, I traveled with a young Russian monk who was visiting one of those saints-in-the-making, a special recluse. The resulting scene was as Dostoyevskian a moment as I've ever known. I remember how he greeted us: he stuck his bulbous nose through the fence and asked what the hell we wanted. When my earnest companion became obsequious and desirous of his wisdom, this wicked old man spoke only to his donkey, making a show of lavishing attention and affection on the perhaps equally confused creature. I've been taken in many times by pretenders to wisdom, but in this case I felt I saw through the whole farce: this old man was very skillful at pinpointing the arrogance and ridiculous attitudes of his supplicants, and I felt his mockery was justified. But I didn't feel he had much more than that, and allowing his disciples to believe there was a great wisdom hidden behind the jokes, was a form of dishonesty. Claiming not to have it, they believe you have it all the more. The ape who mocks the ape seems to transcend apenature, despite utilizing at least two key features of that nature: mockery, and the *falsely false trace*. The holy fool isn't genuinely holy because he's a false fool, he's a genuine scoundrel because he's doubly false. Those who seek human wisdom are fools, and those who embrace foolishness become ape-wise: I've spent too many years on the wrong side of that formula not to know better. It wasn't until I learned the same lesson with women that I got it. It didn't matter that Nietzsche told me so: I couldn't hear until it was too late.

- 446 -

So I've learned to doubt the knight of infinite resignation, the ironic rabbi, the stonewall psychoanalyst, the withholding guru, and any form of the ecstatic slave, the one who needs my confirmation to be complete. He feints, I do a doubletake, then because he respects me more than he lets on, he begins to believe it. The audience acts before the stage, the actors merely imitate, and there is no witness.

- 447 -

I searched for this witness. I played the kind of fool almost no one is willing to play: the earnest unwilling fool – the kind of young man who creates sages and teachers in the wake of his admiration. And in the long aftermath I can tell you this: an earnest thirst is worth more than all quenching answers. I have wished that I was the coolheaded clown, knowing and ironic, but my type is cursed with real foolishness: honesty, yearning, and perseverance. To be too sincere, too motivated, too serious in intent: I know the pain of the child who is already a joke because he is already too old in intent and too young in method.

AFTERWORD:
THE MISANTHROPIC SAGE

- 448 -

What this work demands is not something most of the human race is prepared to give. They neither want it, nor need it, nor think it possible: to seek freedom from those very consolations which appear to give life its meaning and scope. This freedom is an esoteric luxury sought by ascetics with nothing to lose: it costs exorbitant energetic quanta to resist the instinct of mythopoesis – this hydra has no particularly vulnerable locus, and more or less cannot be defeated. What we achieve is not "freedom from delusion", but "freedom for illusion": a little creative room, a little joyful participation, a little less neurosis and compulsion in our dreams. If we can become less reactive, less prone to spasmodic plagiarism, less fixated on childish fantasy, less prone to geriatric moral sentiment, less feeble in imagination and the tolerance of contradiction, less eager to resolve every dilemma and banish every dark premonition that's ever crossed the desk of humanity's collective catalogue of nightmare... then we will have matured, grown deeper roots, and learned receptivity. In the aftermath, comes receptivity: reality as we find it, sparkling wavering reality, like the swirling taste of cinnamon and tamarind, spicy and sweet and bitter all at once – it offers no logical neatness, no curling conclusion, no bedtime story with tucked-away questions and the swallowed seam of unraveling consequence... What we desire is maturity without despair; gratitude without hope; affection without cloying; knowledge without foreclosure.

- 449 -

Disillusionment concerning human nature and the demonstrable pointlessness of all life, is one of the best inducements to that much-sought-after equanimity of the philosopher. Firstly one does not lose as much as one expects: there is no "nothing" for the nihilist to reside in; there is no void waiting to swallow our hopes. These are the fantasies of someone who feels his head will burst from the noise. Disillusionment is a valuable headwound, because it reduces this noise. 毒をもって毒を制す, "Overcome poison with poison", so the ancient Japanese would say. But how could the mythopoetic instinct be poison, since it's obviously part of that core human adaptive package?

In the effort to undo the damage and cumulative error civilization has heaped on us, it was not enough to identify erroneous belief, but to target belief itself. In zealously weeding this garden, we have destroyed the soil. And truthfully since so little remains of the typical Pleistocene nomadic system of belief, and since the forces of credulity and complicitude against which we struggle are so overwhelming and outnumbering, we've had reason enough to always prefer doubt and the most wicked interpretation available. Human wickedness runs a thousand times deeper than human honesty. And since truth is such a weak and tenuous ally in the scope of human delusion, especially where the question of human nature and the meaning of existence is concerned, the only hope of anything like victory is to suspect any interpretation which is not laden with our own *marks of existence*: irony, the absurd, and the uncanny. If an interpretation does not inspire resistance, dismay, and denial, then it is either a banal tautology or it is untrue: nothing less suffices for the guerrilla warfare of good psychology. Anything that doesn't hurt, is unlikely to be true or at least not worth mentioning. Keep in mind that most of the good news also hurts: if you don't know the heartache of joy, you have not yet known joy. Similarly if you don't know the delicious aftertaste of sadness, you have not yet drunk from that cup either.

It's the stultifying insistence on singular valence, that throbbing numbness I detect in the presence of most modern bodies, that dull marching thrum I hear when they gather, which offends me and provokes my misanthropy. It's not merely that the human race lacks beauty – we could forgive that. It's the *cultivated ugliness* of the sedentary slob that offends my taste so deeply. And yet I can trace the logic and the adaptation: to be numb and yet reactive; stupid in the broad scale and extremely clever in minutiae; greedy and yet resigned; narrow and yet obese; slothful and yet frantic; self-satisfied and yet anxious; sure that one possesses the best possible worldview, and yet equally ready to declare that no one knows any more than anyone else. These are all suitable, just, and well-measured adaptations of the creature Homo sapiens to its time and place. He whose pride can accommodate even one or two of these compromises, will find his livelihood much easier. And why are these adaptations ugly? Because they flatten, fatten, dull, and encourage that ugliest of faces the ape can make: moral disapproval. The terse puckered lip, the narrowed beady eyes, the raised eyebrow of warning: the preliminaries of ritual exclusion, which seeks to inspire group cohesion through the fear of anonymous mass violence – the modern body lives within its shadow and is marked by its perpetual threat. Everything which I find so hideous in 21st century humanity can be traced to this cringing, receding cell wall attempting to leave a void precisely where anonymous mass violence draws a bead. – Precisely where we seek to be, we counterphobic antagonists, who for one reason or another have found our satisfaction in *always losing the game*, intentionally, so as to expose it for a game. A most serious game of disguised violence, grotesque absurdity, and nauseating hypocrisy, but a game nonetheless.

- 450 -

"Misanthropist" may not be the right term for what I represent. We don't hate humanity: we hate its degenerate forms, because we love what humanity can be. I suspect that we love humanity's virtues more deeply than most. We are therefore more wounded by its failures. We take seriously in practice what almost everyone actually treats as trivial: the question of virtue, the quest for truth, and its union or divorce from beauty. That I find myself painting such a Boschian scene, with so many butts in the air, heads in the sand, monstrous hybrids and absurd punishments and hideous delights – is only testament to an ability to read both forward and backward, to understand and appreciate contortion and disfigurement for what it is, a record of the determination to find beauty and meaning in the ugliest and most disguised aspects. It's even likely that this superabundant ability to discover beauty is what led me here: there is no other suitable challenge – to look elsewhere is merely self-indulgent and unworthy of my gift. I refuse to debase my poetry with flattery, obsequious hedging, polite silences, polite topics, polite assumptions: this is insulting not to "the truth", but to the almost limitless human ability to *withstand truth*. A reliance on self-deception does not preclude the ability to detect and withstand truth: accurate assessment is a prerequisite to deception. The issue is that the human being chooses the strategy of truth as a last resort, because it is so rarely profitable: it's not deception and delusion we fight against, so much as grindingly accurate calculation of advantage. The "delusion" is only cultivated afterward, as a bumper crop against the disaster of self-discovery: the secret life of neurosis is largely one of wise investment and careful cultivation. Therefore to argue with the impeccable human talent for the unconscious calculation of social strategic advantage, is almost a joke in itself: a psychologist of my ambition must play the fool, or give up psychology. And we are fools: it's foolish to love humanity the way we do, forever upset with its preference for ignoble means, forever dreaming of ways to force it into an unnatural path – and we must also therefore be cruel. There is terrible sadism in the love of truth – that no one can deny. To take away its consolations, to attempt to corner it and block every instinctual escape, and then demand that it be vulnerable enough to tell the whole truth under these conditions: the experiment sounds worthy of B.F. Skinner and every other labcoat inquisition.

Can we therefore forgive humanity? Should we? Perhaps this is what we're groping for: but to do so, would be also to give up on it, wouldn't it? We don't forgive easily, because we prefer to demand: where forgiveness lives, contempt thrives. If I'm forced to forgive, I'm also forced to admit that I was wrong to expect anything else – I'm not yet ready for that wisdom, but perhaps I see it coming over the hill. Once I've arrived there however, I would like to have made the full scope of my vision clear: for the sake of youth, for the sake of stupid hope, for the sake of the fool.

- 451 -

Our ability to tell the truth is derived from our talent for cruelty: there is no nonviolent "love of truth", only innocence itself. Indeed it's largely the inability to prioritize advantageous distortion over plain confession, which characterizes the age-old *idiot*.

And if we instinctual psychologists are masters of subtle cruelty, and if we seek revenge for every loss in a game we refused to play but could not help but be subject to – so be it. The element of revenge is a good bedfellow for truth: it is one of the few human motives which considers truth an asset, a tip of the spear, an ace up the sleeve.

My point is that if I'm correct about the devious depths of apenature, then my own work is only valid because it is itself a devious twist. To conjure truth from out of the depths of the ape heart, would require that one of the fundamental forces of that nature be recruited: either revenge, or self-destruction, or delicious cruelty, or all three – heroism and idealism does not suffice, and in any case can be analyzed further into the former.

- 452 -

As I've already discovered for myself, every exploratory psychologist with bad news to report will find himself in a double bind: if he's correct, then he must be subject to the same critique to the degree that it destroys his validity; if he's wrong, then his critique is only a reflection of his own abject failings. This is the vicious trapdoor established at the frontiers of self-knowledge, and which functions so well that one can count the major psychologists and philosophers who've dared to cross it in the last millennium on one hand. (I'm tempted to believe that the famous difficulties of ontological metaphysics and "first philosophy" are actually an ironic pale parody of the resistances to anthropological self-knowledge: a knowledge of *who one is*, qualifies much more readily as "absolute" and "first" in my reckoning. The history of philosophy as a play within a play...)

But what's even more clever, is that the fruits of that psychological critique will inevitably be absorbed as weaponry anyway: Freud had unconscious neurotic entanglements motivating his theory; Nietzsche was animated by a will to power too colored by resentment; and so on... When cornered, the human creature says: "You're a liar! And even if you're not lying, you're wrong for wanting it to be true." This corresponds to the *second article of ape law*, which as I read it says: "What cannot be destroyed, must be possessed."

- 453 -

If there is cruelty involved in the construction of this labyrinth of mirrors, what of it? It's deeply symptomatic to pathologize every hint of violence as degenerate – and deeply pathologizing to find in violence only another symptom. How ungrateful, to malign the beauty of the *hard heart* as though it were merely impoverished: we are indebted for every safety and privilege to a hard heart, somewhere. Anyway I don't ask any more than I ask of myself: squatting with your head in your hands in the middle of a labyrinth of mirrors, or roaming the halls of a fractalic crystal palace, is merely the difference between the good and the bad days.

- 454 -

If you read carefully the logs of a hermit like Han Shan, you can detect the presence of good and bad days: the oppressive weight of self-observation; the imminent danger that one's carefully crafted contempt will explode in your face; or that you will trip and shatter your amulet of pride; and that danger worst of all for the contemplative nature – that succubus called *regret*. These afflictions strike when loneliness has already weakened the hermit. Loneliness is like a chronic injury to anyone who practices solitude: it flares up when you're tired, when things don't turn out well, when the way forward is unclear. It should be obvious why it spikes in the late afternoon and early evening: this is the instinctual beacon which is supposed to call you home. Loneliness is the plan B of every arrogant ape which has safeguarded our species and ensured our tribality, despite how much difficulty we have in getting along. Therefore what is a hermit? That which in the midst of tribelessness chooses to go without all semblance of it, in the vague hope of recreating a tribe out of himself, his ideals, and his failures. But the recipe is always evolving, because inevitably the hermits will seek to band together, and around someone like Stonehouse or Saint Anthony a little enclave will grow up, and the tribe is reborn under new names, with refreshed goals, and old difficulties.

- 455 -

"The rebirth of the tribe" is probably too much to ask. We merely live as best we can in the mangled aftermath of the agricultural revolution, like warming hands over nuclear ash: our instinctual life is mangled, make no mistake. This perverse path of knowledge and relentless analysis is fit only for a mangled creature, one which seeks power nevertheless and likely forms of combat – a strange afterlife lived prematurely, a battling world of ghosts, a shaman's dream of flight: but I have no other medicine. Only by deepening the nightmare, only by sucking harder at our wounds, only by burning our fuel faster, can I guarantee a brighter light and a cheerier grin. Don't mind my crazed eyes, says the hunter – that's just the look of night overtaking me.

What am I? Just another doofus with a face and a name looking for someone to blame, saying "we're all the same"? Just another overeducated and underutilized superfluity seeking its purpose? Just another cooling shard of ejecta looking back at the molten core with disbelief, awe, and gratitude. Just another consequence of too much and too little: too much confusion and too little chaos, too much despair and too little grief, too much damage and not enough battle, too much vanity and not enough pride, too much conformity and not enough tribe, too much hurt and not enough pain.

But despite the slowly sinking ship of my generation, despite watching my onetime peers succumb one after the other to the diseases I thought we swore a brotherhood to fight – somehow I've managed to avert spiritual disaster and decay. Neither the premature adulthood of a suburban quagmire, nor the prolonged adolescence of an urban princeling have ensnared me – somehow I escaped with my skin of reasons, my self-respect, and my discontent.

Therefore what do I offer? Advocacy of what this world would be, and has been, when the artist and the hunter are united, when the violence of the contradictions within the human condition lead to an exotic sublimation, when a phenotype which was once common, finds a small niche in a hostile new order.

I advocate for what humanity still is, in its deep heart, in its problematic primate nature: still bold, still cunning, still subtle, still indomitable. This epidemic of chronic illness I'm always reminding the reader of, this age of technological dependence and bodily decline, is probably only a superficial episode in the long hominid journey... I want to make it a thrilling tale, even while I spare us nothing, and constantly remind us of the horrors behind and ahead, so that we may be ready, with open eyes, to learn to live the fuller life our ancestors gifted us. Two million years of sacrifice, endurance, and brilliant invention: we refuse to allow our inheritance to amount to a pointless heap of regret and technocratically enhanced fantasy. No matter how sparse the lights, we must find each other in the dark. We must become blind to what we thought we desired, we must learn to see again from out of an inconsolable loss. That is what the hermits mean, when they say that all phenomena are ringed with writhing flame: one learns this by sitting comfortably in the dark... The bleakness and merciless criticality of my vision, which some find unbearable, is for me this kind of comfortable dark. I see it as my vocation therefore, to demonstrate the viability and power of a nihilism which has itself been annihilated: it is the abyss of light which is our destination.

Fool's Bluff, sun in the house of the lion, 2023

ALSO BY BARTHOLOMY

---

bartholomy.ooo/books

THE MORAL DISEASE

Drawing on Foucault, Nietzsche, Arendt, Freud, and many more, this is a study of moral phenomena from the Axial Age philosophical revolutions, to the religious fervor of late antiquity, to the totalitarian movements of the 20th century, to the latest illuminating tales of the "immorality of morality" in our own impotent, absurd, and yet ominous age.

TAPETUM LUCIDUM

CONSCIOUSNESS
AND THE HOSTAGE RESCUE OF MEDITATION

A guide for the spiritually disenchanted. Neuroscience is made to pay up: to yield insight, reasons to be brave, reasons to endure the discipline and comedy that genuine meditative practice entails.

KILL THE BUDDHA

TO THE ASCETIC OF THE FUTURE

Has anyone considered what it means, that the descendants of the world's most devoted *fire cult*, one day wished for "extinguishment"? That a culture does not only grow tired, but *sick* of itself: precisely that which animated the ancestors, is one day experienced as the root of evil.